What Does the Bible Say?

What Does the Bible Say?

A Critical Conversation with Popular Culture in a Biblically Illiterate World

Mary Ann Beavis

AND

HyeRan Kim-Cragg

FOREWORD BY

Catherine Faith MacLean

CASCADE *Books* · Eugene, Oregon

WHAT DOES THE BIBLE SAY?
A Critical Conversation with Popular Culture in a Biblically Illiterate World

Cascade Books
An Imprint of Wipf and Stock Publishers
199 W. 8th Ave., Suite 3
Eugene, OR 97401

www.wipfandstock.com

PAPERBACK ISBN: 978-1-4982-3219-7
HARDCOVER ISBN: 978-1-4982-3221-0
EBOOK ISBN: 978-1-4982-3220-3

Cataloguing-in-Publication data:

Names: Beavis, Mary Ann. | Kim-Cragg, HyeRan. | foreword by MacLean, Catherine Faith.

Title: What Does the Bible Say? : A Critical Conversation with Popular Culture in a Biblically Illiterate World / Mary Ann Beavis and HyeRan Kim-Cragg.

Description: Eugene, OR: Cascade Books, 2017 | Includes bibliographical references and index.

Identifiers: ISBN 978-1-4982-3219-7 (paperback) | ISBN 978-1-4982-3221-0 (hardcover) | ISBN 978-1-4982-3220-3 (ebook)

Subjects: LCSH: Bible—Hermeneutics | Bible—Criticism, interpretation, etc.—History—21st century | Bible—Influence | Popular culture—Religious aspects

Classification: BS538.7 W4 2017 (print) | BS538.7 (ebook)

Manufactured in the U.S.A.

Contents

List of Illustrations

Foreword

BIBLICAL STORIES ARE POWERFUL tools. The Hebrew narratives are so vivid we can smell the river as the girl puts the baby in the basket, and see the stars overhead as a man is challenged to count them. The people in the Gospels are so true to life that we too can hear the wind coming across the lake, and feel tears on the cheek at news of a friend's death. Prayers in the Psalms pull the heart out of your chest with their poignancy, and fill us with righteous anger.

Biblical stories show us truth: contours of good intentions hard-wired into creation, fragilities in human nature, pressure and fallibilities and jealousy, thunderstorms and walking on water, battles and dysfunctional families, judgment and mercy and grace. All these can be read with an eye to affirm and reconcile, or read with a purpose to thwart—or perhaps read in a lonely category of sadness, with no expectation at all but to be dull and dry and then left behind.

Yet biblical literature is not our experience this morning, nor the singular property of preachers, nor a set of ancient and irrelevant texts. It is a living, mystical, puzzling collection that comes as easily into our hand as the opening of an app or the lifting of a book from the shelf.

Mary Ann Beavis and HyeRan Kim-Cragg care how we read Scripture. They have brought the keen eye of a biblical scholar and the good hand of a practical theologian to write this book. "The biblical stories have theological underpinnings and outcomes," they affirm. They open up concepts such as creation and apocalypse, heaven and hell, gender, and God, Christ and Anti-Christ, purity and sex: these are hot topics. HyeRan and Mary Ann take our cultural issues seriously and worry—rightly—about how the Bible is portrayed and interpreted in popular culture. Tools can be dangerous. In their words, "As long as the Bible is being used, abused, and misused to oppress, exclude, and judge, this must be contested and other ways of reading must be offered." This book invites readers "to develop more critical awareness, acumen and confidence in their views of the Bible" with constructive curiosity and practical impact on how we live and move and have our being in an increasingly connected world that is both interfaith and secular.

I possess several dozen Bibles and commentaries. Although I always write my name in the flyleaf to be clear that this collection of Scripture belongs to me, it is more true to say that I belong to it. Those of us who are part of the Christian tradition do—we belong to the sacred stories. Our human nature and faithful orientation to life find deep resonance, even patterned expression, in scripture: national and familial conflicts, soaring hope and jettisoning despair, metanarratives and cosmology. There is power here. Our dreams, our hopes, and the truths in our relationships, theatre, music, and even politics have a backstory in the metaphors found in the Bible.

Mary Ann and HyeRan address themselves to the backstory. They offer lots of useful material. In their discussion of creation and apocalypse, for instance, they refer to not one or two but seven biblical creation accounts. They go on to explore theological themes including the goodness of creation, care of the earth, justice, peace, and liberation. Then they discuss the film *Princess Mononoke*, with questions to engage you and me. Intriguing stuff! The movie *Chocolat* appears in the chapter on suffering and sacrifice; who would have thought? It is a brilliant commentary that moves us beyond "the over-emphasis of many forms of Christianity on the twin themes of suffering and sacrifice" and suggests some alternatives to theologies of atonement to get us thinking about resurrection and life. The movies featured in the chapters are wide-ranging; for example, *Babette's Feast*, *The Virgin Suicides*, *Spiderman II*. When you saw these movies did you notice the biblical elements? This collaboration between two academics whose life work is scripture and theology show us those elements and what the elements mean.

HyeRan and Mary Ann take on biblical understandings of virginity, heavenly tourism, and what they call "culturally pervasive themes" that are treated as biblical truths by popular culture. In accessible language they pierce holes in facile certainties and they offer constructive, educated alternatives. They write, "The problem is that ideologically charged biblical interpretation may have violent and hurtful effects and is very prevalent in this particular modern reality."

Northrop Frye used to test his university students on biblical literacy at the beginning of term. He had been seeing a diminishment in biblical familiarity that he worried would affect our comprehension of culture—and high, low, and in between. *The Great Code: The Bible and Literature*, *The Educated Imagination*, *Anatomy of Criticism*: his work still teaches us. In the forty years since I sat in his classroom, others of us have taken up the torch. We want to light up the metaphors, meaning, and metanarratives of scripture that are worked so thoroughly into our culture that they are invisible in the shadows of everyday life. The bright light of day may reflect our reality as we begin to see biblical truths in fine art, and hear them in rap music, and work them into our politics. Or the torches may shed light on twisted politics, repressive social conditions, and cruel lyrics. Deep understandings illuminate wise decision-making. We need to pay attention.

What Does the Bible Say? A Critical Conversation with Popular Culture in a Biblically Illiterate World is well constructed, a solid gift to the church, and a really good read. It is a robust resource for social studies classes, congregational study groups, neighbourhood ministerial conversations, and students thinking about pursuing religious studies. It is a good gift for newcomers to church, or your great aunt who likes to talk about God's grace at Thanksgiving—tell her what your favorite chapter is, and why. Get talking. Mary Ann Beavis and HyeRan Kim-Cragg hope they have given us a springboard for discussion. Yes. They have given us a book to get us talking, movies to contemplate, and "a critical conversation with popular culture in a biblically illiterate world." The authors say, "this book tries to connect the biblical stories, concepts, and interpretations in conversation with theological issues which address our contemporary cultures and current issues that matter in people's lives." They succeed.

—Catherine Faith MacLean

Introduction

WE NORTH AMERICANS LIVE in a biblically illiterate world. The era when all people grew up as Christian and regularly went to church is gone. The assumption that people know the Bible cannot be taken for granted—even among church-goers. That people no longer go to church much is not the biggest problem. The problem is that ideologically charged biblical interpretation may have violent and hurtful effects and is very prevalent in this particular modern reality. Harmful interpretations have been worsened by a lack of well-informed knowledge of the Bible. People do not know what is in the Bible, therefore, it is easy to be misguided, to submit to an ideology, whether it be of Fundamentalism or Anti-Semitism or of facile rejection of Christianity. The late renowned theologian Edward Farley laments that most adult Christians did not pass the elementary school level in their biblical understanding, thus remain as literalists. Not moving beyond a literal, superficial understanding of the Bible is dangerous because a literalist's position can easily slip into taking a fundamentalist position. We all know how violent fundamentalism can be, given the recent resurgence of fundamentalism and its harmful effects, such as religious intolerance, disregard of human rights, and lack of concern for social justice and ecological health. As long as we continue to live in a biblically and religiously illiterate world, religious violence will be more likely to occur.

A serious effort needs to be made in order to learn what the Bible actually says, and how biblical teachings and narratives have been received, interpreted and reinterpreted throughout history. The critical issue is that while we live in a secular world, a Christian ethos continues to exert a great influence. In short, the number of Christians has been shrinking, but the influence of Christian teaching, grounded in the Bible, has not. As long as the Bible is being used, abused, and misused to oppress, exclude, and judge, this must be contested and other ways of reading must be offered. This book, in a modest way, seeks to offer more positive and accessible readings, not as the authoritative word on biblical meaning, but as a means of inviting readers to develop more critical awareness, acumen, and confidence in their views of the Bible.

The biblical stories have theological underpinnings and outcomes. We need theological conversation partners in terms of how certain biblical stories relate to certain theological themes. For example, based upon the Genesis story of Adam and Eve, a theological theme of original sin developed in western Christianity. And yet, the biblical story of Adam and Eve, when read closely and carefully, does not inevitably lead to this doctrinal outcome. Another conversation partner may be popular culture. Thus, in this book, by looking at some movies that feature certain biblical stories, themes and teachings, we have demonstrated why knowing the Bible is important as an educational tool, as it equips people critically to engage popular culture instead of casually accepting, or simply being unaware of, its interpretations of the Bible.

Learning what the Bible says (or does not say) is of critical importance to Christian faith communities today. Our lack of the knowledge of the Bible becomes a chain that constrains us, makes us docile, and leads us to a cynical (or overly rosy) view of the Bible or the world or both. Perhaps the greatest danger is indifference and the misguided opinion that the Bible does not matter anymore to our faith—or that it contains a deterministic blueprint for Christian life and world history. If we don't care what the Bible says and we don't care what others say about the Bible, or don't know how to respond to uninformed critiques of the Bible, it is because we do not see the power that the Bible and its interpreters still exert in the church and the world. Some will say "the Bible is archaic, why not throw it out?" And yet, knowing what the Bible *really* says or does not say, helps us to slip us out of the chains of misinformation, which may in turn liberate us to find new insights in order to live out the faithful life.

An example of a pop cultural distortion of the Bible is found in a popular Facebook meme, featuring the gay activist Nicholas Ferroni, captioned: "I was born a sinner too. My sin is mentioned in the bible twenty-five times. I tried to change, but I couldn't. Luckily, society learned to accept us left-handed people." At first glance, this is a clever way of comparing the Bible's supposed legislation against homosexuality and the "biblical" teaching that left-handedness is sinful. There are indeed verses in Leviticus that forbid sexual intercourse between men (Lev 18:22; 20:13; cf. Rom 1:26–27); however, these are arguably not prohibitions against homosexuality, but against gender reversal. Since these verses are worded in terms of males lying with other males as if they were females, it is likely that men who engaged in such behavior were deplored not because they were homosexual, but because they were compromising their dominant masculine status, and assuming an inferior feminine role. While this "biblical" way of thinking is problematic in terms of modern conceptions of gender equality and fluidity, it does not define homosexuality per se as sinful. Similarly, the Bible does indeed mention left-handedness many times, but not as sinful. Certainly, several biblical references make the widely-held cultural assumption that the right hand, as the dominant hand of most people, is superior to the left (e.g., Gen 48:13–18; Gal 2:9; cf. Exod 15:6; Ps 118:16). However, in the Gospels, sitting at the right and left hand of Jesus is considered to be an honor (Mark 10:37, 40; Matt 20:21, 23). The judge Ehud is specifically described as left-handed (Judg 3:15–21), and left-handed warriors are mentioned as particularly skilled marksmen (Judg 20:16; see also 1 Chr 12:2). The left hand was used in priestly rituals (Lev 14:15, 16, 26, 27), and in gestures of blessing (Gen 48:13–22). Divine Wisdom holds long life in her right hand, and wealth and honor in her left (Prov 3:15–17). Many of the biblical references to left-handedness are simply neutral (Gen 13:9; Judg 16:29; Neh 8:4; Song 2:6; 8:3; Ezek 39:3; Dan 12:7; Matt 6:3). The only unequivocally negative representation of the left hand is the judgment scene of Matt 25:31–46, where the right hand is associated with heavenly rewards, and the left with eternal punishment. However, the focus of the teaching is on the ethical conduct of the persons being judged, not on whether they're right or left-handed—note that the divine King of the parable has both a right and a left hand! So, although Mr. Ferroni has undoubtedly and unfairly suffered from prejudices against homosexuality and even left-handedness supposedly grounded in the Bible, the Bible arguably does not define homosexuality as a sin, and certainly does not prohibit left-handedness. An unfortunate effect of the Facebook meme, however, is to imply that the Bible is silly and archaic because it outlaws something as harmless and natural as left-handedness.

This book is a collaboration between a biblical scholar (Mary Ann Beavis) and a practical theologian (HyeRan Kim-Cragg) who are concerned with the way that the Bible is portrayed and interpreted in popular culture, including but not limited to the movies. This concern points to a need for a conversation, informing what the Bible *actually* says in order to uncover transformations and distortions of the biblical stories in the wider culture—including Christian culture. At some level, our conversation, then, becomes counter-cultural, not in an oppositional way, but taking an alternative posture that aims to provide different insights by drawing from and closely looking at the Bible. The chapters take a Christian canonical approach, articulating "what the Bible says" with regard to culturally pervasive themes such as sin and salvation, Christ and Antichrist, heaven and hell, and suffering and sacrifice, in contrast and conversation with popular understandings and misconceptions as disseminated in (especially) film, advertising, television, etc. We hope that together we will open up fertile academic, ecclesial, and secular space for disclosing loaded cultural and ideological views. In addition we hope to move the reader towards positive and intriguing insights embedded in the Bible.

As part of this effort, drawing on the popularity of church-based "faith and film" nights, we have selected a movie that engages the biblical theme of each chapter (e.g., *Prince of Egypt* for the chapter on Moses and Jesus), and viewed the movies together with small groups of Christians—church groups, student groups, a women's group—in order to discern and discuss their perceptions of the way that the various biblical themes are expressed in popular culture. Some of the movies have obvious connections to the chapter topics (e.g., *Heaven is for Real* for Heaven and Hell); others less so (e.g., *Agora* for Christ and Antichrist). The films belong to a variety of genres (e.g., animated feature, Japanese anime, superhero, historical drama, romance, art film). Readers may wish to study these chapters in small groups, featuring a showing and discussion of the films suggested for each chapter, or they may choose their own movies. Many of the films discussed in the book contain themes covered in more than one chapter, e.g., all of the movies have perspectives on sin and salvation; several portray the themes of suffering and sacrifice; more than one portrays a Christ figure. Each chapter ends with questions for discussion before and after the movie viewing, and a brief list of resources pertaining to the chapter topic, including other films with similar themes. The information in each chapter, the movie viewing, and the discussion questions are intended to give more substance to the conversation between the bible, theology and popular culture than is usually possible in church-based faith and film events that are aimed for enhancing young people's and adults' teaching ministry.

Finally, there are nuanced biblical insights and new information from cultural, archaeological, anthropological, socio-economic, and political scholarship that have the potential to shed new light on the biblical stories. The average reader may not have access to these or be able to sort through the reams of new information on their own. Religious educator Mary Boys over thirty-five years ago called for accessible but solid materials for biblical teaching. She observed that there has been a tremendous proliferation of knowledge in fields relating to biblical theology. Yet, this very proliferation of knowledge created "an ever-widening gap between, on the one hand, Scripture scholars and, the other, members of the community whom this Scripture ought to nurture, criticize, and reform."[1] Not only is there a gap between biblical scholarship and lack of biblical knowledge in the church but also there is a gap between biblical scholars and theologians. For this reason, recent developments in biblical studies are overlooked by theologians, and biblical scholars, trained to bracket out centuries of theological interpretation of the Bible, are inclined to disregard developments in contemporary theology. In order to reduce this gap, we need a book that can help readers take their first steps into the new avenues of biblical interpretation. Thus, this book tries to connect the biblical stories, concepts, and interpretations in conversation with theological issues which address our contemporary cultures and current issues that matter in people's lives. This collaboration will be a much-needed conversation between two disciplines that are distinct, but often confused in the popular mind. Those who are not strongly acquainted with biblical scholarship, Christian doctrines, teachings, and practices, including young people and post baby boomers, will find the contents interesting, intriguing, and informative.

The topics of the following ten chapters do not exhaust the thematic riches of the Bible, or the many theological issues arising from them. Some readers may find some of the contents of this book to be challenging, and even controversial. As mentioned above, our reflections on these biblical themes are by no means meant to be the final word on the subject, but rather, they are intended as a springboard for discussion, reflection, and further learning.

---

1. Boys, *Biblical Interpretation*, 8.

Note on Terminology

In view of this book's emphasis on Jewish-Christian relations, the long history of Christian anti-Semitism, and the pitfalls of supersessionism, we have opted to use the terms Jewish Scriptures and Christian Testament rather than the more familiar Old Testament and New Testament. This is because the terms "Old" and "New" may carry the connotation that the older is antiquated and outdated, whereas the newer is superior, and replaces the old. The selection of the term "Jewish Scriptures" rather than "Hebrew Bible" is due to the use throughout this book of the larger Christian canon, which includes scriptures regarded as canonical in Catholic and Orthodox Bibles, but that are not in Jewish or Protestant Bibles,[2] variously known as Apocrypha, Deuterocanonicals, or Intertestamentals.

Other Resources

Johnston, Robert K. *Reel Spirituality: Theology and Film in Dialogue*. Grand Rapids: Baker, 2000.
Reinhartz, Adele. *Bible and Cinema: An Introduction*. New York: Routledge, 2013.
———, ed. *Bible and Cinema: Fifty Key Films*. New York: Routledge, 2013.
Stone, Brian P. *Faith and Film: Theological Themes at the Cinema*. St. Louis: Chalice, 2000.

2. For further information, see deSilva, *Introducing the Apocrypha*; Harrington, *Invitation to the Apocrypha*.

1

Creation and Apocalypse

THIS CHAPTER INTRODUCES SEVERAL biblical creation accounts (Gen 1:1—2:4a; Gen 2:4b—3:24; Prov 8:22–32; Job 38–41; Ps 104; John 1:1–5; cf. Heb 1:1–4) in relation to the themes of creation and recreation (Flood and Restoration, Slavery and Exodus, Exile and Return), culminating in Revelation 21–22, which does not look forward to a heavenly afterlife, but envisions the establishment of the reign of God in a "new" earthly realm of justice and peace. It is divided into three parts. The first part shows how the Bible relates the themes of creation and recreation to apocalypse by employing a comparative reading of how these two chapter themes are depicted and understood.

The second part is a theological exploration of the themes arising from creation and recreation as well as restoration. Theological themes that emerge from this discussion include the goodness of creation, care of the earth, justice, peace, and liberation. The presentation of these themes in this chapter contrasts with excessive cultural focus on Adam and Eve, sex and sin, especially in advertising,[1] and with horrific apocalyptic scenarios with deterministic views of history and human destiny that assume that only the violent destruction of the earth can bring about salvation.[2] We critically revisit the book of Revelation in the light of the creation narratives, seeking to learn what the Bible actually says about creation and apocalypse.

Finally, we engage in a conversation with the film, *Princess Mononoke* (dir. Miyazaki, 1997), in order to show how a pop culture presentation of the creation, restoration, and the beauty of the earth can enrich our

---

1. Edwards, *Admen and Eve*.
2. E.g., the *Left Behind* series, http://www.leftbehind.com/.

understandings of the biblical narratives. We argue that this film can be used as a teaching tool that can inform a nuanced reading of creation and recreation and their significance for Christians. Based upon the experience of watching this film with a particular church group, we suggest further discussion questions, and teaching and learning materials for such use.

Creation, Recreation, and Restoration in the Bible

The Christian biblical canon is arranged so that it begins with creation (Genesis 1–3) and ends with recreation (Rev 21:1—22:4). Since they are placed at the beginning of the canon, the first three chapters of Genesis are regarded as the creation story *par excellence*, sketching a grand narrative of the origin of the world, of the human race, and of all living beings, with implications for who we are in relation to the divine as well as about how we live. It delineates a theological anthropology and a relational cosmology.

As students of the Bible know, there are actually two creation stories at the beginning of Genesis. The first of these, Gen 1:1—2:4a, was probably written centuries *after* the second (Gen 2:4b—3:24). This "Priestly" (P) creation account, written during or after the Babylonian exile (587–538 BCE), depicts the creation of "the heavens and the earth" in seven days, corresponding to the days of the week, culminating in the Sabbath. The life of all beings is affirmed as "good" (1:4, 10, 12, 18, 21, 25, 31). This biblical teaching on the affirmation of life is obvious; creation's goodness is repeated seven times as each time God created earthly life, its value is affirmed. In this story, human beings, male and female, are created "in the image and likeness" of the divine, and given a special role in relation to other beings (Gen 1:26–27), rendered in the KJV as "dominion" (*kavash*). As Dianne Bergant explains,

> Despite the fact that they share the same habitat with some of these creatures, they are given a limited jurisdiction over the rest of creation. This is an invitation not to exploit or cause harm to the natural world but to oversee its growth and manage its productivity, for they are representatives of God, meant to govern as God would govern.[3]

The ecological theologian Sallie McFague contends that the intrinsic value of all life is at the heart of the first creation story,[4] and that this same

---

3. Bergant, *Genesis*, 7.

4. *The Earth Chapter*, Principle 1, found at http://www.unesco.org/education/tlsf/

value is spelled out even today in The Earth Charter, a United Nations document:

> Recognize that all beings are interdependent and every form of life has value regardless of its worth to human beings. Affirm faith in the inherent dignity of all human beings and in the intellectual, artistic, ethical, and spiritual potential of humanity.[5]

In its historical context, it is easy to see how this mandate to oversee creation would be meaningful to returning exiles who had enjoyed little control over their lives and environments in foreign territory. In the Priestly account, however, humanity is not God's final word; rather, it is the seventh day, *Shabbat*, when "God finished the work that he had done, and he rested on the seventh day from all the work that he had done. So God blessed the seventh day and hallowed it, because on it God rested from all the work that he had done in creation" (Gen 2:2–3).

The second creation account (the J or Yahwistic account) was written as early as the tenth century BCE, edited together with the Priestly version in post-exilic times almost seamlessly. However, a close reading of Gen 2:4b—3:28 reveals many discrepancies between the two. In Genesis 2, the first (not the last) created being is the human (*ha'adam*), formed out of the earth (*adamah*). Next, the Garden of Eden is planted as an environment for the primal human, so that *ha'adam* will have something to eat. Then, so that the human will not be lonely, God creates the animals and birds, which are named by *ha'adam*. Finally, a woman is created from the side of *ha'adam*, and humanity is divided into man (*ish*) and woman (*isshah*) as fitting partners for one another (2:22–24). As in the P narrative, the human being is given a special task with respect to the garden, "to till it and keep it" (2:15), reflecting the agricultural economy of ancient Israel. Perhaps reflecting its antiquity, the J account is much earthier than P, and presents God (called by the proper name YHWH) in human-like terms, forming the human out of the earth, breathing life into the human's nostrils, planting the garden and placing *ha'adam* there, giving the human every fruit of the garden to eat, except for the fruit of the tree of knowledge (2:15–17). Compared with the cosmic scope of the P account, J is anthropocentric, human-centered. It portrays the relationship between God, humans, and the earth in intimate and relational terms.

mods/theme_a/img/02_earthcharter.pdf.

5. McFague, "Epilogue: Human Dignity," 201.

These ancient stories are the best-known of the Bible's creation narratives, and they have pride of place by virtue of their position at the beginning of the canon and their influence on western culture. They mesh together very well, proceeding from the big picture—the creation of the heavens and the earth in seven days—to the microcosmic focus on the Garden and the first couple. As noted above, however, they are not identical, and reflect the beliefs and needs of their own times and cultural settings. Moreover, they are not the only creation narratives in the Bible. For example, Prov 8:22–32 sketches a very different creation story, where Wisdom (Greek: *Sophia*) is God's firstborn, participating in the divine work of creation:

> When there were no depths I was brought forth, when there were no springs abounding with water. Before the mountains had been shaped, before the hills, I was brought forth—when he had not yet made earth and fields, or the world's first bits of soil. When he established the heavens, I was there, when he drew a circle on the face of the deep, when he made firm the skies above, when he established the fountains of the deep, when he assigned to the sea its limit, so that the waters might not transgress his command, when he marked out the foundations of the earth, then I was beside him, like a master worker [or "little child"]; and I was daily his delight, rejoicing before him always, rejoicing in his inhabited world and delighting in the human race (vv. 24–32).[6]

Job 38–41 presents a sweeping account of God as the divine architect who is mother and father of the universe:

> . . . who shut in the sea with doors when it burst out from the womb?—when I made the clouds its garment, and thick darkness its swaddling band, and prescribed bounds for it, and set bars and doors, and said, "Thus far shall you come, and no farther, and here shall your proud waves be stopped"? . . .
>
> Has the rain a father, or who has begotten the drops of dew? From whose womb did the ice come forth, and who has given birth to the hoar-frost of heaven? The waters become hard like stone, and the face of the deep is frozen (38:8–11, 29–30).

God reminds the defiant Job that for the maker of the monsters Behemoth and Leviathan (40:15; 41:1), who placed the constellations in the heavens (38:31–33), human affairs are only a minuscule part of the picture:

---

6. Cf. Wisd 8:22, where Sophia is called the fashioner of "all things."

"Who has cut a channel for the torrents of rain, and a way for the thunderbolt, to bring rain on a land where no one lives, on the desert, which is empty of human life, to satisfy the waste and desolate land, and to make the ground put forth grass?" (38:25–27). This is a far cry from the human-centred focus of the Genesis accounts. In a similar vein, Psalm 105 praises a divine creation where human endeavors play only a small role:

> O LORD, how manifold are your works! In wisdom you have made them all; the earth is full of your creatures. Yonder is the sea, great and wide, creeping things innumerable are there, living things both small and great. There go the ships, and Leviathan that you formed to sport in it" (104:24–26).

Ps 105:6 reminds us that everything that breathes has the capacity to praise God.

Patterns of creation, and of recreation, recur throughout the biblical narratives. For example, the flood is portrayed as a reversal of creation, where the primal waters held back by the heavens (Gen 1:6–8) are unleashed upon the earth (Gen 7:1–24), and Noah's family is commissioned to "be fruitful and multiply, and fill the earth" (Gen 9:1, 7). The creation of the new nation of Israel begins with Jacob and his family, only to be thwarted by the Egyptian captivity. Under the leadership of Moses, the nation is recreated, and reaches fruition when the people enter the Land of Promise. The pattern is repeated in the Babylonian Exile, where the destruction of Judah is reversed in the "new creation" of the return from exile, portrayed in utopian terms: "For I am about to create new heavens and a new earth; the former things shall not be remembered or come to mind. But be glad and rejoice for ever in what I am creating; for I am about to create Jerusalem as a joy, and its people as a delight. . . . The wolf and the lamb shall feed together, the lion shall eat straw like the ox; but the serpent—its food shall be dust! They shall not hurt or destroy on all my holy mountain, says the LORD." (Isa 65:17–18, 25).

Biblical scholars sometimes use the term "rewritten Bible" to describe the amplification, modification or elaboration of the scriptures to make them more meaningful to later generations.[7] This is a process that begins with the biblical canon itself, as the examples above illustrate. That indicates, in a sense, that the meaning of the biblical text is not fixed, but contextual, depending on the historical, cultural and theological settings

7. See "Rewritten Bible," *Oxford Biblical Studies Online*, http://www.oxfordbiblical-studies.com/article/opr/t94/e1625.

in which it is interpreted. Of course, the Christian Testament writings also reflect this process. For example, the Gospels of Matthew and Luke—and probably John as well—are "rewritings" of the oldest Gospel, Mark. The prologue to the Fourth Gospel boldly reworks the Priestly and Wisdom creation accounts to include the Word (*logos*): "In the beginning was the Word, and the Word was with God, and the Word was God. He was in the beginning with God. All things came into being through him, and without him not one thing came into being. What has come into being in him was life, and the life was the light of all people" (John 1:1–4). For John, this primeval Word is Jesus, who "became flesh and dwelt among us" (1:14).

The most dramatic rewriting of the Genesis creation accounts is found in the Book of Revelation, with its sevenfold scenes of afflictions unleashed upon the earth (Rev 6:1–17; 8:1, 6–13; 9:1–21; 11:15–19; 15:1—16:21), marking the reversal of the seven days of creation. However, in the last two chapters, images from the Genesis creation accounts are reworked in the author's depiction of the recreation of "a new heaven and a new earth" (21:1). As in Genesis 2, God dwells with human beings (21:2–3); the primal light of creation is restored (21:23; 22:5); the river of the water of life flows from the throne of God (22:1), flanked on both sides by the tree of life (22:2), whose leaves are for the healing of the nations. Surprisingly, the disturbing and violent imagery of the earlier chapters culminate in a scene where the nations of the earth are free to enter the holy city and bask in divine light (21:24–27). Like the returning exiles of Isaiah, the author and addresses of Revelation were living in a context of persecution and alienation. The vision of the restoration of creation looks forward to a restoration of the earth, and of right relationships upon the earth. It is a vision of healing from the brokenness resulting from persecution and occupation.

Christian Theology and Creation

Christianity as a religion has recognized creation—the elemental force of life's existence, as a foundational reality. While we may have forgotten it, our religious traditions emerged from Hebraic anthropology and came from non-dualistic incarnational roots.[8] There is no religion or theology as God-talk and God-action without such material bases of creation (i.e., earth, air, water, and fire).[9] To the theologian Catherine Keller, "if God is

8. Nelson, *Body Theology*, 42.
9. Ray, *Theology That Matters*, 2.

immaterial, God doesn't matter."[10] Theology as God-talk and God-action is deeply materialistic and is relevant to and informative of every day experience. If not, Dorothee Sölle asserts, the dichotomy between spirit and flesh, "was and still is a tool of empire and the will to power."[11] This materialistic and elementary necessity of life in creation cannot be reduced to or boxed into dualism which separates the body from the spirit. The dualism not only justifies the separation between body and spirit but also extends its notion to divide nature and culture. Contesting this dualistic notion, the philosopher Glen Mazis contends that human, animal, and machine (as a product of modern culture) are interconnected. Here, machine is understood as the one that is able to communicate and interact with its environment. While the machine is a non-biological living entity, it "embodies a collectivity of human expression, as well as echoes of the biosphere." Thus, Mazis continues, "Human, animal, and machine can enter an ongoing dialogue for creative enrichment."[12] Here, the understanding of machine must be differentiated from mechanism. A Newtonian and Cartesian view of the world as mechanism is opposite of the view of the machine that can interact with the organic environment. Building upon Mazis's effort to connect both biological and non-biological realities, we can further ponder the meaning of and the realm of culture as a way of connecting nature and culture.

Etymologically speaking, culture in Latin is *cultura*, which means "cultivation of soil."[13] We can even take this insight on culture further into the role of education, especially with regards to the concept of *paideia* ("education"). The late Edward Farley who advocated wholesome theological education calls for *paideia* as "the 'culturing' of a human being in *arête* or virtue."[14] Jennifer Ayres, taking his point, argues that those of us who are committed to nurturing the whole person seeking to become cultured persons must pay attention to nature, as she calls for "cultivating ecological faith" by "learning on the ground" as a task for religious education.[15] A grounding work for such education is to have a capacity of investigating the notion of scientific knowledge identified with the power to control nature in addition to a capacity of fueling a view of "nature not as comprising dead

---

10. Keller, "Flesh of God," 91.

11. Sölle, "Between Matter and Spirit," 98.

12. Mazis, "Ecospirituality," 151.

13. Wirzba, *Food and Faith*, 37.

14. Farley, *Theologia*, 152–53.

15. Ayres, "Learning on the Ground," 204.

objects to be exploited, but rather as a totality of active subjects with which they must learn to partner."[16]

Biblically speaking, the Spirit, the inspiring force of breath (Hebrew: *ruach*) is always at once material and spiritual. To use the language of Paul, God as the Spirit is the "one in whom we live, and move and have our being" (Acts 17:28). The key to a non-dualistic theological understanding of creation as the spirit-filled material reality is to recognize that the body and the spirit are different but not separate. The body and the spirit in creation and in every living being are neither the same nor separate. By "difference" we mean "neither separation nor an identity, but a relation—a differential relation of embodiment," Keller explains.[17]

In this sense of relation of embodiment, a biblically based Christian theology is an incarnational theology, meaning God became incarnate in Jesus Christ, who took human flesh and dwelt among us (John 1:14). Using the bold and earthy words of Karen Baker-Fletcher, "Jesus is fully spirit and fully dust. Jesus as God incarnate is spirit embodied in dust. Jesus is God as dust. God as dust is Immanuel, God who is with us in our joy, our suffering, our bodiliness, our spiritual growth, and struggles."[18] All things, all living and breathing things, came into being through this God incarnate and God with us (Hebrew: *Immanuel*; romanized Greek: *Emmanuel*) because this God as the Word (*logos*) and Wisdom (*sophia*) was in the beginning (John 1:2–3). In the Letter to the Hebrews, a similar but not identical view is claimed wherein Jesus as Son of God is the source of life, "through whom God created the worlds. He is the reflection of God's glory and the exact imprint of God's very being and he sustains all things by his powerful word (Heb 1:2; cf. Wisd 7:25–27). In Hebrews, the term translated as "word" (*rhēma*) is used in a way similar to John's *logos* (John 1:1–5). The statement that the Son is the "reflection" of the divine glory (*doxa*) and the "imprint" (*charaktēr*) of God's very being is also reminiscent of God's creation of humanity—male and female—in the divine image (*kat' eikona*) and likeness (*kat' homoiōsen*) (Gen 1:26 LXX).[19]

The incarnational nature of God in the Jewish Scriptures is depicted as God the Creator, who established a relationship with the first human beings

16. Ruether, "Ecofeminist Philosophy, Theology, and Ethics," 91.

17. Keller, "Flesh of God," 101.

18. Baker-Fletcher, *Sisters of Dust, Sisters of Spirit*, 17–18.

19. Beavis and Kim-Cragg, *Hebrews*, 91. LXX refers to the Septuagint, a Greek translation of the Jewish Scriptures often used by the authors of the New Testament.

by forming them. As discussed above, according to the J creation story, God formed the first human from the dust of the ground and breathed into the human's nostrils the breath of life (Gen 2:7). Here, we emphasize the gift of divine breath/spirit (*ruach*) to humanity as prior to the narrative of primal disobedience in Genesis 3 that has dominated Christian theological interpretations of this creation story (see chapter 2).

The incarnational depiction of God as Creator is also found in the book of Job. In an attempt to maintain his own integrity and innocence, Job proclaims the *ruach* of God is in his nostrils: "as long as my breath is in me and the *ruach* of God is in my nostrils, my lips will not speak falsehood, and my tongue will not utter deceit" (27:3). As God created *ha'adam* by breathing into his/her nostrils, the same *ruach* was in Job who desperately argues with God but "sees" God in the end (Job 42:5). In fact, as noted above, Job 38–41 is one of the most bold and creation-centred theological declarations in the Bible. This declaration is far from a dogmatic formula. It is not a doctrinal statement, either. It is rather theological poetry, evoking imagination, enabling us to peek at an undisclosed vision, which we as all living beings seek to behold. After all, "it might take hold of the skirts of the earth" (38:13). Job contains magnificent imagery of all four elements of life, beginning with air in the form of whirlwind (38:1), fire in the form of a boiling pot and burning bushes (41:21), water in the form of the sea (38:8), snow (38:22), rain and dew (38:28), ice and hoarfrost (38:29), and a river (40:23), and finally earth in the form of desert, animals (38:3; 39:1, 5, 9, 13, 19, 26, 27; 40:7, 41:5), grain (39:12), trees (40:17, 21, 22), and mountains (40:20). All of these elemental forces of life captured in Job stir our senses, making bold and tangible claims about the incarnational God as Creator and God's relational nature with all living beings. While God challenges Job (representing humanity), God's ultimate desire is to affirm our life and all creation as good.

In a similarly fleshly vein, God also created a garden, planted every kind of tree that is pleasant to the sight and good for food (2:9). This earthy, sensual, fleshly garden is the Garden of Eden which is also called paradise (Luke 23:43; 2 Cor 12:4; Rev 2:7). We came from this paradise and we yearn for this paradise, but our yearning is neither a fantasy nor a nostalgia. This yearning for paradise means "yearning persistently for the beloved," feminist educator Rosemary Carbine argues, "that is, for better mutual relations and ways of life."[20] We seek to bring this paradise into our ways of life here

20. Carbine, "Erotic Education," 324.

and now. Jesus taught it this way, "Repent, the Kingdom of God has come near" (Mark 1:15). In the words of the prophet Isaiah, God is about to create "new heavens and a new earth" (65:17). In the vision of Revelation, the paradise is depicted as "the river and the tree of life" (22:1–2). Peter Short, the past Moderator of The United Church of Canada, puts it this way, "the residual memory of paradise is still in you . . . You are a paradise-haunted creature. If it were not so, why would you expect so much of the world? Why would you expect so much of yourself?"[21]

We expect so much of ourselves not because we as humans are better than other creatures but because we are part of the creation and as beings in creation and with God we are precious and valued. "Deck yourself with majesty and dignity, clothe yourself with glory and splendor" (Job 40:10). If we expect so much of the world and ourselves, in terms of our accountability and our responsibility for the sake of our majesty and dignity, how can we understand the biblical apocalypse? Are we not obliged to care for the earth, and care for our life since the end of the world is coming? Do we have to "remain faithful to the earth?"[22]

To respond to these questions, it may be fruitful to go back to the etymology of the word, "apocalypse." It comes from the Greek word, *apokalypsis*, which means to "unveil, to disclose, to reveal." It is a disclosure of something hidden. That is why the last book of the New Testament is called "Revelation" as it vividly reveals the end time in terms of destruction, fall, and God's wrath. The popular media, certainly movies and TV series, successfully market the apocalypse script, painting a certain Christian message with a harshly judgmental tone. For example, the TV mini-series *The Stand* featured a Christ-figure who opposes a New Age style Antichrist group. A blockbuster film *Terminator* (1984), followed by *Terminator 2: Judgment Day* (1991), presents a second coming of Mary and Jesus figures.[23] Of course, not all movies dealing with apocalyptic themes are uncritically violent and vindictive. For instance, *Apocalypse Now* (1979) discloses the hidden truth of the Vietnam War, depicting its inhumane militarist US imperialism and its effect on ordinary people, both American and Vietnamese. Popular culture can play a role in questioning unexamined events and concerns. Such cultural scripts provide a critical lens through which to read "the signs of the time" (Matt 16:3). Wearing this lens, one may also

21. *Emmanuel College Newsletter* (Toronto: Emmanuel College, Autumn 2004).
22. Nietzsche, *Thus Spoke Zarathustra*, Prologue, §3.
23. Keller, *Apocalypse Now and Then*, 4.

notice that the binary and dualistic line of good and evil, us and them, friend and enemy is blurred since both groups fall victim to the tangled spiral of violence.[24]

How, then, do creation and apocalypse go together? The life of creation precedes the death of creation and vice versa. In the cycle of life, a beginning goes hand in hand with an end or a closure. Even if creation is a beginning, taken as a new life, and apocalypse means an end, a destruction of that life, this order is not inevitable. Conversely, an apocalypse may usher in a new creation. "'The End,' may, paradoxically, dis/close an opening."[25] In fact, elementary forces of life in creation effectively teach this paradox. *The Nature of Things*, a TV science documentary series produced by The Canadian Broadcasting Corporation, uses the origin of the ocean to explain how the world began.[26] The ocean, the fundamental source of life for the entire planet earth, began in the midst of great volcanic activity six billion years ago. The beginning of life was and is linked to the end, the destructive movement of the volcanic dis/closure. The beginning of one life is the end of another life. The end is the beginning and the beginning is the end—this is the paradox of life and death and the paradox of creation and apocalypse. After all, we came from the dust, and to dust we shall return (Gen 3:19). The Bible affirms this paradox.

What this biblical teaching of paradox also implies is that the creation and the apocalypse, the beginning and the end, the birth and the death of life, do not negate one in order to affirm the other. Rather, they are interconnected, like a web. While the old must die, the Bible, culminating in Revelation, does not regard this as negative and undesirable. For all its reputation for fire and vengeance, the book ends on a remarkably conciliatory note of hope for reconciliation and healing; the leaves of the tree of life in the New Jerusalem are "for the healing of the nations" (Rev 22:2). Like other apocalyptic writings, Revelation presents a message of hope for believers suffering religious persecution (Rev 1:9; 2:3, 10; 6:9–11; 14:12–14). In short, the beginning and the end, the creation and the apocalypse are not linear. The Bible does not have an absolute ending, but instead leaves

---

24. Horsley, *Jesus and the Spiral of Violence*. Horsley helps us see this interlocking identification of the victims and the victimizers during Jesus's life and ministry in this book.

25. Keller, *Apocalypse Now and Then*, 2.

26. http://www.cbc.ca/geologic/eg_atlantic_coast.html.

room for hope and healing, pointing to multiple webs of incarnated Spirit, dynamic, often involving disruptions, irruptions, and instability.

On a concluding note, the question of "What does the Bible say?" with respect to Creation and Apocalypse points to the question of biblical literacy, implying that the Bible has been, sometimes, misunderstood and the wisdom of the biblical teaching has been lost in church and society. In this regard, this chapter also has to do with ecological literacy, which according to David Orr, is "the knowledge necessary to comprehend interrelatedness, and an attitude of care or stewardship."[27] When such knowledge is properly taught, those who learn it will have a "life lived accordingly."[28] For this purpose, we now turn to the movie.

Creation and Apocalypse in Popular Culture

Watch: *Princess Mononoke* (1997)

Discussion Questions

Before the viewing

What kinds of images do the terms "creation" and "apocalypse" raise in your mind?

Do you think of creation and apocalypse as opposites?

How do you see these biblical themes in relation to the present ecological crisis?

After the viewing

What are some of the main themes of the movie?

Does it have any significance for Christians?

How does the movie address the issue of religious violence upon environment?

27. Orr, *Ecological Literacy*, 92.
28. Ibid., 87.

What are the insights of human responsibility as stewardship and repentance upon our creation?

Discussion Notes

Princess Mononoke is not a movie that engages with the Bible in an obvious way, like the films discussed in some of the following chapters. It is easy to see how a film like *Heaven is for Real* relates to the themes of Heaven and Hell, or how *Prince of Egypt* pertains to Moses and Jesus. The director, Hayao Miyazaki, is famed for his animated productions, including *The Wind Rises* (2013), *Howl's Moving Castle* (2004), and *Spirited Away* (2001). Its religious framework is Shinto, the indigenous religion of Japan, which sees divinity in nature, and where gods are represented in both human and animal form. The genre of the movie is anime, a distinctively Japanese style of animation, ranging from children's programming to pornography. Compared to western-style animated TV and film, it is often highly emotionally charged, violent, sexual, spiritual, mystical, supernatural, running the gamut from pure innocence to utter depravity, perversion, and darkness. However, anime often combines western religious images and themes with Shinto elements: angels, demons, apocalyptic, crosses, trees of life, Armageddon, Mary Magdalene. A very popular video/manga (anime-style comic book genre) is the post-apocalyptic *Neon Genesis Evangelion* ("New Creation Gospel"), set in a near-future earth whose population has nearly been wiped out by a meteor, with mysterious alien beings called "Angels" and female savior figures called "Evangelions" (Gospels)—"Evas" (Eves) for short. A recent anime film, *Saint Young Men*, portrays a scenario where Jesus and Buddha live as roommates in present-day Tokyo.

As an example of the blending of traditional Shinto and "biblical" elements in *Princess Mononoke*, consider the figure of Prince Ashitaka. The name Ashitaka is from Japanese folklore; according to the director, Ashitaka is a mythological hero who was defeated and killed by the first emperor of Japan; however, in a variant of the story, he survives and escapes the northwest part of Japan. There is also a Mount Ashitaka in southwestern Japan, which, like Mount Fuji, is a sacred mountain, currently home to a nature conservation center. As a hero, Ashitaka doesn't seem at first glance to resonate much with biblical archetypes; however, he is a royal figure from a small, tribal people, persecuted by an evil emperor, who goes off to fight a decisive battle between good and evil. That is, in general, he is portrayed as a messianic figure.

More specifically, the story of Ashitaka is remarkably similar to the medieval, European, Christian, Arthurian legend of the Fisher King (note the presence of a kingfisher by the lake at the beginning of Ashitaka's travels). In Christian legend, the Fisher King is also called the Grail King and the Wounded King; in some forms of the story, he is descended from Joseph of Arimathea, who donated the tomb of Christ (traditionally, the uncle of Christ who brought the Holy Grail to England). The name "Fisher King" comes from the tradition that, like Christ, the king fed many people from one fish caught in the river by his castle; however, the name may also be a play on the French *roi pecheur*, which means both "fisherman-king" and "sinner-king." The "fish" symbolism connects him with Christ, but, like Ashitaka, the fisher-king is a tainted hero.

According to most forms of the grail legend, the fisher-king, like Ashitaka, receives a terrible wound (the "dolorous blow"); thus he is also called the Wounded King. The wounding impairs the King's "sacred marriage" with the Land (in the medieval understanding, Lady Sovereignty), thus threatening his country with infertility (i.e., his wound is a threat to Nature). The only way for the King to be healed is for him to find the Holy Grail (the cup used at the Last Supper, which held the sacred "blood of Christ" and has magical healing properties and takes many forms)—the equivalent in *Princess Mononoke* is the casket containing the head of the Night Walker (remember that Lady Eboshi has heard that the blood of the Great Spirit/Shishigami can cure any illness). When the King finds the Grail, he must answer the Grail Question, which is "What is the purpose of the quest and what will it mean?" Only the Grail King who is qualified to attempt the quest will know the question and answer it for everyone to hear. In the movie, Ashitaka is only healed when he understands what the Forest Spirit (the Deer God/Night Walker) wants for the world: "He wants us to live." The twofold nature of the Fisher King/Ashitaka (the good king tainted by an evil wound) is similar to the Taoist idea of *yin* and *yang*, where light and dark, good and evil are seen not as mutually exclusive, but as intermingled and interdependent (no light without darkness, no goodness without evil). Even the demonic boar-god Nago, who inflicts the wound on Ashitaka, is a good kami (Shinto nature-spirit or god) gone bad; despite his being poisoned by hatred and fear, he is respected as a god by Ashitaka and the villagers.

Figure 1: Scene from *Princess Mononoke*

In the Christian Bible, the Tree of Life and the sacred waters appear *both* in Genesis *and* in Revelation (the End recapitulates the Beginning). In Rev 22:1–2, the prophet sees "the river of the water of life, bright as crystal, flowing from the throne of God and of the Lamb; . . . also, on either side of the river, the tree of life with its twelve kinds of fruit, yielding its fruit each month; and the leaves of the tree were for the healing of the nations." The primeval Garden becomes a holy city, where the marriage of the Lamb and his Bride is consummated; the holy couple ("the Spirit and the Bride," recapitulating the primal couple, Adam and Eve) invite everyone who is thirsty freely to drink the priceless water of life (Rev 22:17). The Garden and the City, nature and civilization, are unified and integrated.

In the film, the city, Iron Town, symbolizes the forces of civilization/industrialization pitted in a "last battle" against Nature/the gods, perceived by the townspeople as threatening and uncontrollable, and vice versa. The US version of *Princess Mononoke* was released in 1999, at around the same time when "apocalyptic/millennial" films and TV series were particularly popular. In all of these, the message was that the world as we know it was about to be destroyed, and only heroic action on the part of humanity could avert the disaster (killing the aliens, destroying the comet/asteroid, interpreting the apocalyptic signs). In contrast with traditional Christian eschatology, which holds that everything will inevitably get worse and worse, Christ will return to judge the world, and establish a perfect, eternal reign of peace and justice for the elect, in the "neo-millennialism" of popular culture, ultimate disaster can be dealt with once it is properly understood and decisively addressed (through science, military action, heroism, diplomacy, magic, technology, cooperation, etc.).

This neo-millennial theme that "ultimate disaster can be averted" is at work in *Princess Mononoke*, but within the context of the less linear notion (Hindu, Buddhist) that time is cyclical and endless, involving great cycles of creation, destruction and recreation. The main combatants in the "Last Battle" are not completely good or completely evil. Ashitaka is tainted by the poisonous wound; Mononoke, like her wolf/god/mother, is filled with hatred for humanity; the Lady Eboshi wants to "kill" nature/the gods (perceived as hostile and unpredictable) in order to ensure the survival of the lives of the people of Iron Town, especially "her" prostitutes and lepers. There is no simple "choice" to be made between the "simple" tribal lifestyle in harmony with nature/the gods and the harsh industrialization represented by the townspeople. The real enemies, who threaten Iron Town, the tribal peoples, and the realm of nature/the gods are the Samurai—representing the forces of militarism and imperialism—and the cynical monk, Jigo, whose only "value" is himself: "Everybody wants everything—that's the way the world is . . . but I just might get it!"

Miyazaki films are known for their ecological themes, and *Princess Mononoke* is no exception. The ultimate message of the film is that cutting Nature off from its "Head" leads to disaster. This is a critique of technology for its own sake, without regard for ecological processes and principles. The "life" that the Great Spirit wants for the world is only achievable when nature and civilization are no longer seen as opposites; when the city's *dependence* on nature is recognized, and the forces of nature are no longer "harnessed" without regard for their ecological interconnectedness; the townspeople finally realize that it is the Forest Spirit that "makes the flowers grow." When the "head" is restored to the "body" of the Night Walker transformed by the decapitation into "a brainless, swollen, life-sucking god of Death"—technology not informed by ecological processes—the Great Spirit is "resurrected" in a new form, as the divine force that pervades and integrates everything; the world is infused with "holy spirit."

The idea that the ostensibly violent and vengeful Christian Apocalypse could have an ecological message seems far-fetched, but as in this movie, the Last Battle in Revelation is waged against Babylon/Rome, personifying the forces of militarism, imperialism, and economic exploitation (Revelation 18); the judgement on the nations is for the reward of the "prophets and saints," but also for "destroying the destroyers of the earth" (11:18).

However, unlike the Christian Apocalypse, which relishes the destruction of the enemy, the "last battle" in *Princess Mononoke*, more realistically, is sad, tragic and destructive, and does not solve anything. Rather, it is the resolution to Prince Ashitaka's quest—the restoration of the Great Spirit's "head" and the answering of the "Grail Question" ("the Great Spirit wants us to live")—that leads to healing, reintegration and resurrection/renewal of nature and the city, and the initiation of a new age in the great cosmic cycle of creation and destruction.

Other Resources

Apocalypse: The Puzzle of Revelation. The History Channel, 1994.

McFague, Sallie. *Life Abundant: Rethinking Theology and Economy for a Planet in Peril*. Minneapolis: Fortress, 2001.

Parker, Rebecca Ann, and Rita Nakashima Brock. *Saving Paradise: How Christianity Traded Love of This World for Crucifixion and Empire*. Boston: Beacon, 2008.

Ray, Darby Kathleen, ed. *Theology that Matters: Ecology, Economy, and God*. Minneapolis: Fortress, 2006.

2

Sin and Salvation

In the mid-twentieth century, the German biblical scholar Hans Conzelmann coined the term *Heilsgeschichte*, "salvation history," to refer to the conception of history found in Luke-Acts. For Conzelmann, the author of the two volumes viewed history as comprised of three periods or ages: the time of the Law and Prophets, culminating in John the Baptist; the "center of time," the time of Jesus; and the time of the church.[1] This time scheme presupposes that the Jewish Scriptures (the Law and the Prophets) are preparatory to the revelation of Christ (the Gospel), who brings salvation to the world, a message to be spread by the church "in Jerusalem, in all Judea and Samaria, and to the ends of the earth" (Acts 1:8). For many Christians, this way of conceiving history seems very familiar, with Jesus as a savior figure who brings salvation to the world. But what does "salvation" mean in the Bible—and what does it mean to twenty-first century Christians? If Jesus saves, what does Jesus save from? This question leads to the question of sin. How does salvation relate to sin or does salvation relate to sin? This chapter explores these questions.

Surprisingly, the word translated as "salvation" (*sotēria*) is not used much in the Gospels, except for the Gospel of Luke (1:77; 2:30; 3:6; 19:9; the only other Gospel usage is in John 4:22). The Book of Acts carries through the theme (4:12; 13:26, 47; 16:17; 28:28). Similarly, Luke-Acts distinctively refers to Jesus as "savior" (*sotēr*) (Luke 1:69; 2:11; Acts 5:31; 13:23).[2] As Mark Allan Powell notes,

---

1. Conzelmann, *Theology of St. Luke*.
2. In the other Gospels, the term only appears in John 4:42.

Salvation, according to Luke-Acts, is available to all. Salvation is broadly conceived in these writings as participation in the reign of God, and, thus, as a present experience of life as God intends. This salvation is available because God has granted the Lord Jesus Christ the right to bestow salvation on whomever he chooses. People who wish to participate in the reign of God and desire to live as God intends receive this salvation when, through God's grace, they respond to the proclaimed word about Jesus with faith.[3]

For Luke, salvation is not connected with sin—in fact, the term sin (*hamartia*) only appears once in Luke (17:2), and only once in Acts, where the dying Stephen prays that God will not hold "this sin" against his persecutors (Acts 7:60).

As we will see below, Luke's understanding of salvation is consistent with the perspective of the Jewish Scriptures insofar as Luke does not connect salvation with sin. This chapter will explore biblical meanings of salvation, and discuss how these have been interpreted in Christian theology, especially in the light of the teachings of Paul—and how sin became connected with the idea of salvation. We will also show how the connection between sin and salvation was fully developed by Augustine of Hippo in the doctrine of original sin.

Biblical Meanings of Salvation and Sin

As Powell observes, "The Jewish world typically associated salvation [*yeshua*] with deliverance from enemies, while Greco-Roman society thought of salvation [*sotēria*] more in the bestowal of various blessings."[4] In the Jewish Scriptures, when the term salvation is used, it most often refers to the salvation of Israel, or of an individual, from danger. For example, in 1 Samuel 22, David thanks God for his salvation from his enemies, including the old king Saul:

> The LORD is my rock, my fortress, and my deliverer,
>
> my God, my rock, in whom I take refuge,my shield and the horn of my salvation, my stronghold and my refuge,
>
> my savior; you save me from violence.
>
> I call upon the LORD, who is worthy to be praised,
>
> and I am saved from my enemies. (2 Sam 22:3–4)

3. Powell, "Salvation in Luke-Acts," 5–11.

4. Ibid., 7.

Isaiah prays that God will see to the salvation of Israel every day, and especially in difficult times: "Be our arm every morning, and our salvation in the time of trouble" (Isa 33:2). Although it is assumed that God's salvation may be withheld if Israel is persistently disobedient (e.g., Deut 32:15), salvation is not particularly associated with sin; nor is it connected with afterlife beliefs (see chapter 5).

Christian readers may be puzzled as to why the story of Adam and Eve, and their fateful eating of the fruit of the knowledge of good and evil (Gen 3:1–24), is not front and center in this discussion. In Christian theology, the succumbing of the first couple to the temptation to disobey the divine command has become the explanation for the origin of sin in the world, and thus the need for salvation. As Elaine Pagels observes, the Hebrew creation account of Genesis tells the story otherwise: God granted humans the authority to rule in this royal dwelling place, the paradise ("pleasure-garden") of Eden. The God who created the world gave humanity moral freedom and free will.[5] It is no surprise, then, that there is no explicit mention of sin in Genesis story; the "curse" on Adam and Eve (3:16–17) can be interpreted, in its ancient socio-economic context, as explaining why women suffer in childbirth, and why men must toil in the fields in order to feed their families.

The well-known messianic interpretation of Gen 3:15, that Christ is the "seed" (offspring) of the woman who would crush the serpent's head, thus conquering sin, does not actually appear anywhere in the Bible; it is first attested in Irenaeus (second century CE).[6] Rather, the curse on the serpent (3:14–15) explains why snakes crawl on the ground ("upon your belly you shall go, and dust you shall eat all the days of your life"), why snakes bite people, and why people fear snakes ("I will put enmity between you and the woman, and between your offspring and hers; he will strike your head, and you will strike his heel"). Like the identification of the "offspring" with Christ, the idea that the serpent was Satan is only found in much later, mostly apocalyptic, writings.[7] In Genesis, as James L. Kugel observes, the serpent is simply one of the "beasts of the field," a clever animal with the power to lead people astray.[8] The presence of a talking animal in this

---

5. Pagels, *Adam, Eve, and the Serpent*, 98.

6. *Against Heresies* V.21.

7. See Kugel, *Bible As It Was*, 73–75.

8. Ibid., 72.

tale—one of only two in the Bible (cf. Num 21:22–39)—points to its literary genre as a fable: a story that conveys a moral (much like a parable).

Salvation in Christian Theology

Luke's understanding of salvation differs significantly from Paul's. As Powell observes:

> Surprisingly, Luke does not link salvation to Jesus' death on the cross (except, perhaps, in Acts 20:28). There is no reference in Luke to Jesus giving "his life as a ransom" (cf. Matt 20:28; Mark 10:45) or shedding his blood "for the forgiveness of sins" (cf. Matt 26:28). Instead, Luke finds the basis for salvation to be manifest in Jesus' life and in his resurrection/exaltation.[9]

As discussed in chapter 5, Paul is the Christian Testament theologian who tends to interpret salvation as deliverance from sin and death, personified as supernatural forces that only the power of Christ can conquer:

> Therefore just as one man's trespass led to condemnation for all, so one man's act of righteousness leads to justification and life for all. For just as by the one man's disobedience the many were made sinners, so by the one man's obedience the many will be made righteous. But law came in, with the result that the trespass multiplied; but where sin increased, grace abounded all the more, so that, just as Sin exercised dominion in Death, so grace might also exercise dominion through justification leading to eternal life through Jesus Christ our Lord (Rom 5:18–21).

Although Paul does sometimes use the term "salvation" to describe divine deliverance (Rom 1:16; 13:11; 2 Cor 1:6; 6:2; 7:10; Phil 1:28; 2:12; 1 Thess 5:8–9), he usually frames his arguments in Jewish terms of righteousness and justification.

Christian readers may not appreciate how ingenious, and rather strained, Paul's argument with respect to the relationship between the law, sin and justification is. During Paul's career as a Pharisee (Phil 3:5; Acts 23:6; 26:5), like his Jewish contemporaries, he fervently believed that the law (Torah) was adequate to deal with sin (violations of Torah) and impart righteousness to the Torah-observant. This does not mean that Jews of Paul's (or Jesus') time regarded Torah obedience as imparting permanent

---

9. Powell, "Salvation," 8.

moral perfection; rather, keeping Torah was a way of leading one's life in relationship with God, with provision for forgiveness when one fell short. As a Pharisee, like many (but not all) other Jews, Paul would have believed that as a righteous Jew, he would have a share in the resurrection in the world to come (see chapter 5). However, in the light of his intense mystical relationship with the exalted Christ, whom he experienced as savior (Phil 3:2), he was motivated to find a way to understand Jesus' role in the divine plan. His solution, as illustrated in the quotation above, was to substitute Christ for the law, and argue that the justification offered by Jesus was permanent and eternal. He was so fervently convinced that Jesus was the only means of justification before God that he vigorously opposed missionaries who taught that, like Jesus and the disciples, Christians, whether Jewish or Gentile, should remain obedient to Torah (Phil 3:1–3; Gal 2:15—3:15).

The Christian doctrine of original sin is not fully developed in the Christian Testament. Paul's teaching that Christ was a "second Adam" who rectified the sinfulness of the first human and thus made possible decisive spiritual salvation through the medium of faith in divine power to save was not shared by all early Christians for many centuries. For example, the Jewish-Christian Letter of James, addressed to "the twelve tribes of the dispersion" (1:1) admonishes its recipients that faith is only manifested when "works" of the "royal law of liberty" are part of one's everyday practice (2:14–26; see also 1:19–27), and recommends fervent prayer and mutual assistance as remedies against sinfulness and death (5:13–19).

The theologian who decisively formulated the Christian understanding of original sin was Augustine (354–430). Prior to his conversion to Christ, Augustine belonged to the sect of the Manicheans, a religion that sharply divided good from evil, light from darkness, spirit from matter. Even as a Christian, his worldview was shaped by the Manichean dualism that divided the world into good and evil/sinful.[10] This worldview also influenced his theological understanding of God (good) who was over and against the world (evil). Augustine believed that the human race belongs to this "evil" world because of the "fall" of the first humans, and that, beginning with Adam and Eve, sinfulness was transmitted through sexual reproduction to the whole human race throughout the generations. In Augustine's words, every human being is born with sin because of "the nature of the semen from which we were to be propagated."[11] Such an extreme

---

10. Heyward, *Saving Jesus*, 172.

11. Augustine, *The City of God*, cited in Pagels, *Adam, Eve, and the Serpent*, 109.

argument further strengthened his doctrine of the birth of Jesus as the sinless One who can thus save fallen humanity, since he was born without the medium of semen (through the virgin Mary). Issues of sexual politics and of the sexual body come to the fore here. Chapter 9 will deal with this issue extensively in connection with purity and sex.

As mentioned above, Paul was the first to connect salvation with the concept of sin in the Christian Testament. But Augustine's reading of Paul in Romans took a radically different stance from his predecessors and contemporaries including John Chrysostom. Pagels points out Augustine's idiosyncratic interpretation of Romans 5:12, contrasting it with that of Chrysostom. She writes,

> The Greek text reads, "Though one man [or "because of one man"] sin entered the world, and through sin, death; and thus death came upon all men, *in that* all sinned." John Chrysostom, like most Christians, took this to mean that Adam's sin brought death into the world, and death came upon all because "*all* sinned." But Augustine read the passage in Latin, and so either ignored or was unaware of the connotations of the Greek original; thus he misread the last phrase as referring to Adam. Augustine insisted that it meant that "death came upon all men, *in whom* all sinned"—that the sin of that "one man," Adam, brought upon humanity not only universal death, but also universal, and inevitable, sin.[12]

Augustine's teaching was forged in opposition to the argument of the Celt Pelagius, for whom the sin of Adam was merely a bad example, and who taught that human beings were capable of leading morally upright lives pleasing to God. The doctrine of original sin took many years to gain acceptance, and sparked riots in the streets of the city of Rome and throughout Africa and Europe. Christians were divided in their support of Augustine versus Pelagius. Those who advocated Pelagius, often influenced by Greek science and philosophy, argued that humans are given free will to make moral choices. History teaches us that Augustine and his supporters won the battle, and his views still prevail today. The message of human dignity and moral freedom that was taught by many ancient theologians was changed in the late fourth century and early fifth centuries into a doctrine of humanity's enslavement to sin. Augustine's radical argument that humans were incapable of goodness apart from divine grace, and that baptism was essential to wash away original sin, became highly influential in many

---

12. Pagels, *Eve, Adam, and the Serpent*, 109.

denominations in the Christian tradition, although it is interpreted differently in different confessions.

Certainly the understanding of sin has been far from unanimous. There has always been a spectrum from heavily individualistic understandings of sin that see it as something strictly personal, to a corporate notion that sees sin as structural, something that effects everything in systematic ways. Both ends of the spectrum and in-between spectrums can be found in most church denominations today. Generally a balance is sought by trying not to take one side at the expense of the other side. One such balanced perspective is found in The United Church of Canada's most recent theological statement of faith. It states, "We surrender ourselves to sin, a disposition revealed in selfishness, cowardice, or apathy. Becoming bound and complacent in a web of false desires and wrong choices, we bring harm to ourselves and others. This brokenness in human life and community is an outcome of sin. Sin is not only personal but accumulates to become habitual and systemic forms of injustice, violence, and hatred."[13]

Holding together both individual and corporate as well as personal and systemic aspects of sin is important when we pray. As long as we understand the world as marked by power differentials, we know there will be people who commit sins and people who are sinned against. Feminist liturgical theologian Marjorie Procter-Smith warns us that univocal prayer, the prayer that does not allow to hold both spectrums, assumes consent, as if there is only one possible response. "Prayer of confession in particular," she writes, "makes this presumption" and can thus be problematic.[14]

It is true that Augustine's theology of "original sin" prevailed and dominated in the western Christian traditions for centuries. But the Bible neither speaks of nor affirms such theology. In fact, many scholars and theologians from early on in the church have taken a more biblical stance. For example, Julian of Eclanum, the bishop of a provincial town in southern Italy who argued with Augustine in his later life, points out that Augustine's reading of Genesis and other readings including those of Paul in the Bible are misguided. With regards to Genesis 3, Julian argues, "nothing remains of all Augustine's arguments and propositions that has not been refuted . . . I proved that many things in his invention are false, many foolish, and many are sacrilegious."[15]

---

13. *Song of Faith: A Statement of Faith of The United Church of Canada L'Église Unie du Canada* (2006). http://www.united-church.ca/beliefs/statements/songfaith.

14. Procter-Smith, *Praying with Our Eyes Open*, 42.

15. Pagels, *Adam, Eve, and the Serpent*, 136.

Despite the criticism of many of our theological ancestors it remains the case that after 1600 years, Augustine's views are still prevalent in many churches and particularly in North American Christian culture.

Readers may, therefore, wonder why Christians cannot move beyond his teaching on "original sin" but continue to stumble over it. To answer this question, we need to locate the political and social contexts of the first four centuries in which Augustine lived as well as our own human state of mind. The pivotal change was the endorsement of Christianity as a legitimate religion of the Roman Empire in 313. Up until then, Christians were persecuted because Roman civil authorities regarded them as a subversive sect. In the context of religious oppression, many early Christians persevered and exercised their moral freedom and human dignity. This perseverance was manifested in their proclamation of human freedom as the heart of the Gospel and their continued faith in Jesus Christ, even though it cost their lives.[16] When Christians were no longer persecuted but received "magnanimous benefits" from the Christian emperors, things changed.[17] Such benefits had unintended consequences because the privilege came with strings attached. Willingly or not, church and state became inextricably interdependent. Christian theologians, including Augustine, began to justify the rule of the emperors as being divinely sanctioned. Christian emperors used military force to stamp out pagan worship. Augustine endorsed the emperor's rule as permanent and ineradicable, while acknowledging that that same rule was limited and corrupt. Such contradictory endorsements made sense to Augustine who entirely believed that nothing holy and perfect could issue from humanity or from this world. In this regard, Pagels' conclusion is persuasive:

> Augustine's theory of original sin could make theologically intelligible not only the state's imperfections but the church's imperfections as well. . . . It is Augustine's theology of the fall that made the uneasy alliance between the Catholic churches and imperial power palatable—not only justifiable but necessary—for the majority of Catholic Christians.[18]

Of course the current Christian context of North America is different from that of Augustine and Roman Empire era. Yet Christianity since the fourth century has enjoyed its privilege and inserted its political, economic,

16. Ibid., 99.

17. Ibid., 100.

18. Ibid., 119, 126.

and cultural power, certainly in Europe, for over a millennium. Even though Europe has become secular and Christianity is a becoming minority, it is far from being in a state of persecution. North American Christianity is not much different. While mainline Christian churches are dwindling and struggling, they still enjoy their own privilege and receive social and cultural benefit more than any other religious groups in society. Paul Kivel, researching the history of Christian hegemony, reveals how such social concepts as truth, judgement, and charity are shaped by Christian beliefs. He also notes how Christian ideas manifest in our lives consciously and subconsciously and influence the way we think and behave, even impacting large-scale institutional and public policy.[19] In this regard, the Christian reality of privilege has not changed much. That is why the discourse of original sin from privileged positions free from persecution may still make sense in the twenty-first century.

Another plausible reason why original sin has become so central to Christian tradition may be that uncontrollable and unexplainable events (death, disaster, illness) happen in human lives and that people tend to feel guilty or feel the need to assign blame to someone else, rather than feel completely helpless in the face of such events. Although the logic of an original sin that came from Adam does not make sense and it is neither rational nor scientific, this logic eases the feeling of pain and even comforts those who feel punished (as a result of sin). It is appealing to fragile and vulnerable people to know that it is not their fault but that they can blame their ancestors and attribute suffering to sinful human nature. The question of why bad things happen to good people haunts us when we are faced with unexpected suffering, as Rabbi Harold Kushner's popular book points out.[20]

Inevitably and admittedly as humans, we need to make sense out of suffering. Liturgical homiletic scholar Kathy Black provides six possible theological explanations of our effort to making sense of accidents that result in disabilities: 1) it is God's punishment for the sin of the disabled or for the sin of their parents; 2) it is God's test of their faith and character; 3) it is an opportunity for God to relate to persons with disabilities; 4) it presents an opportunity for the power of God to be made manifest; 5) suffering is redemptive; and 6) the mysterious omnipotence of God's will which we cannot know.[21] These explanations not only include this chapter's theme

---

19. Kivel, *Living in the Shadow of the Cross.*

20. Kushner, *When Bad Things Happen to Good People.*

21. Black, *Healing Homiletic*, 23.

of sin and salvation but they are also closely related to other themes of suffering and sacrifice. In chapter 10, the final chapter, we will deal with these latter themes further.

Jesus Christ, Superhero

As noted above, Paul portrayed Sin and Death as irresistible evil spiritual forces, and Christ as the only one with the power to destroy them in the resurrection:

> When this perishable body puts on imperishability, and this mortal body puts on immortality, then the saying that is written will be fulfilled:
>
> "Death has been swallowed up in victory."
>
> "Where, O death, is your victory? Where, O death, is your sting?"
>
> The sting of death is sin, and the power of sin is the law. But thanks be to God, who gives us the victory through our Lord Jesus Christ. (1 Cor 15:54–57)

The heroic portrayal is intensified in the Book of Revelation, Christ is portrayed as the mighty "rider on a white horse," portrayed in supernatural, militaristic terms:

> Then I saw heaven opened, and there was a white horse! Its rider is called Faithful and True, and in righteousness he judges and makes war. His eyes are like a flame of fire, and on his head are many diadems; and he has a name inscribed that no one knows but himself. He is clothed in a robe dipped in blood, and his name is called The Word of God. And the armies of heaven, wearing fine linen, white and pure, were following him on white horses. From his mouth comes a sharp sword with which to strike down the nations, and he will rule them with a rod of iron; he will tread the wine press of the fury of the wrath of God the Almighty. (Rev 19:11–15)

This is a far cry from the rabbi of Nazareth. It should be noted that, like other ancient apocalyptic writings, Revelation was written in the context of the oppression of believers; this portrayal of Christ as a heroic savior who will bring justice to the suffering people of God was meant to encourage the persecuted churches of Asia Minor.[22] The Apocalypse does not encourage

22. See, e.g., Schüssler Fiorenza, *Book of Revelation.*

its audience to engage in violent resistance against their Roman oppressors, but to await divine vindication.

In western culture, Christ is often understood as the ideal human being, the ultimate savior figure. In view of the kinds of biblical presentations of Jesus as a supernatural hero surveyed above, it is not altogether surprising that the pop culture figure of the superhero partakes in many characteristics of the Christ figure: powerful, yet self-sacrificing men with mysterious origins, dual identities and special destinies (divine and human, Superman and Clark Kent, Spiderman and Peter Parker).[23] Recently, this cultural tendency to portray superheroes in Christ-like terms was deliberately capitalized upon by the makers of the Superman movie *Man of Steel* (dir. Zack Snyder, 2013), which was marketed to pastors as a movie whose hero could be sermonically compared to Jesus Christ.[24] The scene illustrated in Figure 1 takes place in a church, where Clark Kent ponders his destiny to fight against evil in dialogue with his pastor, a stained glass Gethsemane scene framing his head.

Figure 1: *Man of Steel*, 2017

23. See, e.g., Jewett and Lawrence, *The Myth of the American Superhero*; Koslovic, "Structural Characteristics of the Cinematic Christ Figure."

24. See "'Man of Steel' marketers target Christians by sending pastors prepared sermons that compare Superman to Jesus Christ," http://www.dailymail.co.uk/news/article-2343165/Man-Steel-marketers-target-Christians-sending-pastors-prepared-sermons-compare-Superman-Jesus-Christ.html. See also "'Man of Steel' director Zack Snyder on Superman's Christ-like parallels," http://www.cnn.com/2013/06/14/showbiz/zack-snyder-man-of-steel/. A similar marketing strategy was used for the *Narnia* films and *The Passion of the Christ* (see http://www.christianitytoday.com/le/2013/june-on-line-only/man-of-steel-in-den-of-thieves.html).

In turn, the superhero figure has informed the presentation of Jesus in film. Most notably, Mel Gibson's *The Passion of the Christ* has been criticized not only for its extreme violence, but also for its portrayal of Jesus in the heroic terms familiar from films like *Braveheart* (1995):

> In many ways Gibson's passion movie has more in common with Gibson's own action movies than with previous Jesus films. Gibson knows that violence sells. While Gibson's focus on violence obscures the witness of the gospel writers, the main problem with his film lies in its interpretation of violence itself. For Gibson, Christ's love is measured by the amount of suffering he endures, namely: *more pain.*[25]

Armfriður Gudmundsdóttir argues that the effect of isolating the passion from the rest of the Gospel narrative is simply to glorify abuse, suffering and violence as necessary to salvation. Rita Nakashima Brock and Rebecca Ann Parker similarly contend that the claim that we are saved by the cross, the execution of Jesus, isolates Jesus. They write, "When the victims of violence are made singular, solitary, unprecedented in their pain, the power of violence remains."[26]

Far from looking at Jesus as superhero, there are a number of Christian theologians who elaborate the communal, and not the singular, nature of redemption, with respect to Christology. Carter Heyward views the cross of Jesus as the cost of seeking mutual relationship. She sees resurrection as the power of mutual relationship, a power which is stronger than sin and death. Rita Nakashima Brock names the power of Christ as "erotic power of Christa/Community," arguing that it is the communal relationship that enables Christ's redeeming act. Andrew Sung Park contends that salvation must be "relational and dynamic" in order to be liberative and reconciling. Don Schweitzer writes, "Jesus saves people, but people can also save Jesus through their response to him."[27] What these theologians claim in common is that the self-giving power in Christ is not unilateral or un-relational power. It is powerful because people in relationships, the followers of Jesus, believe in that power and push the power into activity. The power of redemption in general and of Christ or motherhood in particular does not come from one (extraordinary) individual, as if s/he exists out of context or out of history. It exists in many ultra-masculinized heroic movies where the

25. Gudmundsdóttir, *"Passion of the Christ,"* 205.
26. Brock and Parker, *Proverbs of Ashes*, 250.
27. Schweitzer, *Contemporary Christologies*, 45.

male fantasy of saving a woman or the whole world is lifted up and ideal-ized in the case of *The Passion of Christ*. Subsequent to the viewing of the Gibson film, a remark often made by audience members is that it helped them to understand how much Jesus had suffered for their salvation—an equation that is rarely made in the Christian Testament (the only reference that associates Jesus' suffering with the remission of sin is 1 Pet 3:18; see also 1 Pet 4:1). Gibson's portrayal of the suffering of Jesus goes far beyond anything in the Gospel passion narratives.

This fantasy of heroic masculinity operates in many ways in today's world, particularly through technologies that are given "near-salvific status" at the expense of the distortion of humanity as the image of God, Joyce Ann Mercer muses.[28] Therefore, it is important to emphasize the relationality of salvation, as a self-giving and self-receiving act, which requires responsibil-ity and accountability to the community. When a saving act is viewed as an individual selfless act of giving, it may seem that one person did all the work, without communal support. In contrast, when a saving act is viewed at a relational level, those unnamed and often regarded as unimportant can once again be seen as present and as instrumental in this act. Darby K. Ray says that one man's heroic self-sacrificial redemption of love is problematic because "it undermines the agency of women and children."[29] Even with Jesus, it was not a one-man show; there was community involvement. So circling back to the question at the beginning of this chapter, does salvation relate to sin in the Bible? The answer is "not very much," except in Paul's writings. The Bible rarely relates salvation to sin. Instead it is, the theology of original sin beginning with Augustine that relates salvation to sin that is still well and alive in churches and popular culture. The following movie attempts to challenge the view of the heroic solo salvation and that of a passive human sinful nature.

28. Mercer, "Virtual Sex, Actual Infidelity?," 74.
29. Ray, *Deceiving the Devil*, 105.

Sin and Salvation at the Movies

Watch: *Jesus of Montreal* (1989)[30]

Discussion Questions

Before the viewing

If you could make the ideal Jesus movie, what would it be like?

What meanings do the terms "sin" and "salvation" raise in your mind?

Have you seen any movies where the themes of sin and salvation are prominent?

After the viewing

How are the notions of sin and salvation represented in the movie?

How are the themes of sin and salvation worked out in the lives of the main characters?

How do the themes of this chapter relate to the film's critique of Montreal society in the late twentieth century? Or to twenty-first-century North American society?

Discussion Notes

A Jesus film that provides a very different perspective on salvation than *The Passion of the Christ* is Denys Arcand's *Jesus of Montreal* (1989). In this movie, set in 1980s Montreal, the main character, an unemployed actor named Daniel Coulombe, is invited by a priest to update the Lenten passion play. Daniel gathers together a band of four actors, two men and two women, and radically

---

30. Note: this movie was filmed in French; for best effect, we recommend watching the French version with English subtitles, rather than the dubbed version.

rewrites the old play in the light of historical research on the Gospels. The play is a dazzling success, and as the story of Daniel and his friends unfolds, they—and especially Daniel—begin to mirror the Gospel stories in their lives outside the play. The decision of church authorities to close down the play because of its "dangerous" portrayal of Jesus ends in tragedy, although there is a salvific aftermath that we will leave our readers to discover.

Although both are inspired by the medieval passion play genre, Gibson's *Passion of Christ* and *Jesus of Montreal* are very different. Unlike Gibson's film, *Jesus of Montreal* does not claim to be a historically accurate account of Jesus life—or, in Gibson's case, Jesus' last days, though such claim is not accurate, which we will discuss further in chapter 10.[31] The passion play staged by Daniel and his friends is clearly an outdoor dramatic performance, where the audience, and the security guard who ushers them from station to station, are very much in evidence. Despite its mysterious and challenging content, it is not the play, but the effect of the Jesus story on the actors where salvation resides in the film—not just for Daniel and his friends, but for the people of Montreal. Arcand portrays Montreal society of the late 1980s—especially the cultural and media elites—as shallow, superficial and cruel, out of touch with the simple, Christian values that were rejected—along with the Catholic Church—after the "Quiet Revolution" of the 1960s that brought secularization to Quebec. The values acted out by Daniel and his "disciples" are those that, Arcand implies, need to be revived:

> Daniel preaches a return to the holiness of human existence: salvation must be found within; don't give up on the meaningfulness of life; walk in solidarity; forget yourself and love one another; live simply.[32]

Daniel's preaching recalls and echoes the teaching of the early Christian theologians who believed that God had given humans free will, the will to choose goodness, the will to choose life and love without succumbing to sinful acts leading to death and hatred. *Jesus of Montreal* does not demand a wholesale return to the church, and the values modeled by Daniel are human values, portrayed by a very human and vulnerable Christ figure. Love, whether human or divine, is not demonstrated by suffering, or by superhuman heroism, but by mutual respect, caring and hope lived out in

---

31. Gudmundsdóttir, "*Passion of the Christ*," 203–4.

32. Beavis, "*Jesus of Montreal*," 150.

community. The response from the church group that viewed this film together in the winter of 2014 was that Arcand's film "got" Jesus in a way that other Jesus films do not.[33] Love, embodied as mutual care and communal hope, overcomes violence. This love is conducive to healing when "healing is neither a solitary nor simple journey. There is a synergy to grace."[34]

Figure 2: Scene from *Jesus of Montreal*

Other Resources

Craigo-Snell, Shannon, and Shawnthea Monroe. *Living Theology: A Pastoral Theology for Today*. Minneapolis: Fortress, 2009.
MacLean, Catherine Faith, and John H. Young. *Preaching the Big Questions: Doctrine Isn't Dusty*. Toronto: United Church Publishing House, 2015.
Man of Steel (dir. Zack Snyder, 2013).

33. This is a conclusion amplified by several generations of students in Mary Ann Beavis's Bible and Film course, taught at St. Thomas More College, The University of Saskatchewan.

34. Brock and Parker, *Proverbs of Ashes*, 248.

3

Moses and Jesus

THIS CHAPTER DISCUSSES MOSES in relation to Jesus, and Jesus in relation to Moses. It is divided into three parts. The first part shows how the Bible relates the two figures by employing a comparative reading of how they are depicted and understood. This is important to show that they are not separate but closely related, since each is the pre-eminent figure in the religious traditions of Judaism (Moses) and Christianity (Jesus), and the presentation of Jesus in the Christian Testament often echoes the role of Moses in the Jewish Scriptures.

The second part is an examination of Christian anti-Judaism in a religious tradition that claims to be founded on the teachings of the Jew, Jesus. We identify anti-Judaism and anti-Semitism as among the most critical issues that face Christians when we seek to learn what the Bible says. We will return to this theme in chapter 4 from another perspective.

Finally, we engage in a conversation with the film *Prince of Egypt*, in order to show how a pop culture presentation of the life of Moses can enhance our understanding of the Exodus story and its meaning for Christians. We argue that this film can be used as a teaching tool that can inform a nuanced reading of Moses and his significance for Christians. Based upon the experience of watching this film with a particular church group, we suggest further discussion questions and learning materials for such use.

Moses and Jesus: An Inter-Textual Reading

For Christians, what is the significance of Moses, apart from being one of many admired biblical characters who children learn about in Sunday

School? How can an understanding of the figure of Moses enhance our understanding of the Bible, of Jesus and the Gospels? In our church group viewing of the film *Prince of Egypt*, one woman commented that Moses was a Jew, so he must have had something to do with the Law. This is an understatement—and it also applies to Jesus! Technically, Moses was not a Jew; he was a descendant of Jacob/Israel (Gen 3:28), of the tribe of Levi, born in Egypt. He died before entering the Promised Land of Canaan, many centuries before the people of Judea started being called Jews. In Exodus, in fact, they are often called Hebrews, or the children of Israel. Scholars believe they were not one unified ethnic group, but many different groups who were fleeing oppression within the Empire of Egypt[1]—a "mixed multitude" (Exod 12:28).

As the great mediator of the Law (Torah), Moses is the most important human figure in the Jewish Scriptures, mentioned repeatedly in the Christian Testament as lawgiver, hero of faith, and prototype of Christ:

> By faith Moses was hidden by his parents for three months after his birth, because they saw that the child was beautiful; and they were not afraid of the king's edict. By faith Moses, when he was grown up, refused to be called a son of Pharaoh's daughter, choosing rather to share ill-treatment with the people of God than to enjoy the fleeting pleasures of sin. He considered abuse suffered for the Christ to be greater wealth than the treasures of Egypt, for he was looking ahead to the reward. By faith he left Egypt, unafraid of the king's anger; for he persevered as though he saw him who is invisible. By faith he kept the Passover and the sprinkling of blood, so that the destroyer of the firstborn would not touch the firstborn of Israel. (Heb 11:23–28)

In the Gospels, Jesus mentions Moses more often than any other human figure (Matt 8:4; 19:8; 23:2; Mark 1:44; 7:10; 10:3; 12:26; Luke 5:14; 16:29, 31; 20:37; 24:44; John 5:45, 46; 6:32; 7:19, 22, 23). Both the Jewish Scriptures and the Christian Testament mention Moses and the Exodus frequently, in different contexts. At the beginning of the book of Joshua, the crossing of the Jordan River into the Promised Land is compared to the crossing of the Red Sea (Josh 3:14–17; 4:21). The prophets often compare the return from exile in Babylon to the Exodus (Isa 40:1–33; Isa 43:15, 19; Jer 2:5–7; 31:31–33; 32:20–22; Ezek 20:5–19; Dan 9:14–16; Amos 2:10):

---

1. Gottwald, *Jewish Scriptures.*

Then they remembered the days of old, of Moses his servant. Where is the one who brought them up out of the sea with the shepherds of his flock? Where is the one who put within them his holy spirit, who caused his glorious arm to march at the right hand of Moses, who divided the waters before them to make for himself an everlasting name, who led them through the depths? (Isa 63:11–12)

In the rabbinic literature, it is said that heaven and earth were created only for the sake of Moses,[2] a very exalted statement about a human being in a religious tradition as monotheistic as early Judaism. It is also similar to early Christian statements about Jesus, like "for in him all things in heaven and on earth were created, things visible and invisible, whether thrones or dominions or rulers or powers—all things have been created through him and for him" (e.g., John 1:3; Col 1:16; Heb 1:2). Although Jews do not regard Moses as divine in the way as (most) Christians see Jesus, Moses is the most highly revered person in Jewish tradition. For Jews, he is *Moshe rabbenu*, "Moses our Teacher"—"The greatest of the prophets who saw God through a clear glass, while the other prophets saw him through a darkened glass."[3]

As a Jewish teacher, Jesus took the authority of the God-given Law of Moses seriously, as many of his sayings illustrate:

Then Jesus said to him, "See that you say nothing to anyone; but go, show yourself to the priest, and offer the gift that Moses commanded, as a testimony to them." (Matt 8:4).

For Moses said, "Honor your father and your mother"; and, "Whoever speaks evil of father or mother must surely die." (Mark 7:10)

And as for the dead being raised, have you not read in the book of Moses, in the story about the bush, how God said to him, "I am the God of Abraham, the God of Isaac, and the God of Jacob"? (Mark 12:26)

In fact, some of the earliest usages of the term *rabbi* ("my teacher") appear in the Gospels, where Jesus' disciples sometimes address him as such.

Then Peter said to Jesus, "Rabbi, it is good for us to be here; let us make three dwellings, one for you, one for Moses, and one for Elijah." (Mark 9:5)

2. *Leviticus Rabbah* 36.4.

3. "Moses," *Dictionary of Jewish Lore and Legend*, 141.

When Jesus turned and saw them following, he said to them, "What are you looking for?" They said to him, "Rabbi" (which translated means Teacher), "where are you staying?" (John 1:38)

Nathanael replied, "Rabbi, you are the Son of God! You are the King of Israel!" (John 1:49)

Although in Jesus' time the title may not have had the later, full-blown Jewish meaning of expert in Torah interpretation, as rabbi, Jesus the Jewish teacher is asked questions concerning the interpretation of the Law, and he answers them with reference to Moses. He warns a group of Pharisees not to circumvent Moses's command to honor one's parents by withholding support from them, even on religious grounds (Mark 7:9–13); he uses the "book of Moses" to support the belief in resurrection (Mark 12:18–27); he answers a question about the legitimacy of divorce, which he admits the Law of Moses allows, by referring back to the first book of Torah:

But Jesus said to them, "Because of your hardness of heart [Moses] wrote this commandment for you. But from the beginning of creation, "God made them male and female." "For this reason a man shall leave his father and mother and be joined to his wife, and the two shall become one flesh." So they are no longer two, but one flesh. Therefore what God has joined together, let no one separate." (Mark 10:5–9)

By using Torah to explicate Torah (Deut 24:1; Gen 2:24), Jesus offers an interpretation of the Law that strictly limits a man's right to divorce, and that expresses the radical opinion that a man could commit adultery against his wife (Mark 10:10–12). His summary of the Law in answer to the scribe's question (Mark 12:28–34) is echoed in stories of rabbis who are able to express the essence of Torah in a single commandment:

One of the scribes came near and heard them disputing with one another, and seeing that he answered them well, he asked him, "Which commandment is the first of all?" Jesus answered, "The first is, 'Hear, O Israel: the Lord our God, the Lord is one; you shall love the Lord your God with all your heart, and with all your soul, and with all your mind, and with all your strength.' The second is this, 'You shall love your neighbour as yourself.' There is no other commandment greater than these." (Mark 12:28–31)

In a similar story, when Rabbi Hillel was challenged to recite the entire Torah while standing on one foot, he replied with a version of the Golden

Rule: "What is hateful to you, do not do to your neighbor. That is the whole *Torah*. The rest is commentary. Go and learn it!"[4] (cf. Matt 7:12). This does not mean that Jesus—or his older contemporary Hillel—taught that his followers could cut corners in their observance of the Law, as this passage from the Sermon on the Mount illustrates:

> Do not think that I have come to abolish the law or the prophets; I have come not to abolish but to fulfil. For truly I tell you, until heaven and earth pass away, not one letter, not one stroke of a letter, will pass from the law until all is accomplished. Therefore, whoever breaks one of the least of these commandments, and teaches others to do the same, will be called least in the kingdom of heaven; but whoever does them and teaches them will be called great in the kingdom of heaven. For I tell you, unless your righteousness exceeds that of the scribes and Pharisees, you will never enter the kingdom of heaven. (Matt 5:17–20).

In Matthew's Jewish-Christian Gospel,[5] the fulfillment of the Law and the Prophets—with the Writings, two of the three divisions of Jewish scripture—is taken very literally. As Aaron M. Gale observes, stipulating that the disciples' righteousness in fulfilling the Law must exceed that of the scribes and Pharisees sets the bar high, since the Pharisees were known for their righteousness.[6] Jesus was not attempting to break away from Judaism, or even to purify it, but to engage with Torah in dialogue and debate with other Jewish teachers. This does not mean that Jesus had all the answers and that "the Jews" were wrong about Torah; rather, Jesus was a Jewish teacher in conversation, debate and disagreement with other Jewish teachers.

In the Book of Acts, Peter delivers a sermon in the Temple in which he cites an ancient prophecy that God will raise up a prophet like Moses to deliver his people (Acts 3:22, citing Deut 18:15–18), whom he interprets as Jesus, the Messiah. The Gospels carefully portray Jesus not only as an authoritative interpreter of Moses, but as a prophet whose words and deeds echo and even surpass those of the great Lawgiver. In the Gospel of Matthew, Jesus, like Moses, is born during the reign of a wicked king, and narrowly escapes being massacred at the king's command (2:16–28). Also

---

4 Stern, *Jewish Christian Testament Commentary*, 33.

5. By "Matthew's Jewish-Christian Gospel," we mean the Gospel that was written primarily for Jewish-Christians as the intended audience; the Gospel of Luke, in contrast, was primarily written for Gentile, meaning non-Jewish, Christians.

6. Gale, "Matthew," *Jewish Annotated New Testament*, 10.

in Matthew, Jesus and his family replicate Israel's migration to Egypt and their return to the Promised Land by divine intervention (2:19–23). While Moses grew up in Egypt, he fled the country after murdering an Egyptian and settled in Midian (Exod 2:15). Later, he returned to Egypt to face Pharaoh (Exod 4:18). The Gospel of Matthew, especially, suggests a similarity between Moses and Jesus in the theme of forced migration to and from Egypt. Not only is their experience of displacement shared, but so is the cause of that experience, namely the threat from authority.

The parallels go on. In Matthew, Jesus climbs up a mountain and delivers authoritative teaching that fulfills the Law and the Prophets (5:1–7:29), reminiscent of Moses on Mount Sinai. All four Gospels contain stories of miraculous feedings where God provides bread for his people in the desert, echoing the manna in the wilderness (Mark 6:30–44; 8:1–10; Matt 14:13–21; 15:32–39; Luke 9:10–17; John 6:1–14; cf. Exod 16:1–3; Num 11:1–9). John's Gospel underlines and interprets the parallel: "Then Jesus said to them, 'Very truly, I tell you, it was not Moses who gave you the bread from Heaven, but it is my Father who gives you the true bread from heaven. For the bread of God is that which comes down from heaven and gives life to the world'" (6:32–33). In the Gospel transfiguration narratives, Jesus appears together on a mountaintop with Moses and Elijah (Mark 9:2–8; Matt 17:1–8; Luke 9:28–36; cf. 2 Pet 1:16–18); in Jesus' time, two prophets whose appearance was associated with the Day of the Lord (Mal 4:4–6; Deut 18:15–18). These many similarities and overlaps suggest that not only do Moses and Jesus have a lot in common, but the faiths in which they are revered as founding figures were born of similar experiences and stand for similar things: justice, integrity, the reign of God. There is an obvious parallel between Moses and Jesus and the faiths they represent.

As reflected in Matthew's Gospel, some early Christians followed Jesus' example of Torah observance, and lived in accordance with the demanding traditions of Torah interpretation that he had left them, to "be perfect, as your heavenly father is perfect" (Matt 5:48). For these disciples, as for other Jews of the time, to fulfill the Law was to obey it, to live it out wholeheartedly, in accordance with the divine command of the *Shema* (Deut 6:4–9), which is quoted in all three Synoptic Gospels (Mark 12:28–34; Matt 22:34–40; Luke 20:25–28):

> Hear, O Israel: The LORD is our God, the LORD alone. You shall love the LORD your God with all your heart, and with all your soul, and with all your might. Keep these words that I am commanding

you today in your heart. Recite them to your children and talk about them when you are at home and when you are away, when you lie down and when you rise. Bind them as a sign on your hand, fix them as an emblem on your forehead, and write them on the doorposts of your house and on your gates.

Today, some Christian educators and scholars of religious education call the *Shema* the core and the foundation of Christian education.[7] This means that Christian formation is bound up with Jewish religious formation and education. If that is the case, one may wonder where the Christian problem of anti-Semitism and anti-Judaism came from and why such problems continue. For Christians, a self-critical examination is in order.

Christianity and Anti-Judaism

As more and more non-Jews ("Gentiles") were attracted by the missionary preaching, the question of the status of the Law for converts became a live issue in the early Christian communities. Should non-Jews be required to convert to Judaism, and become Torah-observant—like Jesus and the disciples (Acts 15:5)? Should Gentiles be released from full Torah observance, but required to follow some minimal requirements out of respect for the Law of Moses, and out of regard for the sensitivities of Jewish Christians (Acts 15:19–21)? Or, as Paul taught, should Christians, both Jewish and Gentile, be released from Torah observance since believers had been "justified" (made righteous before God) in Christ? In the early church, debates on these matters persisted for many years, but for most Christians, Paul's lenient teaching prevailed, leading to the development of a new religion that became profoundly different from Judaism, and, tragically, often anti-Jewish, founded on the conviction that Christianity had "replaced" Judaism, and, ironically, that only Christians understood the true meaning of the Jewish Scriptures!

Since then, Christians (unconsciously and consciously) have attempted to dismiss and even to demonize Judaism. For example, the text mentioned above dealing with the divorce law in the Torah has been used and abused to prove how oppressive and outdated Judaism is, while in contrast, following Jesus' "Christian" teaching is liberating. Even in the Christian Testament, the debates of Jesus with Pharisees, Jewish religious scholars, sometimes paint Jesus as merciful and righteous and the

7. Tye, *Basics of Christian Education.*

Pharisees as harsh and unrighteous. The Gospel of Matthew even calls them "hypocrites"—"play-actors" (Matt 15:7). The long-standing anti-Jewish reading of the Christian scriptures and its theology of supersessionism, the idea that (new=superior) Christianity "replaces" (old=obsolete) Judaism, are problems that Christians must face. Here, a critical and transformative Christian education is necessary. Although Moses was not technically and chronologically a Jew, the comment from our focus group that Moses was a Jew, and as such, must have had something to do with the Law, offers a pedagogical moment for further learning and deeper understanding.

For such learning, we turn to the Jewish feminist scholar Judith Plaskow as a pedagogical example, teaching us how the Bible has been interpreted with an anti-Jewish bias, even by a group of scholars who would publicly deplore the denigration of Jews—Christian feminist theologians. This interpretive tendency is not confined to feminist theologians, but goes back to the earliest decades of the church, and that is deeply embedded in Christian theology. Anti-Jewish themes and strategies can be traced back as early as the Christian Testament (e.g., Matt 27:25; John 8:43–47; Acts 7:51–53; 1 Thess 2:14–16; Titus 1:1–14). Christian feminist anti-Judaism can be dated as early as 1885 when Elizabeth Cady Stanton's *Woman's Bible* was published.[8] For example, in her commentary on Exodus, Stanton remarks that the only value of much of the Jewish Scriptures "is to show us the character of the Jewish nation, and make it easy for us to reject their ideas as to the true status of woman, and their pretension of being guided by the hand of God, in all their devious wanderings."[9] In her commentary on Numbers, Stanton comments that "such records are enough to make the most obstinate believer doubt the divine origin of Jewish history and that claim of that people to have been under the special guidance of Jehovah."[10]

Katharina von Kellenbach identifies three signs of the anti-Jewish tendency operative in Christian thought. The first is the sign is the use of *antithesis*. Antithesis is the setting up of a dualistic opposition, Judaism as negative and Christianity as positive. Our discussion of the divorce law is a good example. The text is taken to mean that the teaching of Moses and that of Pharisees are bad, while that of Jesus is good, when in fact it reflects an inner-Jewish dialogue regarding the intention of the Torah's marriage legislation. The second sign that anti-Judaism is at work is in the use of a

8. Plaskow, "Anti-Judaism in Feminist Christian Interpretation," 117.

9. Stanton and the Revising Committee, *The Woman's Bible*, 72–73.

10. Ibid., 119–20.

scapegoat, making the Jews to blame for something. For example, Jews have been blamed for the death of Jesus. More examples of this Jew-blaming can even be found in the Gospels (e.g., Matt 27:25). More recently and most disastrously it was deployed by Hitler and the Nazis. This use of a scapegoat has a more modern example as well. It can also be found, Plaskow contends, in Christian feminist discussion, blaming Jews for patriarchy.[11] Jews are made responsible for inventing and inflicting patriarchal religion on the world, which Christianity is seen as either remedying, or callously perpetuating, contrary to the feminist intent of Jesus.

The third sign indicating the presence of anti-Judaism is the use of *prologue*, that is, seeing "Judaism," conflated with the "Jewish Scriptures," as a preparation for Christianity, as opposed to a living and growing religion. The Christian theology of supersessionism—Judaism is replaced by Christianity—is a prime example.[12] The very terminology of "Jewish Scriptures" and "Christian Testament" illustrates this anti-Jewish tendency; here, "old" implies antiquated, whereas "new" implies fresh and relevant. Little wonder, then, why Moses has been downplayed in Christianity, since he is interpreted as the "prologue" of Jesus, who as fulfillment of prophecy, replaces him.

All of these tendencies are found in Christian writings throughout church history. As noted above, even Christian feminists have unintentionally promoted anti-Judaism when seeking to prove how liberating and feminist Jesus was in contrast to how sexist and constraining Judaism was—as if Jesus was not a Jew, who likely gained his pro-woman attitudes from his tradition. Plaskow extensively examines various Christian European and American White feminists' antithetical interpretations of the Christian Testament marriage and the divorce teachings against Judaism.[13] In the search for proto-feminist Christian Testament writings, Christian feminists stumble over Paul, who cannot be wholeheartedly painted as feminist, unlike Jesus, with his allegedly unique and consistent feminist stance. Thus "the many contradictions that plague Paul's work" appear to create a split

11. Plaskow, "Blaming Jews for the Birth of Patriarchy."

12. von Kellenbach, "Anti-Judaism in Christian-Rooted Feminist Writing," 57, cited in Plaskow, "Anti-Judaism," 118–19.

13. Plaskow, "Anti-Judaism," 119–24. She examines the work of Leonard Swidler who first claimed that Jesus was a feminist, along with the writings of Elisabeth Moltmann-Wendel and Rosemary Radford Ruether, who falls into the trap of painting Judaism as oppressive towards women "after warning that Jesus' iconoclasm toward women's subordination should not be used as the basis of a new anti-Judaism" (121).

identity, "a Jewish and a Christian Paul" where the "Jewish Paul" is "un-relievedly misogynist," while "Christian Paul" is non-sexist thanks to "the revelation of God in Christ."[14] Thus Christian feminists seek to sanitize Jesus and Paul from their Jewish ways to the point that their very Jewishness is downplayed or even denied. This is a dangerous move for Christian feminists—or for any Christian—to make, for it can lead to anti-Judaism, opposition to the Jewish religion, or even anti-Semitism, that is social, ethnic, and racial hatred toward Jews. Plaskow's advice for Christian feminists is instructive for all Christians: "Clearly the dilemma for feminist interpreters is that acknowledging the Jesus movement as a movement within Judaism would undercut claims about Jesus' *Christian* uniqueness. If he was simply a Jew, his attitudes towards women would represent not as a victory *over* early Judaism but a possibility *within* it."[15]

Since Plaskow's sharp and thorough criticism of white Christian feminist anti-Jewish interpretation in the 1980s, there have been many writings in the same vein, among which is the work of Amy-Jill Levine, a Jewish feminist Christian Testament scholar.[16] Her work is particularly worth examining because it names the problem of anti-Judaism in non-white, non-western women's writings for the first time.[17] Levine unapologetically critiques these writings as perpetuating anti-Jewish interpretations, while challenging women scholars from non-European and non-North American nations with the statement that "a history of marginalization need not grant a moral high ground."[18] Her critique is poignant for those of us non-white scholars and teachers who address the interlocking oppressions of women related to gender, class, race, and colonialism. We are "cognizant of the dangers of dividing marginal from marginal in the struggle for liberation" which is how a colonial logic of divide and conquer works.[19] For those of us who are of white, European or European descent, the work of revealing the anti-Judaism embedded in non-white, non-western feminist work is also not an easy path to take since we can be easily "perceived to be silencing those who previously had been silenced," and be vulnerable to the

14. Plaskow, "Anti-Judaism," 122–23.

15. Ibid., 124.

16. Levine, "Lilies of the Field and Wandering Jews," 229–252.

17. Kwok comments on this fact. See "Roundtable Discussion," 99.

18. Levine, "Disease," 99.

19. Ibid., 92.

charge of racism.[20] Not surprisingly, therefore, Levine's critiques have provoked heated debates, some of which bore helpful and constructive fruit. Here we present the work of Kwok Pui-lan as an example of such fruit to conclude this section on Christian anti-Judaism.

Fully mindful of the anti-Judaism that is sometimes embedded not only in white feminist theology but also in the work of some non-white feminists, Kwok states that "anti-Semitism was an integral part of the colonialist discourse used to oppress colonized people."[21] Her critique is important because she successfully names the intersection between anti-Judaism, sexism, and colonialism. She acknowledges that anti-Semitism, women's subordination, and colonialism all operate within the nineteenth-century European religious framework: "The imperial impulse of cleansing the Jews as the Others within Europe had much to do with the universalizing of Western culture and homogenizing the Others from without."[22] It is critical in Christian education about anti-Judaism that we expose and dislodge the Eurocentric and ethnocentric biases that are so entrenched in Christian theology and biblical interpretation. This work is something that both non-White, non-European Christians and Jewish people may mutually benefit from as they strive towards a wider Jewish-Christian dialogue. As Kwok convincingly argues, "If we were to see the Jesus movement not as an innovation of Jesus, but as a reform or emancipatory movement within Judaism, Christian feminists from the Third World could dialogue with Jewish feminists about how to assess the emancipatory nature of this movement."[23] Such dialogue is not limited to Christian women in the developing world but extended to all Christians who yearn for learning and reading the Bible in ways that are free from the biases of anti-Judaism and anti-Semitism. As Levine has remarked with respect to the anti-Judaism disease: "all we can do is alleviate the manifest symptoms and continually apply booster shots where needed."[24] We think that is a good goal for this chapter as well, where we now turn to the final section.

---

20. Ibid., 98–99.

21. Kwok, "Roundtable Discussion," 101.

22. Kwok, *Postcolonial Imagination*, 49–50.

23. Ibid., 94.

24. Levine, "The Disease," 132. The five responders are Kwok Pui-lan from Hong Kong and the United States, Musimbi Kanyoro from Africa, Adele Reinhartz, a Jewish Canadian, Hisako Kinukawa from Japan, and Elaine Wainwright from Australia.

Moses and Jesus in Dialogue

Watch: *Prince of Egypt* (1998)

Discussion Questions

Before the viewing

What do you know about the figure of Moses?

What is the significance of Moses for Christians?

Did it ever occur to you to relate the figures of Moses and Jesus?

After the viewing:

What are some of the main themes of the movie? Is it just a simple retelling of the Book of Exodus? Does it have any significance for Christians?

Does the character of Moses remind you of Jesus in any way? Does Jesus remind you of Moses?

What stereotypes about Judaism and the Jewish Scriptures does the movie challenge?

How does the movie address the issue of religious violence?

Discussion Notes

While it seems contradictory to claim Christian superiority over Judaism while at the same time citing Jewish Scriptures as foundational for Christian faith, such claims continue to be made. We can find them in many places, including televised sermons and modern efforts at converting Jews to Christianity. In this dangerous and unfortunate situation, viewing *The Prince of Egypt* together with a church group was illuminating and encouraging. Here we would like to share some of the perspectives and

45

interpretations that viewing and discussing the film can offer towards more biblically and theologically informed approaches.

The movie *The Prince of Egypt* was made with care and research. While Steven Spielberg, an American diaspora Jew, did not direct the movie, he was behind the movie as one of its executive producers from its very beginning, together with another Jew, Jeffrey Katzenberg.[25] As such, they strove for "historical and theological accuracy" when dealing with the Exodus story. They were also concerned with its interfaith and religious implications. In the process of making it they invited "Bible scholars, Christian, Jewish and Muslim theologians, and Arab American leaders to help his movie be accurate as well as excellent. After previewing the developing animated Bible story, all these leaders noted that the studio executives listened and responded to their ideas, and praised the studio for reaching out for comment."[26]

Contrary to anti-Jewish sexist stereotypes, this film portrays women as strong leaders and teachers who nurture Moses to find his identity and vocation. The figure of Miriam stands out in this regard. As the sister of Moses, she is resilient, persistent and prophetic from the moment she meets the adult Moses who is himself confused about his own identity as a Prince of Egypt. This important role continues all the way through the crossing of the Red Sea. In the movie, the woman who rescues Moses from the river and allowed Moses's birth mother to nurse him is portrayed as the wife of the Pharaoh rather than his daughter. Though seemingly incorrect from the standpoint of the canonical Bible, the identification of Moses's foster-mother as Pharaoh's wife follows Muslim scripture (Qur'an 28:9). Jewish tradition praises Moses's Egyptian mother Batya, "daughter of God," for her role in the salvation of Israel.

25. See http://www.assistnews.net/strategic/s0000023.htm. The director of this movie, Jeffrey Katzenberg, was sitting at the living room of the Spielberg's home, posing this idea of making an animated movie. Katzenberg recalls that Spielberg looked at him for two seconds and said, "Good, you ought to do the Ten Commandments."

26. See http://www.assistnews.net/strategic/s0000023.htm.

Figure 1: Moses and his foster mother, *Prince of Egypt*

In the case of Moses's call from the burning bush to lead his people, the Bible does not describe his inner struggle, or his possible unwillingness to be part of the events that involve so much killing of the people of Egypt. While many interpreters of the Bible have endorsed such violence as "holy war" and justified it as "God's victory," *Prince of Egypt* shows Moses's tormented emotions in contemplating the death of his own Egyptian friends and family, although they were oppressors and enemies of the Hebrews. This allows those of us who know the story to further critically investigate our own wrongdoings, including religiously sanctioned violence that Christians have committed against other religious groups and other people throughout centuries.

During our small group discussion, one person commented on how violent some of the scenes in the movie were, and asked if this was a good movie to show to children. This question prompted a further discussion about Christian education with respect to children and youth.[27] The movie powerfully depicts the ambiguous view of the violence enacted on the Egyptians by God under Moses's leadership. The focus group discussion also touched on the danger of teaching the Bible as if it contains nothing bad, ugly or violent. The group strongly felt that because it is a difficult story to watch, we must not avoid the challenge of viewing it. The ugly face of violence should not be ignored in Christian education but shared

27. Dalton, *Video, Kids, and Christian Education*.

openly with care, honesty, and integrity.[28] In fact, the focus group consisted of adults and children (mostly under thirteen years of age), and we were able to share our feelings of horror, this unresolved feeling about what we and/or God had done. Theologian Fumitaka Marsuoka calls this "holy insecurity." He argues that the ability to reside in the unsettled and unsettling space within the biblical narrative is a discipline that we must cultivate. He further suggests that the discipline of holy insecurity is necessary if transformative learning is to occur.[29]

Finally, this movie offers ways to engage in Jewish-Christian dialogue. Since the movie-making process was highly inter-religious, as mentioned above, it may be fruitful to encourage this aspect of learning in congregational levels. Given that the church where our discussion took place has a connection with a nearby synagogue, such a suggestion was definitely a viable option to pursue further. It may be interesting and illuminating to hear what Jewish sisters and brothers think of the movie, as we continue to explore the role of Moses in Judaism in relation to that of Jesus in Christianity together.

Other Resources

Boys, Mary C. *Has God Only One Blessing? Judaism as a Source of Christian Self-Understanding*. New York: Paulist, 2000.

Levine, Amy-Jill. *The Misunderstood Jew: The Church and the Scandal of the Jewish Jesus*. San Francisco: HarperCollins, 2009.

Levine, Amy-Jill, and Marc Zvi Brettler, eds. *The Jewish Annotated New Testament*. Oxford: Oxford University Press, 2011.

---

28. Kim-Cragg raises this issue in *Story and Song*, 47.

29. Matsuoka, *Out of Silence*, 62.

4

Jews and Christians

THIS CHAPTER NOT ONLY follows, but builds upon, the last chapter on Moses and Jesus. Here, we explore the reasons why it is so common for Christians to assert that "Jesus was a Jew," while at the same time holding naively anti-Jewish views—such as that "the Jews" didn't recognize their own Messiah, or that the "new covenant" has made the "old covenant" with Israel obsolete, or by mistaking the "Jewish Scriptures" for "Judaism." Here, we will investigate anti-Jewish attitudes embedded in the Christian Testament with special reference to the work of Jewish scholars who study the Christian Testament, exploring the implications of such material for Jewish-Christian relations. Since many Christians know little about Judaism as it is practiced by Jews in modern, as opposed to biblical, times, the movie feature for this chapter is *The Chosen* (1981).

Jesus the Jew

What does it mean to say that Jesus was Jewish? Not that he was a Jew who opposed Judaism, or who meant to found a new religion. Jesus was born as a Jew, was brought up as a Jew, died as a Jew, and, Christians believe, rose to new life as a Jew. As discussed in chapter 3, he was Torah-observant. Jewish scholar Paula Fredriksen observes:

> Jesus . . . if we can judge by some synoptic passages and from the Q material surviving in the Sermon on the Mount, extended and intensified the Torah's commandments. But—as we should expect from a lay leader of a lay movement—he focused on the moral aspects of these. . . . It should be noted here that his teaching in

the Sermon on the Mount is not presented as an alternative to Torah, despite the way we might hear Matthew's rhetoric ("You have heard it said. . . . But I say. . . . "). Jesus here does what later rabbis will term "building a fence around the Torah"; that is, he prescribes rules of behavior that extend the prohibition, thus ensuring that the biblical command cannot be broken.[1]

Jesus lived during a period of Jewish history known by scholars as the Second Temple period. This period saw the development of multiple religious renewal movements. The era of Second Temple Judaism can be described as a period of plural "Judaisms"—think of the Pharisees and Sadducees mentioned in the Gospels, or the Essenes, sometimes identified with the authors of the Dead Sea Scrolls. In Egypt, the Jewish intellectual, Philo of Alexandria, an older contemporary of Jesus, sought to interpret the Jewish Scriptures in the light of Platonic philosophy. Jesus grew up in this fertile religious context, a fruitful, fluid time, open to many religious possibilities.

Jesus was baptized by John the Baptist, a charismatic Jewish teacher and leader. Since Jesus is by far the dominant figure in the Gospels, it is surprising to see Jesus portrayed as undergoing baptism, a ritual of repentance (Mark 1:4; Matt 3:11; Luke 3:3), by another Jewish prophet. Many scholars think that Jesus was initially a disciple of John, who carried on this mission of preaching repentance in view of the imminent arrival of the Reign of God. Thus, John's influence on Jesus should not be underestimated. As Christian theologian Don Schweitzer observes:

> Both John and Jesus were Jews. Neither departed from underlying assumptions shared by the divergent movements within Second Temple Judaism and thus by the other Jewish religious leaders and institutions they criticized. Their criticisms and denunciations were part of an inner Jewish debate at that time about the nature and purpose of God. They were in no way a criticism of Judaism per se.[2]

Another aspect of Jesus' Jewish identity is suggested by his geographical location. The Gospels refer to him as from Nazareth in Galilee. The Galilean context suggests that Jesus, like many Jews of his time, grew up in a broad and diverse cultural context in which encounters with people other

---

1. Fredriksen, *Jesus of Nazareth*, 104.
2. Schweitzer, *Jesus Christ for Contemporary Life*, 15.

than Jews were very possible.[3] It also means that while he was faithfully Jewish, he had dealings with non-Jews, a fact that is indicated in the record of his ministry. The Gospel stories tell how Jesus connected with various non-Jews ("gentiles") to heal their sickness and save them from their suffering (e.g., Mark 5:1–20; 7:24–30, 31–37; Matt 8:4–12; Luke 7:1–10). Ultimately Jesus mediated God's acceptance, while proclaiming the Reign of God. Here the Reign of God is a concept offered in contrast to the Roman Empire. That is to say, the Reign (Kingdom) of God exists for the sake of the "well-being and freedom for all," similar to the Jewish concept of *tikkun olam*, "restoration of the world."[4]

Theologically, Christians affirm the Gospel of John's teaching, "The Word became flesh" (John 1:14). Christians believe in God incarnate in the person of Jesus, a Jew. St. Augustine taught that this claim is ultimately incomprehensible because speaking of God in Jesus is "to speak in some way about that which we cannot fully express in any way."[5] Knowing this limit, the understanding of Jesus as the Word of God incarnate points to the historical reality of God's lived history on earth. God is expressed in history rather than beyond or outside history. That is why Jesus's teaching of the Reign of God is important because this Reign of God is not about a reality beyond this world but instead one right here on this earth, in this life rather than the next. It also affirms the beauty and the goodness of creation, the material, the bodily, and the incarnational elements of life.[6] As discussed in chapter 1, creation's intrinsic value is in line with and compatible with the incarnational nature of Jesus as imaging God, the cosmic source of life for all.

The Christian Testament and Anti-Judaism

There are numerous passages in the Christian Testament that may easily lend themselves to anti-Judaism and antisemitism (e.g., 1 Thess 2:14–16; Matt 27:22–23; Luke 3:7; Matt 27:7; 12:34; 23:33).[7] Here, "anti-Judaism" is defined as prejudice against Jewish people based on religion, an attitude

3. Crossan, *Historical Jesus*, 16–19.

4. Schüssler Fiorenza, *Jesus: Miriam's Child, Sophia's Prophet*, 89–90.

5. Augustine, *The Trinity* 7.4.7.

6. Moltmann, *Theology of Joy*, 50–51.

7. For a more complete discussion of potentially anti-Jewish material in the Christian Testament, see Levine, *The Misunderstood Jew*, 87–118.

that Christians throughout history have, regrettably, often harbored. "Antisemitism" refers to the racist belief that Jews as an ethnic group are inferior to non-Jews, an ideology that led to the atrocities of the Holocaust.[8] Both should be decisively repudiated by contemporary Christians. As Pope Francis recently reconfirmed: "We hold the Jewish people in special regard because their covenant with God has never been revoked, for 'the gifts and the call of God are irrevocable' (Rom 11:29)."[9]

Among the four Gospels, John is most notorious for its anti-Jewish passages. Instead of distinguishing different Jewish groups such as Pharisees, Sadducees, priests, elders, scribes, crowds, etc., John, unlike the other Gospels, opts for the generalized use of "the Jews" about sixty times. In most cases, the Jews are portrayed negatively: they persecute Jesus (5:16), disapprove of him (6:41), and seek to kill him (7:1). They are impervious to his teaching (7:35), guilty of unbelief (8:24), and it is even asserted that they are the offspring of the devil:

> Why do you not understand what I say? It is because you cannot accept my word. You are from your father the devil, and you choose to do your father's desires. He was a murderer from the beginning and does not stand in the truth, because there is no truth in him. When he lies, he speaks according to his own nature, for he is a liar and the father of lies (8:43–44).

Passages like this have provided the "mythic foundations" of historic Christian claims that Jews are evil. It is important to realize, however, that John's fierce anti-Jewish rhetoric originated in the historical circumstances in which the Gospel was written. Quite possibly, the audience he had in mind was Jewish-Christian believers who had recently been expelled from the synagogue due to their growing conviction that Jesus was divine (John 9:22; 12:42; 16:2; cf. John 20:28).[10] Sometimes family feuds can be the most bitter and hard to resolve.

The other Gospels contain similar material, or passages that can be read in anti-Jewish ways. For example, the synagogue setting of Jesus' healing of a man with an "unclean spirit" (1:21–27) could lead to the conclusion that the Jewish house of prayer was a haunt of demons, although the text says nothing of the kind. Rather, Jesus is in the synagogue because it is the

---

8. See Kienicki and Wigoder, *Dictionary of the Jewish-Christian Dialogue*, 9–15.

9. *Evangelii gaudium* (2013), n. 247.

10. For a list of historically plausible reasons why Jesus' followers might have been expelled from the synagogue, see Levine, *Misunderstood Jew*, 108–9.

Sabbath, so the possessed man likely went to the synagogue to look for relief. The other people in the congregation are impressed by Jesus' teaching, and by his power over the spirits (1:22, 27); they do not reject him, or his power. As noted above, in many stories, Mark, Matthew and Luke single out specific groups of Jewish leaders and teachers for criticism as opponents of Jesus,[11] but not the Jewish people as a whole, and certainly not all Jews for all time! Moreover, the fact that in some of these stories, members of various Jewish factions are portrayed as questioning, testing and challenging Jesus does not always mean that they were hostile to Jesus; sometimes, they are simply shown asking him difficult questions concerning the interpretation of Torah, which he answers authoritatively. For example:

> One of the scribes came near and heard them disputing with one another, and seeing that he answered them well, he asked him, "Which commandment is the first of all?" Jesus answered, "The first is, 'Hear, O Israel: the Lord our God, the Lord is one; you shall love the Lord your God with all your heart, and with all your soul, and with all your mind, and with all your strength.' The second is this, 'You shall love your neighbor as yourself.' There is no other commandment greater than these." Then the scribe said to him, "You are right, Teacher; you have truly said that 'he is one, and besides him there is no other'; and 'to love him with all the heart, and with all the understanding, and with all the strength,' and 'to love one's neighbor as oneself,'—this is much more important than all whole burnt-offerings and sacrifices." When Jesus saw that he answered wisely, he said to him, "You are not far from the kingdom of God." After that no one dared to ask him any question. (Mark 12:28–34)

When John the Baptist castigates his audience as a "brood of vipers" (Luke 3:7; Matt 3:7; 12:34; 23:33), he is evoking the Jewish prophets and wisdom teachers who harshly denounce the sins of their contemporaries (cf. Isa 59:4–6; Ps 140:3; Job 20:15–16; Sir 39:29–31). Luke, particularly, exalts the Jewish prophetic tradition, lifting up not only John but other prophetic Jewish figures such as Mary (1:38), Elizabeth (1:42), Zechariah (1:67), Simeon (2:25–32), and Anna (2:36), taking pains to match the Gospel's literary style, especially in the infancy narrative (chs. 1–2), to the style of the Jewish Scriptures.

11. E.g., Pharisees (Mark 7:1–13; Luke 5:17; 14:3); Sadducees (Mark 12:18–27; Luke 20:27); Herodians (Mark 12:13–17); scribes (Luke 20:46); chief priests and elders (Mark 14:43; Matt 21:23; Luke 22:4).

It is important when considering this material to distinguish the text of the Gospels from interpretations that have been imposed on them by Christian theologians. For example, as a document on Christian-Jewish relations published by The United Church of Canada observes, many of the Luke's parables have been interpreted in anti-Jewish ways:

> Luke accuses the Jewish leaders of rejecting God's initiatives, not allowing themselves to be baptized by John (7:30). In Luke's account, Jewish leaders become more hostile to Jesus when he comes to Jerusalem. According to one interpretive approach, many parables seem to extend this accusation and rejection to the whole of the Jewish people, contrasted with gentiles who accept Jesus (the prodigal son 15:11–32; Lazarus and the rich man 16:19–31; the Pharisee and the tax collector 18:9–14; the talents 19:11ff. especially v. 27; the tenants of the vineyard 20:9–19).[12]

While the evangelist likely intended the parables to be read allegorically in Lucan context, it is more likely that in the story of the Prodigal, for example, the elder son represents God's ongoing relationship with the Jewish people, with the younger, rebellious son representing Gentile latecomers to the covenant. It is an interpretive stretch to read stock figures such as the Pharisee and the tax collector, Lazarus and the rich man, the nobleman and his slaves, or even the landowner and his hostile tenants, simplistically in terms of "Jews" and "Gentiles"; each needs to be interpreted on its own terms, both within the ministry of Jesus, and in Gospel context.

Turning to the letters of Paul, it is clear that Paul was a proud Jew (Phil 3:4–6; Rom 11:1; 9:3). In fact, as the Jewish scholar Pamela Eisenbaum puts it, in a very real way, Paul was not a Christian.[13] In fact, the term "Christian" had probably not yet been coined in Paul's time; the term appears only three times in the Christian Testament, in books written toward the end of the first century (Acts 11:26; 26:28; 1 Pet 4:16). For Paul, the same God who is righteous and faithful brings gentiles to God through Christ, "apart from Torah, but not in contradiction to it."[14] For Paul, becoming an evangelist for Jesus Christ did not mean giving up his Jewish identity. In fact, his apologetic arguments proclaiming the Gospel of Jesus as the Messiah are derived from Jewish wisdom, applying a Jewish style of interpretation to the scriptures. That is why many Jewish scholars, although they may not

12. Davies, *Bearing Faithful Witness*, 27–28.

13. Eisenbaum, *Paul Was Not A Christian.*

14. Davis, *Bearing Faithful Witness*, 34.

agree with his conclusions, recognize that "Paul had no alternative but to rely on the Jewish Scriptures—the only Bible he knew or could imagine—and to utilize exegetical [i.e., interpretive] procedures that the rabbis would use, with at least equal dexterity."[15] In fact, as Fredriksen observes with respect to converts, "Paul demanded of his gentiles a much greater degree of Judaizing than either the synagogue or the Jerusalem temple ever required or presupposed of theirs."[16] For Paul, the Jewish people enjoyed many advantages with respect to salvation history: "They are Israelites, and to them belong the adoption, the glory, the covenants, the giving of the law, the worship, and the promises; to them belong the patriarchs, and from them, according to the flesh, comes the Messiah, who is over all, God blessed for ever" (Rom 9:4–5).

In the Christian Testament, some of the most problematic passages implying a supersessionist view of Judaism are found in the Letter to the Hebrews, where the anonymous author argues that the law, while good, was only a shadow of the good things to come (10:1). Christ is the mediator of a better covenant than Moses (8:6), because that first covenant was faulty (8:7); he abolished the first in order to establish the second (10:9). In speaking of "a new covenant," Hebrews asserts, Christ made the first one obsolete (8:13). Jesus is "the mediator of a new covenant" (12:24). However, as Richard B. Hayes notes,

> Hebrews nowhere speaks of Jews and gentiles, nowhere gives evidence of controversies over circumcision or food laws, criticizes nothing in the Mosaic Torah except for the Levitical sacrificial cult, and contains no polemic against Jews and Jewish leaders. . . . Nowhere does Hebrews suggest that the Jewish people have been replaced by a new and different people of God.[17]

In fact, as the authors of this book have argued in a recent commentary, the "new covenant" of Hebrews is seen not only as the fulfilment of prophecy (Jer 31:31–34; Heb 8:8–12), but as the realisation of the eternal covenant with David (Ps 89:3–4; Isa 55:3; Jer 33:20–22), the basis of early Jewish messianic expectations that a descendant of David would rule again in Israel.[18]

---

15. Levenson, *Death and Resurrection of the Beloved Son*, 219.

16. Fredriksen, "Why Should a 'Law-Free' Mission," 637.

17. Hayes, "'Here We Have No Lasting City,'" 154.

18. Beavis and Kim-Cragg, *Hebrews*, 100; see also Beavis, "New Covenant and Judaism," 24–30.

The Christian Testament, then, undeniably contains texts that lend themselves to supersessionist, and even anti-Jewish, interpretations by Christians. However, the Christian scriptures also affirm Jewish teachings, honor Torah, and respect prophetic wisdom and traditions. We should also remember the particular contexts in which the problematic passages were written, often by those enduring persecution as Jewish believers in Christ, threatened by both Jews and non-Jews. It is critical to know that some of the writings of the Gospels and letters in the first few centuries bear the marks of an insecure religious minority. The Christian Testament writings, particularly, belong to a period when believers experienced themselves as living in the end times, when the prophecies of old were being fulfilled, and the "present form of this world" was "passing away" (1 Cor 7:31; cf. Heb 12:25–29; Mark 13:35–37).

It is also important to note that the critique of Judaism from the educated elite of Christianity in the early centuries of its development bears a Greco-Roman polemical style, which includes the practice of defaming the other. Even after Christianity became the state religion of the Roman Empire, and thus was no longer persecuted and in no need of defending their faith, many Christian scholars still focused on apologetics, justifying their beliefs and teachings to critics. Some of these critics were Jews,[19] who, understandably, were highly critical of some emerging Christian doctrines. However, at the same time, groups like the followers of Marcion were arguing that Christians should drop the Jewish Scriptures, and the Jewish God, from the canon altogether[20]—a measure firmly rejected by the apologists. These contextual factors must be considered when we read and interpret the Christian Testament lest we once again fall into the old and familiar patterns of anti-Judaism and supersessionism. Jewish scholar Amy-Jill Levine wisely recommends, "Christians need to recognize the impact that the problematic verses . . . and other texts as well have had on Jews. In turn, Jews should be aware that most Christians do not consciously read the texts anti-Jewishly and even resist anti-Jewish implications. . . . We need to imagine how our words sound to different ears."[21]

19. For examples of early Christian anti-Jewish polemic, see Ehrman, *After the New Testament*, 95–130.

20. Boys, *Has God Only One Blessing?* 46, 49. Marcionism continued in the West for 300 years, although Marcionite ideas persisted much longer.

21. Levine, *Misunderstood Jew*, 117.

Anti-Judaism in the History of Christianity

For many centuries, Christians thought of their tradition as the fulfillment of Judaism. Because it was commonly understood that the Gospels portray "the Jews" as killing Jesus (in fact, crucifixion was a Roman punishment), later generations came to believe that the Jews were accursed. Thus began the history of "the world's oldest hatred," and this "enduring problem" continues to evolve in the post-Holocaust era.[22] Can this ancient history of hatred be reversed?

Mary Donovan Turner, in teaching how to preach the Jewish Scriptures with a focus on the account of the Exodus narrative, claims that the key to reading and understanding the Bible lies in the interpretive lens of "reversal of fortune," which might otherwise be called God's blessing.[23] While it is impossible to review a long Christian history in this limited space, we will trace some of the broad outlines of Christian history in light of its relationship with Judaism and the Jewish people. We will employ Turner's interpretive lens, reversal of fortune, to help us understand it.

"The Jews were portrayed as the enemies of Jesus, blind to his fulfillment of God's promises."[24] This view of Jewish blindness is represented in many Christian writings and probably draws from the Gospel of John.[25] But as opposed to the scriptural basis of anti-Judaism, it is the symbols inspired by these texts and created over the centuries that speak louder than words. The power of symbols and visual presentation cannot be underestimated. One such presentation is found in the Strasbourg Cathedral in France. There are a few sculptures of iconic importance in this cathedral. One of these is called *Ecclesia* ("Church") and another is called *Synagoga* ("Synagogue") (see Figure 1). As might be inferred from the names, *Synagoga* symbolizes Judaism, while *Ecclesia* stands for Christianity. The *Synagoga* sculpture is of a downcast woman, blindfolded. It conveys the implication of John that Jews are "blind" to the teaching of Jesus (7:35), shamed by

22. Davies, "Antisemitism: An Enduring Problem in Western Society," 6.

23. Turner, "Reversal of Fortune," in *Performance in Preaching*, 87–98. Here she uses the word "fortune," also containing the meaning of God's love, mercy, and forgiveness.

24. *Bearing Faithful Witness: United Church-Jewish Relations Today*, 6.

25. For instance, Synagoga and Ecclesia first appeared in the ninth century in Northern France and Southern Germany, where they were intended as representations of the Old and Christian Testaments and personifications of Judaism and Christianity, respectively. See http://beyondborders-medievalblog.blogspot.ca/2013/02/the-equivocal-woman-shifting.html.

their resistance to the Christian truth. *Ecclesia* stands upright, wearing a crown, and bearing a cross and a chalice, representing the triumph of the church over the synagogue. Mary Boys, a Catholic religious educator who has written extensively on Jewish-Christian relations, makes the following comments regarding this sculpture: "Christian iconography of the Middle Ages provides a vivid image of rivalry in the figures 'Synagoga' and 'Ecclesia,' two representative women who graced many a cathedral, chapel, and Book of Hours in sculpture. . . . Typically, they portray Ecclesia as standing erect and triumphant, symbol of the church of the victorious Christ. Synagoga, in contrast, is a conquered figure, symbol of Judaism's defeat and obsolescence."[26]

Visual art like these sculptures is powerful in teaching Christian faith and remembering Christian stories. Visual presentation and representation have been used to teach the Bible from as early as the third century. In the medieval period, the visual presentation of the Bible flourished.[27] The sculptures of Ecclesia and Synagoga were created during this period and are part of a cultural legacy known as "Bibles in stone."[28] Given that most Christians during this time were illiterate and the written Bible was not available to them, the educational influence through the visual representation of the Bible and its teaching spoke volumes. "Seeing" became "believing" and this belief was considered as truth, even as the historical and scientific fact. One may see the dangerous consequences of this pious, uncritical acceptance.[29]

26. Boys, *Has God Only One Blessing?*, 5.
27. Kim-Cragg, *Story and Song*, 18.
28. Weber, *Experiments with Bible Study*, 25.
29. Westerhoff III, *A Pilgrim People*, 8.

Figure 1: Ecclesia and Synagoga, Strasbourg Cathedral
(source: Wikimedia Commons)

Not only does visual art convey anti-Jewish messages, but myth in the modern age suffers from the same problem. Historian of religion Alan Davies argues that antisemitism has "mythic foundations." According to Davies, the myth of the Jew as a cosmic demonic figure came to be accepted under the guise of scientific race theory. That is why, he suspects, antisemitism occurs and reoccurs throughout the twentieth century and into the twenty-first century.[30]

The Christian version of this mythic history began to cast a long shadow in the late Middle Ages.[31] Images of Jews as enemies swept across Europe during this time. "Christ killers" was a name used to brand them. Jews came to be regarded as a living threat to society.[32] In any society undergoing rapid social change, minority groups who are different from the societal norm often suffer stigmatization. Jews along with non-Whites, homosexuals, and lepers, to name a few, were prime targets during the

30. Davies, "Antisemitism," 81.

31. Boys, *Has God Only One Blessing?*, 62.

32. Chazan, *Medieval Stereotypes and Modern Antisemitism*, 72–73.

Middle Ages. The Fourth Lateran Council in 1215 banned interracial marriage (with Jews), and copies of the Talmud were burned in Paris in 1242 and 1244, an action which was repeated more publicly in Rome in 1553.[33] In the context of uncertainty and chaos, the notion of ethnic purity was emphasized. So began Christians' obsession with so-called purity of blood and fear of "tainted blood" which justified expulsion of Jews from the community. In Spain, for example, under the leadership of Thomas Torquemada, a Dominican priest and confessor to Queen Isabella, Jews were expelled from the nation in 1492. Those who left Spain and landed in Portugal were chased down and expelled from that country in 1497.[34] These are ominous foreshadowings of what would happen in Nazi Germany 440 years later.

The Reformation did not change much for the Jews in Europe. Reformers including Martin Luther and Martin Bucer regarded Jewish people as the enemies of society and opponents of God. Jews were damned along with the Popes, Turks, sophists and monks. But the reformers did not go as far as Catholics in their ill-treatment of the Jews. In fact, the Catholic scholar Boys argues that "Protestantism benefitted the Jews."[35] The Protestant theological claim of collective human responsibility for the death of Jesus took the edge off claims by the Catholic Church at that time that Jews were solely responsible for the crucifixion.

The notion of collective sin also opened up a new view of religious tolerance, freedom of conscience, and paved the way for Enlightenment thought. Ironically, however, the Enlightenment ushered in a new wave of antisemitism. With the rise of capitalism and under new legal equality, Jews achieved remarkable economic prosperity, with many becoming successful bankers, doctors, politicians and business people. This brought jealousy and a need for European Christians to prove their superiority over Jews. Germans took this issue most seriously under the flag of nationalism, with the help of pseudo-scientific theories of racial purity. Jews were blamed for economic and social problems during the economic depression of the 1870s.[36] Jews might not have been considered as Christ-killers any longer, but they were still a problem in the eyes of most European Christians. So it is not coincidental that the term "semite" from which the notion of "antisemitism" came into use during this depression, when the German

33. Stow, "Burning of the Talmud," 64.

34. Boys, *Has God Only One Blessing?*, 65.

35 Ibid., 70.

36. Perry, "Radical Nationalism," 241–68.

Wilhelm Marr coined it in 1878. The term swept all over Europe during the early 1900s, leading to the historically unprecedented tragedy of the Holocaust (known by Jews as the *Shoah*, "calamity," or "disaster") in the middle of the twentieth century.

No other religion is as closely related to Christianity as Judaism. Whether members of the two religions like to admit it or not, they are siblings. Indeed, according to Christianity's own interpretive tradition, they are even closer than most siblings; they are twins. Christians have long been fascinated by the story of the twins Esau and Jacob, seeing themselves and their religious tradition represented by Jacob in contrast with his older twin Esau (e.g., Rom 9:13; Heb 12:16). The story in Genesis tells how Jacob tricked his brother and stole a blessing from their father. When he learned of Jacob's deceit Esau cried out to his father, "Have you not reserved a blessing for me? Have you only one blessing, father? Bless me, me also, father!" (Gen 27:36; 38) Mary Boys argues that Christians need to take their estranged relationship with Judaism seriously. We must learn to confront the terrible and horrifying violence committed by Christians on Jews. However, the weight of this confrontation should not be too heavy or impossible to carry. While the shadow side of Christian history may overwhelm contemporary Christians, its history is not "synonymous with a history of antisemitism." We should not, Boys continues, "avoid reducing the history of our relationship to hostility and hate. It is a far more complex reality."[37] We are twins, after all, equally worthy of blessing.

This complex history of both groups also tells us that Jews and Christians have lived side by side. The boundaries between these groups have often been fluid rather than rigid. Even in the First Crusade of 1096, according to Robert Chazan, "Christians attempted on many occasions to offer assistance to their beleaguered Jewish neighbors, in some instances at considerable danger to themselves."[38] Chazan, the author of this claim, is a Jewish scholar whose research focuses on Jewish-Christian relations in the Middle Ages. Another renowned Jewish scholar makes a similar claim that there has often been admiration (and not hostility) between Jews and Christians, with Christians expressing their respect for Jewish commitment to the Sabbath and their excellence in education as well as their devotion to their faith, and Jews respecting Christian dedication to learning, their

---

37. Boys, *Has God Only One Blessing?*, 40.

38. Chazan, *In the Year 1092*, 13. Cited in Boys, *Has God Only One Blessing?*, 41.

excellence in preaching, and their commitment to their church.[39] Even in the twelfth century when Christian hostility against Jews began to intensify, there is evidence that some significant Christian scholars were taught by rabbis. One may contend that there have been some wholesome relationships (however fragile and frangmentary) between Christians and Jews for much of the past two thousand years.[40] Religion alone is not the cause of Jewish-Christian enmity. When other socio-economic and political difficulties surface and socio-economic problems intensify conflicts, different groups may resort to religion as a means of blaming the other. In reality, religion is only one part of a toxic brew in such situations, as it is obvious that the mix includes factors such as rage, racism, xenophobia, and nationalism.[41]

In this chapter we have attempted to show a reversal of fortune. While this reversal is a long process, it has nonetheless begun. There is no God who condemns one group of the faithful in order to choose the other. God blesses all. However, although the blessedness of the Jewish people may be affirmed by many Christians today, as Levine points out, Christian teachers and leaders unintentionally continue to perpetuate anti-Jewish attitudes by using Judaism as a foil for Christianity:

> Church homilies and sermons, daily and weekly Bible study, and even respected academic monographs depict, both explicitly and implicitly, a Judaism that is monolithic, mired in legal minutiae, without spiritual depth, and otherwise everything that (they hope) Christianity is not. Pastors, priests, and religious educators, Christians well aware that the New Testament has been interpreted in an anti-Jewish manner, wind up perpetuating anti-Jewish teaching nonetheless.[42]

One of the authors of this book was shocked when recently, at a national theological conference, a distinguished Christian theologian made the contrast between "Law and Gospel" shortly after expressing his sensitivity to the dangers of supersessionism. His easy assumption that "Law" (Torah, Judaism) is inferior (and in opposition) to "Gospel" (the Christian message)

---

39. Saperstein, "Christians and Jews—Some Positive Images." Cited in Boys, *Has God Only One Blessing?*, 41.

40. The phrase "a persecuting society" was coined by Moore in his *The Formation of Persecuting Society*.

41. Boys and Lee, *Christians and Jews in Dialogue*, 2.

42. Levine, *Misunderstood Jew*, 119.

was a vivid example of the naïve anti-Judaism that too often characterizes Christian discourse.

In conclusion, what does the Bible, especially the Christian Testament say about Jews? A lot but it is not clear cut! A nuanced and informed reading of the Bible is required, given that the dangers of supersessionism and anti-Jewish prejudices are widespread and strong in today's culture, church, and academia.

Jews and Judaism in Film

Watch: *The Chosen* (1981)

Discussion Questions

Before the viewing

What do you know about Judaism?

What is the significance of Judaism for Christians?

What does it mean to say that "Jesus was a Jew"?

After the viewing

What did you learn about Judaism from watching the movie?

Does watching the film make any difference to your understanding of the Bible? Of Jesus?

Very few Christians are portrayed in this movie. Which characters would you identify as Christians?

Does the parable told by Reuven near the end of the movie remind you of anything in the Gospels?[43]

---

43. "There is a story in the Talmud about a king who had a son who went astray. The son was told, 'Return to your father.' The son replied that he could not. The king then sent a messenger to the son with the message . . . 'Come back to me as far as you can, and I will meet you the rest of the way.'" See http://www.imdb.com/title/tt0082175/quotes.

Discussion Notes

In order to begin to become conscious of negative caricatures of Judaism, our church group watched the movie *The Chosen*. The film is based on Chaim Potok's novel of the same name, published in 1967. Surprisingly for a film in a chapter about Jews and Christians, the story focuses on very Jewish themes: biblical interpretation, Torah obedience, attitudes to the state of Israel, and relations between different kinds of Jews. The decision to view a film set in the twentieth century, rather than in biblical times, was deliberate. Rather than portraying Jews as biblical characters, as Christians are sometimes apt to see them, the Jewish characters, and the communities they belong to, are shown as modern people, struggling to remain faithful to their tradition amid the turbulent events of World War II and its aftermath. This movie challenges the stereotype of Jews as archaic and unchanging, which is at the heart of Orientalism;[44] in Christian terms, the tendency to see Jews and Judaism as the exotic "Other," and especially as a foil for Christianity. Instead it offers a heterogeneous view of Jews whose identities are fluid and changing. The movie demonstrates the struggles of finding Jewish identities as relevant to the contemporary society in the midst of a changing world. Such struggles can easily resonate with all of us, including Christians. This may be why, despite its lack of explicitly Christian content, the members of the church group, none of whom had seen the movie before, spontaneously broke into applause at the end of the showing for its powerful depiction of Jewish life and spirituality.

The teenagers who are the main characters in the film are Reuven Malter, a modern Orthodox Jew and son of an academic biblical scholar, and Danny Saunders, the son of a Hasidic Rebbe (rabbi). Rebbe Saunders is a highly regarded leader in his highly traditional Jewish enclave in New York. The two are thrown together when at a baseball game between their two high schools, Danny accidentally bats a ball into Reuven's eye, which lands him in the hospital with an eye patch, and the fear of vision loss. Although Rueven is initially resentful when Danny visits him to apologize, and somewhat contemptuous of Danny's old world appearance and limited experience, the two become close friends. Eventually, the mysterious and

---

44. Said, *Orientalism*. The postcolonial Christian biblical scholar R. S. Sugirtharajah argues that the description of labeling the Other in Orientalism is to view the Other as "eternal, timeless, static, and incapable of any change." See Sugirtharajah, *Asian Biblical Hermeneutics and Postcolonialism*, 105.

dignified Rebbe Saunders allows Reuven to visit their home and participate in Hasidic synagogue services.

The relationship between the two young men allows each of them to explore their own identities as Jews and as members of the larger society. Reuven has a close relationship with his father and wants to follow in his academic footsteps, and Danny, as the eldest son of a distinguished Rebbe, is destined to succeed him, although his relationship with the Rebbe seems strained and distant. However, when the time comes for the boys to go to college, Rebbe and Mrs. Saunders allow Danny to join Reuven at Hirsch College, named after the founder of contemporary Orthodox Judaism, rather than attending the Hasidic Yeshiva (rabbinical college). At Hirsch, both boys study Torah in the mornings, and take academic university classes in the afternoons. There, Danny is allowed to pursue his secret love of psychology, and Reuven, initially the more "secular" of the two, decides to become a rabbi.

Figure 2: Chaim Potok with Robbie Benson (Danny)
and Barry Miller (Reuven) in *The Chosen* (1981)

Some members of the church group were surprised that both Danny and Reuven were Orthodox Jews, pointing to the diversity within contemporary Judaism. This led to a discussion of Jewish diversity in the time of Jesus—would Jesus be more like the Hasidic Danny than the Sunday school versions of him in Christian art? Or would Jesus, with his more liberal attitude to Torah interpretation, be a Reuven to the Pharisees, with their strictly observant ways?

As portrayed in the film, the Hasidic and Modern Orthodox communities differ both in their understanding of Torah and, significantly for the two main characters, in their attitudes to the founding of the State of Israel, which takes places towards the end of the movie. As Professor Malter puts it, as a Jewish academic, he sees the Bible as inspired by God, but as written by human beings, whereas the Hasidic Rebbe sees Torah as purely divine. More importantly for the relationship between Reuven and Danny, the two communities differ sharply in their attitudes to the founding of Israel in 1948. For Professor Malter and Reuven Malter, a Jewish state is necessary to the survival of the Jewish people in the wake of the Holocaust, but for Rebbe Saunders and his community, Israel can only be restored by the Messiah; to try to do otherwise is sacrilegious, even in the face of the dreadful events of the war. It is the Malters' support for Israel and Danny's respect for his father's anti-Zionist views that leads the two friends to part ways, at least for a time.

In keeping with the title of the film, "chosen-ness" resonates throughout the story at many levels. The Jews are the chosen people, but their chosen status has exposed them to genocidal persecution. All the main characters are Jewish, and yet they live out their "chosen" status in very different ways. Danny, like his father, is chosen by virtue of being the eldest son to succeed the Rebbe, but his interests lie elsewhere, inspired by the writings of a secular Jew, Sigmund Freud. Reuven chooses a career as a rabbi, which provokes some mockery by his secularized friends. Reuven and Shaindel, Danny's sister, are attracted to one another, but as the smitten Reuven learns from Danny, she has been betrothed to a Hasidic boy for years. The viewer is left wondering if perhaps the intelligent and spirited Shaindel might eventually follow her brother's example and choose her own path in life, rather than accepting the marriage imposed on her by her parents. Throughout the movie, it appears that to be chosen does not mean that the characters are predestined to their life paths but that they make choices within the constraints of time, place, and identity.

Other Resources

Levine, Amy-Jill, and Marc Zvi Brettler, eds. *The Jewish Annotated New Testament: New Revised Standard Version.* Oxford: Oxford University Press, 2011.

Levine, Amy-Jill. *The Misunderstood Jew: The Church and the Scandal of the Jewish Jesus.* San Francisco: HarperOne, 2006.

Salmon, Marilyn J. *Preaching without Contempt: Overcoming Unintended Anti-Judaism.* Minneapolis: Fortress, 2006.

5

Heaven and Hell

IN CASUAL CONVERSATIONS ABOUT religion, the topic inevitably turns to life after death. A common assumption in the western world is that a blissful afterlife is the payoff for believing in God, and that Christianity is all about "going to heaven" (and, presumably, avoiding hell). The cultural fascination with afterlife beliefs is illustrated by the many books and movies about the near-death experiences of people as diverse as a three-year old and a neurosurgeon,[1] television "reality" shows about psychics who can communicate with deceased loved ones, and paranormal investigators who never seem to find anything much. While it is true that historically, Christianity has become a religion where afterlife beliefs are prominent, the Bible, especially the Jewish Scriptures, has surprisingly little to say about life after death, and where the terms "heaven" and "hell" have meanings that are a far cry from the way they are used in popular culture—including contemporary popular Christianity. Both words are translations of Hebrew and Greek words and concepts that changed and developed over time in biblical times and afterward.

This chapter will trace how concepts of heaven and hell relate to the Bible. It will show how the understanding of heaven and hell changed in the course of the history. It will call for a rediscovery of the biblical meaning of heaven as the promise and the glory of God.

---

1. Burpo, *Heaven is for Real*; *Heaven is For Real* (dir. Randall Wallace, 2014); Alexander, *Proof of Heaven*.

Heaven and Hell in the Jewish Scriptures

The ancient Israelite religion represented on the pages of the Jewish Scriptures was very this-worldly, with little interest in, or hope for, a life beyond this one. The term usually translated as "heaven" is *hashamayim*, literally, "the heavens" or "the skies." Like other Ancient Near Eastern people, the Israelites thought of the cosmos as three-storied—the heavens/skies, where the sun, the moon and the stars were placed, the earth, the place of human beings, animals and plants, and the underworld, in Hebrew, *Sheol*, the abode of the dead. The creation story in Genesis 1 and many other references portray the heavens as a solid dome (KJV: "firmament") over the earth to hold back the primal waters of chaos:

> And God said, Let there be a firmament in the midst of the waters, and let it divide the waters from the waters. And God made the firmament, and divided the waters which were under the firmament from the waters which were above the firmament: and it was so. And God called the firmament Heaven. (Gen 1:6-8a, KJV)

The realm of God and the angels was "the heavens" (e.g., Gen 21:17; 22:11, 15, 17; 24:7; 28:12, 17) to the point that the term "heaven" was synonymous with God, especially in early Jewish Scriptures (e.g., 1 Sam 5:12; Ps 73:9; 1 Macc 3:19; 4:50, 60; 2 Macc 7:11). That may explain why Jesus prayed "*Abba* (Aramaic, translated as 'Our Father' in English) in heaven," because heaven is associated with the divine sphere. This biblical view took roots in other missionized cultures in China and Korea; for example, God in the Chinese and Korean languages is referred to as "*Cheon-Joo*," literally meaning, "Lord in Heaven." The dome of the heavens was a barrier that held back and contained the primal waters so that they would not inundate the earth (cf. Gen 7:11). For the Israelite authors, the purpose of existence was to live a long, prosperous and righteous life in accordance with the precepts of Torah, and to leave behind a large and healthy family. A person's "afterlife" was their posterity lived out in covenant with their people and their God: "I will establish my covenant between me and you, and your offspring after you throughout their generations, for an everlasting covenant, to be God to you and to your offspring after you" (Gen 17:7, 9). This-worldly prosperity and contentment were the rewards of living in accordance with the divine commandments: "They are like trees planted by streams of water, which yield their fruit in its season, and their leaves do not wither. In all that they do, they prosper" (Ps 1:3; cf. Deut 28:11; Deut 30:9; 2 Chron 26:6; Prov 13:21).

Throughout the Jewish Scriptures, the hoped-for culmination of a long and happy life was a peaceful death, not a blissful afterlife. Job's youthful friend Elihu expresses the standard Israelite expectation that the righteous would "complete their lives in prosperity, and complete their years in pleasantness" (Job 36:11). The suffering Job is not so sure, but he expresses the standard worldview when he observes that sometimes the wicked seem to enjoy the happiness and security that the upright should inherit: "They spend their days in prosperity, and in peace they go down to Sheol. . . . one dies in prosperity, being wholly at ease and secure" (Job 21:13; 23). Whether the person is good or bad, the final destination of the human spirit is Sheol; the reward of a righteous existence was to face death in the knowledge of a life well-lived, and, ideally, to be buried together with one's ancestors (e.g., Gen 15:15; 24:29; 47:30; Deut 31:16; 2 Sam 7:12; 1 Kgs 2:10; 11:43; 14:32; 15:8; 2 Chr 32:33; Neh 2:10; Jdt 8:3; 1 Macc 9:19). Sheol, later translated as "Hell," is not located in another world. The world view of the Hebrew Bible is non-dualistic, focusing on this world. While death is the end of the life in this world, one does not have fear death since as "the home of the dead, Sheol does not stand outside God's presence. . . . Sheol itself lies within God's wisdom and guidance."[2]

Nonetheless, for a contemporary Christian reader, the ancient Israelite concept of *Sheol* seems foreign and forbidding. As Andrew B. Perrin observes:

> Although the OT does not present a formal doctrine concerning the fate and destination of the dead, Sheol is described through various metaphors and images concerning what existence beyond the grave entailed. Characteristically, Sheol is presented as a pit (Isa 14.15; Ezek 31.16), a deep abyss shrouded in darkness (Job 14.13; 17.13) and a realm of destitution (Prov 30.16) in which the dead remained in a shadowy existence.[3]

Despite its forbiddingness, *Sheol* was not regarded as a punishment for misdeeds, but as the inevitable destination of the living: "Remember how short my time is—for what vanity you have created all mortals! Who can live and never see death? Who can escape the power of Sheol?" (Ps 89:47–48). The sage of Ecclesiastes advises his pupils: "Whatever your

---

2. Jensen, *Living Hope*, 74.
3. Perrin, "Sheol," 488.

hand finds to do, do with your might; for there is no work or thought or knowledge or wisdom in Sheol, to which you are going" (Eccl 9:10). Being dispatched to Sheol prematurely was the punishment for the wicked (e.g., Num 16:31–35; Ps 49:10–15; 2 Sam 2:5–9), but all would eventually share in it. Nor was there any notion of resurrection or an end-time judgement where the righteous would be rewarded and the unjust be punished; the righteous Job laments: "The eye that beholds me will see me no more; while your eyes are upon me, I shall be gone. As the cloud fades and vanishes, so those who go down to Sheol do not come up; they return no more to their houses, nor do their places know them any more" (Job 7:8–10). Ecclesiastes expresses agnosticism regarding life after death: "For who knows what is good for mortals while they live the few days of their vain life, which they pass like a shadow? For who can tell them what will be after them under the sun?" (Eccl 6:12). In early Jewish tradition, the only figures who escape Sheol are the righteous Enoch, who "walked with God, and then he was no more, because God took him" (Gen 5:24), and the prophet Elijah, who ascended to the heavens in a whirlwind at the end of his career (2 Kgs 2:1–12)—the exceptions to the rule articulated by the Jewish sage Sirach (second century BCE):

> Remember that death does not tarry, and the decree of Hades [Sheol] has not been shown to you.
>
> Do good to friends before you die,
>
> and reach out and give to them as much as you can.
>
> Do not deprive yourself of a day's enjoyment;
>
> do not let your share of desired good pass by you.
>
> Will you not leave the fruit of your labors to another,
>
> and what you acquired by toil to be divided by lot?
>
> Give, and take, and indulge yourself,
>
> because in Hades one cannot look for luxury.
>
> All living beings become old like a garment,
>
> for the decree from of old is, "You must die!"
>
> Like abundant leaves on a spreading tree
>
> that sheds some and puts forth others,
>
> so are the generations of flesh and blood:
>
> one dies and another is born.
>
> Every work decays and ceases to exist,

and the one who made it will pass away with it. (Sir 14:11–19)

Heaven and Hell in Early Judaism
and the Christian Testament

Obviously, the early Jewish tradition accepted by Jesus and the authors of the Christian Testament presupposes afterlife beliefs—notably, resurrection and last judgment—that are foreign to the religion of ancient Israel. Here, we are making a distinction between pre-exilic Israelite religion (pre-586 BCE) and post-exilic Jewish religion (post 538 BCE), when the people of Judah (Judea) were allowed by the Persian king to return to their homeland. It is in the post-exilic period that biblical historians begin to speak of "Judaism," a religion grounded in, but distinct from, ancient Israelite ways. This emergent Judaism is represented literarily by the later books of the Hebrew scriptures (1–2 Chronicles, Ezra, Nehemiah, Haggai, Zechariah, Esther, Daniel), the Deuterocanonical scriptures (1–2 Maccabees, Judith, Tobit, Sirach, Wisdom, Baruch, additions to Daniel, additions to Esther), and other early Jewish writings. The Book of Ezekiel, written during the Babylonian exile, contains a precursor of the resurrection doctrine in the famous vision in which a valley full of dry bones is transformed by God into a vast multitude of people, brought back to life (37:1–10). It is clear from the interpretation in Ezek 37:11–14 that the vision is not to be taken as a literal account of a future resurrection, but as symbolic of the restoration of the people of Israel to their homeland: "I will put my spirit within you, and you shall live, and I will place you on your own soil; then you shall know that I, the LORD, have spoken and will act, says the LORD" (37:14).

Some scholars think that early Jewish beliefs changed during and after the exile as a result of exposure to the Persian religion of Zoroastrianism, which posited a cosmic battle between good and evil deities, a messianic figure, an end-time resurrection, and a last judgment—all elements that begin to appear in post-exilic Judaism.[4] One of the earliest expressions of Jewish belief in a bodily resurrection (c. 100 BCE) appears as a response to persecution and martyrdom. 2 Maccabees 7 relates the story of a pious Jewish mother and her seven sons who are executed by the Greek-Syrian king of Judea, from oldest to youngest, followed by their mother, after "extreme tortures" (2 Macc 7:42), for the crime of refusing to eat pork. Throughout

---

4. E.g., Hinnels, "Zoroastrian Influence," 1–23.

the ordeal, the sons and their mother repeatedly affirm their confidence that "the King of the universe will raise us up to an everlasting renewal of life, because we have died for his laws" (7:9, 11, 14, 23, 29, 36). The mother encourages her youngest son with the assurance that the God who created heaven and earth and breathed life into the human race has the power to restore him to life, along with his brothers (7:28–29). Another text from this era, the Book of Daniel, prophesies: "Many of those who sleep in the dust of the earth shall awake, some to everlasting life, and some to shame and everlasting contempt. Those who are wise shall shine like the brightness of the sky, and those who lead many to righteousness, like the stars for ever and ever" (Dan 12:2–3). Here, the hope of resurrection is a consolation for Jews suffering loss of national sovereignty and religious persecution.

It is important to remember, however, that there was no unified belief about the afterlife in the so-called "intertestamental" period, a Christian term for the gap of time between the period covered by the Jewish Scriptures and the period covered by the Christian Testament. As noted above, the author of Sirach maintained a traditional ancient Israelite belief that the spirits of the dead reside in the underworld. His translator, his own grandson, translated the Hebrew term *Sheol* with the similar Greek word Hades, "a dark and indistinct place where the deceased dwell in near-oblivion, regardless of their actions in life."[5] In contrast, the Book of Wisdom (first century BCE), probably influenced by Greek philosophy, adopted the radical new notion (for Judaism) of the immortality of the soul: "For God created man to be immortal, and made him the image of his own immortality" (Wisd 2:3); "But the souls of the righteous are in the hand of God, and there shall no torment touch them. In the sight of the unwise they seemed to die: and their departure is taken for misery, and their going from us to be utter destruction: but they are in peace. For though they be punished in the sight of men, yet is their hope full of immortality" (3:1–4). "To know [God] is perfect righteousness, and to know [God's] power is the root of immortality" (15:3). Even in the time of Jesus, the Jewish sect of the Sadducees rejected the notion of resurrection (Mark 12:18; Luke 20:27), while the Pharisees affirmed it: "The Sadducees say that there is no resurrection, or angel, or spirit; but the Pharisees acknowledge all three" (Acts 23:8).

Obviously, Jesus, as represented in the Gospels, agreed with the Pharisees on the resurrection doctrine, and his followers came to believe that Jesus himself had risen from the dead as a prelude to the final judgment that

5. De Crom, "Hades," 198.

would fulfill the words of the prophets (e.g., Matt 10:15; 11:22, 24, 36, 41; Luke 10:14; 11:31). The righteous would be resurrected by God as a reward for their faithfulness (e.g., Mark 12:18–27). He expresses the Jewish belief of his time that the unrighteous would be punished in the underworld (Greek: *Gehenna, Hades, Tartarus*), a place of fiery torment (e.g., Matt 5:22, 29, 30; 10:28; 18:9; 23:33; Mark 9:43, 45, 47; Luke 12:4–5). These Greek terms, along with *Sheol*, were later rendered as "hell" in English translations.

Some of these ideas are summarized in the parable of the Rich Man and Lazarus (Luke 16:19–31). The righteous Lazarus is rewarded by being taken to be with his ancestors ("Abraham"), where he lies waiting for the end-time resurrection. The rich man is consigned to *Hades* (not "hell"), conceived as a dry and fiery place. He wants Abraham to send Lazarus (presumably in ghostly form) to his brothers to warn them to repent, but Abraham refuses, since they (like everyone else) have the Law and the Prophets to guide them. However, it is important to remember that this is a parable, a fictional story meant to illustrate a moral. It can't be taken as a literal map of the afterlife. The point of the story is to live a moral and upright life in the light of divine judgment. As Leander E. Keck explains:

> It was not [Jesus'] aim to provide information about death and afterlife, but to call people to a new way of life on earth. He frequently calls attention to the coming judgement, as in some of his stories, the parables. Some of them end with a warning about people being thrown into "outer darkness" where they will "weep and gnash their teeth" (e.g., Matthew 8;12; 22:13). So, too, he urges people to deal decisively with whatever causes them to sin. "If your hand causes you to sin, cut it off; it is better for you to enter life maimed that with two hands go to hell [*Gehenna*], to the unquenchable fire" (Mark 9:43). In all such sayings, Jesus is not providing instruction about life after death, but is referring to the future to say that the consequences of not acting rightly now are serious.[6]

The "good news" ("gospel") that Jesus preached was not about himself (not "I am the messiah," or "I am the savior"), but about/from God; the message is about the kingdom or "reign" of God, which is near (Mark 1:14–15). In the Gospels, the synonymous terms "kingdom of God" or "kingdom of heaven" do not refer to an otherworldly realm where God reigns, but to the eternal rule of God over the universe, both the heavens and the earth (e.g.,

---

6. Keck, "Death and Afterlife," 86–87.

Ps 93:1–2; 47:7; 74:12; 97:1). The Gospels presuppose that God has always reigned, that God's reign is especially present in the ministry of Jesus, and that it will be powerfully manifested in the near future. Jesus preaches "repentance"—turning away from disobedience to the Law of Moses—in the face of this urgent message.

Although the writings attributed to the apostle Paul dominate the Christian Testament, Paul never met Jesus personally. He began his career as a Pharisee (Phil 3:5), committed to the persecution of the earliest church in Jerusalem after the death of Jesus. As a result of a visionary experience of the risen and exalted Christ, he repented of his opposition to the gospel, and became devoted not just to the spread of Jesus' message, but to preaching the good news that Jesus was risen and exalted to heavenly status as the son of God (Gal 1:13–17). Unlike Jesus and his disciples, Paul was not from the traditional land of Israel, but from Tarsus in Asia Minor. He spoke and wrote Greek, as well as (probably) Hebrew and Aramaic. As a Pharisee, he would have been educated in the Jewish legal tradition, and he would have shared a belief in an end-time resurrection and last judgment, but as a Greek-educated Jew, he would also have had exposure to Greek culture and ideas, especially the body-spirit dichotomy.

For Paul and other Jews of his time, resurrection was associated with the end times, so if Jesus had been vindicated by being raised from the dead and subsequently taken up into heaven to be with God, this meant that the last judgment was near, and that Jesus would play a special role in the judgment and the world to come. In Paul's preaching, anyone who believed in this message would be justified before God when they were judged, and would share in the resurrection.

As a Pharisee, Paul would have been firmly committed to observance of the Torah (Law of Moses) as his means of justification before God. However, as a follower of Jesus, he became convinced that the good news of imminent salvation was for the entire world, not just for Jews. He began to preach that non-Jews (Gentiles) did not have to become Jewish and obey Torah in order to achieve righteousness. Rather, righteousness was now available by simply believing in Christ's triumph over death through resurrection. For Paul, Christ replaces the Law, and makes it possible for everyone to be judged as righteous before God.

In developing his distinctive teachings on the relationship between the Law and Christ, Paul places a great deal of emphasis on Sin and Death, which he personifies as evil, supernatural forces that exert an irresistible influence on human beings, and that will ultimately be destroyed by Christ. For example, in Rom 5:18–21 he presents an argument that culminates in the proclamation that as "Sin exercised dominion in Death, so grace might also exercise dominion through justification leading to eternal life through Jesus Christ our Lord." The eternal life that Paul preaches is resurrection in the world to come, when the Lord will appear to judge humanity: the dead will be raised to imperishability, and the mortal will assume immortality (see 1 Cor 15:52–53). The bodies of the resurrected righteous will not be material human bodies, but "spiritual bodies," imperishable and glorious (1 Cor 15:42–57). For Paul, the physical body is weak and mortal; the spiritual (resurrection) body is glorious and eternal. However, unlike the Greek philosophers, the Jewish Paul insists that the afterlife is *both* bodily and spiritual, not purely immaterial.

Paul does not say much about what the reign of God would be like after the last judgment, or about what happened to the souls of the dead in the interim period before the resurrection. However, in 2 Cor 12:1–4, he reports a visionary experience of being caught up to the third heaven ("whether in the body or out of the body I do not know"). There, he says, he was "caught up into Paradise and heard things that are not to be told" (v. 4). The term "paradise" is a Persian loan-word that is synonymous with the Garden of Eden in early Judaism and Christianity. In Luke 23:43, Jesus tells the "good thief" on the cross that he would join him in Paradise. The Book of Revelation refers to the Tree of Life that is in the "Paradise of God" (Rev 2:7). These references reflect a belief that the souls of the righteous dead reside in a heavenly region until the resurrection and last judgment. A similar image is found in the Book of Revelation where the visionary sees the souls of those martyred for their faithfulness to God who are located under the altar of the heavenly temple, awaiting their final vindication: "They cried out with a loud voice, 'Sovereign Lord, holy and true, how long will it be before you judge and avenge our blood on the inhabitants of the earth?' They were each given a white robe and told to rest a little longer, until the number would be complete both of their fellow-servants and of their brothers and sisters, who were soon to be killed as they themselves had been killed" (Rev 6:10–11).

The only extensive description of the world to come subsequent to the Last Judgement is found in Rev 21:1—22:5. A new heaven and a new earth will replace the old cosmos, which is passing away. The holy city, the New Jerusalem will descend from above, the righteous will be rewarded by the eternal presence of God, but the wicked will perish in a lake of fire. There will be no need for a temple in the city, as God and the Lamb (Christ) will be there. There will be no need of a sun and moon, because it will be illuminated by divine light:

> The nations will walk by its light, and the kings of the earth will bring their glory into it. Its gates will never be shut by day—and there will be no night there. People will bring into it the glory and the honor of the nations. But nothing unclean will enter it, nor anyone who practises abomination or falsehood, but only those who are written in the Lamb's book of life. (Rev 21:23–27)

In a scene reminiscent of the Genesis creation accounts, the apocalyptist depicts "the river of the water of life" flanked by the tree of life, whose twelve fruits are for "the healing of the nations" (Rev 22:22). For all its reputation for fire and vengeance, the book ends on a remarkably conciliatory note of hope for reconciliation and healing. Like other apocalyptic writings, Revelation presents a message of hope for believers suffering religious persecution (Rev 1:9; 2:3, 10; 6:9–11; 14:12–14).

The early Christians had a strong expectation that the resurrection and the Last Judgment were about to happen imminently. However, as time went by and the world did not end, Judgment Day was pushed forward into the remote future, and theologians began to focus more on ideas of otherworldly salvation or damnation, heaven and hell. Heaven was viewed as a place that was open to all the faithful, free from sorrow and pain, a blissful state of communion with God. Hell was seen as the opposite of heaven, a place of punishment and torment, used by preachers to encourage good behavior in this life. Rita Nakashima Brock and Rebecca Ann Parker have shown that scenes of paradise, depicted not as the locus of life after death, but as the transformation of life in this world, dominated early Christian art for a thousand years.[7]

In conclusion, what is the biblical teaching on life after death? What does the Bible say about "heaven" and "hell"? The answer is that there are several: the ancient Israelite belief in *Sheol* as the final destination of all living things; the notion of the resurrection of the body at the last judgment; the Greek concept of immortality of the soul. Another related concept is "eternal life," especially as represented in the Gospel of John. In keeping with Jesus' message of the arrival of the reign of God, John emphasized that eternal life (*zoēn aiōnion*) is the life of the "age to come" in the here-and-now:

7. Brock and Parker, *Saving Paradise.*

"Very truly, I tell you, anyone who hears my word and believes him who sent me has eternal life, and does not come under judgement, but has passed from death to life" (John 5:24). Believers experience eternal life in the present: "They have already passed the eschatological judgment and have received the eschatological blessing."[8] As Brenda B. Colijn observes, this does not mean that John has no end-time expectation: "Eternal life is powerful and dynamic, bringing life in the present and culminating in the resurrection of the dead."[9] Whatever awaits us after death, the time of salvation is always now.

Theologically, the key teaching that cuts across these diverse biblical beliefs on heaven and hell is about relationship. Rather than conceiving heaven and hell only as literal afterlife destinations, they emphasize relationship with God and one another. Jesus' call for repentance as the core Gospel message indicates that "heaven," as "the promise of eternal communion with God,"[10] points to the necessity of faithful living based upon right relationships with fellow human beings and creatures. "Hell," however it is conceived, is the opposite way of life. Understood this way, heaven and hell can be experienced as everyday realities in the here-and-now.

Heaven and Hell in Popular Culture

Watch: *Heaven is for Real* (2014)

Discussion Questions

Before the viewing

What role do afterlife beliefs play in your faith life?

Which biblical afterlife concepts are most relevant to you?

How would you sum up biblical teaching on life after death?

---

8. Colijn, *Images of Salvation in the New Testament*, 90.

9. Ibid., 90 n. 8.

10. Jensen, *Living Hope*, 83.

After the viewing

How does the movie portray the afterlife?

What do you think of the criticism that the movie's portrayal of heaven is "unbiblical"?

Is the Bible the "last word" on Christian afterlife beliefs?

Discussion Notes

It could be said somewhat facetiously that the ancient Israelite notion that all spirits sink down into *Sheol* at death is not that different from the revelation of the life's purpose at the end of *Monty Python's The Meaning of Life*: "now here's the Meaning of Life. Well, it's nothing special. Try and be nice to people, avoid eating fat, read a good book every now and then, get some walking in and try and live together in peace and harmony with people of all creeds and nations."[11] However, Monty Python is remarkably close to the ancient opinion that "there is nothing better for people under the sun than to eat, and drink, and enjoy themselves, for this will go with them in their toil through the days of life that God gives them under the sun" (Eccl 8:15). When it came to discussing the theme of heaven and hell with a group of students in a university chaplaincy setting, there was broad agreement that it was difficult to pin down what the Bible actually says about life after death, as opposed to understandings from popular preaching and teaching.

The movie *Heaven is for Real* represents the afterlife in terms that reflect Christian hopes that go far beyond anything the Bible has to say. The film is based on a book by the same title, written by Todd Burpo, based on his three-year-old son Colton's near-death experience while in surgery for a ruptured appendix.[12] Burpo, a struggling pastor and part-time contractor, is astonished when his small son begins to relate details of his journey to heaven, where he claims to have met deceased relatives his parents had never told him about, including his paternal grandfather and unborn sister. Little Colton also mentions having met Jesus, hearing angels sing, and seeing the marks of crucifixion of Jesus' hands and feet. After initial skepticism

11. *Monty Python's The Meaning of Life*, dir. Terry Jones and Terry Gilliam, 1983, transcribed by Jason R. Heimbaugh. See http://sfy.ru/?script=mp_meanlife.

12. Burpo and Vincent, *Heaven is for Real*.

on the part of both his family and church members, the little boy's innocent confidence in the reality of heaven strengthens everyone's faith, and public interest in Colton's account of heaven leads to the improvement of the family's fortunes. In fact, the book became an immensely profitable bestseller.

Heaven is for Real is part of a popular genre of Christian literature known as "heavenly tourism," containing testimonies about life after death by people claiming to have experienced the afterlife during life-threatening episodes. One of these is *The Boy Who Came Back From Heaven*, published at about the same time as Burpo's book, which was disavowed two years later by the subject of the book, Alex Malarkey, as a fraud.[13] The controversy sparked by this scandal was one of the factors that led to the decision of a large Christian book store chain in the United States, LifeWay Christian Resources, to discontinue the sale of "experiential testimonies about heaven."[14] The reason given was a 2014 Southern Baptist Convention resolution on "the sufficiency of Scripture regarding the afterlife." Any account of a near-death experience that went beyond the biblical account was judged to be misleading.

Compared to the book, the movie version of *Heaven is for Real* is restrained in its depiction of Colton's experiences in heaven; unlike the film, the book describes Jesus as wearing a crown adorned by a big pink jewel, and Colton prophetically sees Jesus lead a war in heaven against "monsters," where only men fight in the cosmic battle, and the women and children look on. When his father asks what weapons he will carry in the Battle of Armageddon, the little boy assures him that it will either be a sword or a bow and arrow, but that God is sure to win.[15] The film has the virtue of avoiding much of the heavy-handed sermonizing interspersed throughout the book.

In addition to the story of Colton's accounts of heaven, the book contains a section about a painting of Jesus by a young girl who claims to have visited heaven repeatedly; the well-groomed portrait of a handsome young Caucasian man with blow-dried brown hair and a neatly trimmed beard printed in the book seems too much like a Sunday school illustration to be taken seriously as an authentic image of the historical Jesus. The film ends with this image, but places less emphasis upon it. A critical reader might surmise that such elements in the book were shaped more by the

13. Malarkey, *Boy Who Came Back from Heaven*.

14. Roach, "Heaven Tourism Books Pulled."

15. Burpo, *Heaven is for Real*, 138.

father's cherished religious beliefs and evangelical intent than by the little boy's memories. Unlike the book, the movie emphasizes the role of the church community in supporting the struggling Burpo family, and the role of Colton's simple conviction that he has experienced heaven in the faith development of the church. One of the final scenes in the movie portrays the interior of the church as a sort of gateway to heaven—a place of relation to God, and to one another.

Figure 1: Scene from *Heaven is for Real*

Other Resources

Jensen, David H. *Living Hope: The Future and Christian Faith.* Louisville: Westminster John Knox, 2010.

Moreman, Christopher. *Beyond the Threshold: Afterlife Beliefs in World Religions.* Lanham, MD: Rowman & Littlefield, 2008.

90 Minutes in Heaven (dir. Michael Polish, 2015).

Parker, Rebecca Ann, and Rita Nakashima Brock. *Saving Paradise: How Christianity Traded Love of This World for Crucifixion and Empire.* Boston: Beacon, 2008.

Pearson, Patricia. *Opening Heaven's Door: Investigating Stories of Life, Death, and What Comes After.* Toronto: Random House Canada, 2014.

6

God and Satan

THE IDEA THAT CHRISTIANITY, like its sister-religions Judaism and Islam, is monotheistic, goes without question for Christians: "We believe in one God" (Nicene Creed); "Hear O Israel: The Lord is our God, the Lord alone" (Deut 6:4); "There is no God but God; Muhammad is his messenger" (*Shahada*). Many Christians also assume that Satan figures throughout the Bible as the arch-enemy of the one God, and that the two powers and their troops have been engaged in a battle between good and evil since the dawn of creation. This chapter will uncover what the Bible actually says about God and Satan, and show how these archetypes figure in popular culture, using the film *Spiderman II* (dir. Mark Webb, 2004) as an example.

God in the Bible

Human language about the divine is limited, metaphorical and multifaceted (see chapter 8). As theologian Elizabeth A. Johnson puts it, the divine is fundamentally unknowable; all speech about God is analogical and metaphorical; and no one image or name is sufficient to comprehend the divine mystery.[1] From the very beginning, the Bible presents the divine in terms of multiplicity; the word translated as "God" in the Priestly creation account (Gen 1:1—2:4a) is *elohim*, literally, "gods" (the singular is *el*). This is why, in Gen 1:26, God proclaims, "let *us* make humankind in *our* image, according to *our* likeness." The use of the first-person plural is a hint that the Priestly author is thinking in terms of a divine council where the God

---

1. Johnson, *She Who Is*, 104–17.

of Israel confers with other deities, as in Ps 82:1: "God has taken his place in the divine council; in the midst of the gods he holds judgment" (see also Job 1:6; 2:1; 15:8; 1 Kgs 22:19–23; Ps 89:5–7). The term "sons of God" (*bene elohim*, literally "sons of gods") is sometimes used to refer to the divine beings of the heavenly council; in the Jewish Scriptures, these "sons" are usually portrayed as subordinate to the God of Israel (Gen 6:2; Job 1:6; 38:7; Ps 29:1). Traditionally, they are understood as messengers ("angels") of God: "Ascribe to the LORD, O heavenly beings [*bene elohim*, 'sons of gods'], ascribe to the LORD glory and strength" (Ps 29:1).

In English translations of the Jewish Scriptures, the other significant term used to identify the deity is the Lord, introduced in Gen 2:4b: "In the day that the LORD God made the earth and the heavens," the introduction to the second (Yahwist) creation account. From this point on, Lord, spelled with small caps, refers to the proper (personal) name of God, YHWH. In Hebrew, this name is always printed without vowels to indicate that the divine name is so sacred and powerful, it must not be pronounced. Some English translations, notably the KJV, render the name as Jehovah (Exod 6:3; Ps 83:18; Isa 12:2; 26:4, KJV), or, in some more recent versions,[2] Yahweh.

Although the divine name was likely spoken by ancient Israelites, nobody today knows how it was actually pronounced. YHWH is a form of the Hebrew verb "to be" (*ehyeh*—"I will be"), as indicated in the divine words to Moses in Exod 3:14: "God said to Moses, 'I am who I am.' He said further, 'Thus you shall say to the Israelites, "I am has sent me to you."'"

> God provides three forms of the divine name: "ehyeh asher ehyeh," (one meaning of which is *I Am Who I Am*); "ehyeh" (I am) and "yhwh" (probably pronounced Yahweh, it may mean "he who causes to be" . . .).[3]

This name is often combined with *Elohim* in a phrase often translated as the LORD God (YHWH Elohim). In addition, the God of the Bible is known by many other designations, e.g., the Most High (*El Elyon*) (Gen 14:18);[4] Num 24:16; 2 Sam 22:14; Acts 16:17); the Lord (*Adonai*); the God who Sees (*El Roi*) (Gen 16:13–15); God Almighty (*El Shaddai*) (Gen 17:1–4);[5] Father

---

2. E.g., the *Names of God Bible* (NOG).

3. *New Oxford Annotated Bible Ecumenical Study Bible*, 87, nn. 14–15.

4. Biblical references here are illustrative, not exhaustive.

5. Sometimes translated as "the God with Breasts." See Biale, "The God with Breasts."

(Isa 64:8); Spirit (Gen 1:2; Ps 51:11; Isa 61:1; 11:2); Word (John 1:1–4); Wisdom (Wisd 7:21b–8:1).

The multiplicity of divine names in the Bible originates in the history of ancient Israelite religion. As Shawn W. Flynn explains,

> Likely at the earliest point in Israel's history, Yahweh was one god among many who had his own place in the divine council of the gods. Like Baal, at an earlier period Yahweh was subservient to the head god El (Deut. 32.8–9). While the Canaanite god El was a part of early Israelite worship (hence the name Israel), Yahweh eventually became Israel's primary deity. Later Yahweh was conceived as head of the divine council (Ps. 82) and in the exilic period Israel embraced monotheism (Isa. 53.10; 44.6–8).[6]

The ancient Israelite tendency toward polytheism is illustrated by the many disapproving biblical references to the worship of Canaanite deities such as Baal and Asherah (e.g., Judg 3:7; 1 Kgs 18:19; 2 Kgs 23:4; Num 25:3–5; Deut 4:3; Judg 2:11, 13; 1 Kgs 15:13; 2 Kgs 23:6–7; 2 Chr 15:16). However, in pre-exilic Israel, the devotion to the "one God" of Israel, YHWH Elohim, was a sort of henotheism, devotion to one God, YHWH, among others; the famous commandment "you shall have no other gods *before me*" (Exod 20:3) implies the existence of "other gods." As Barry Bandstra explains, even the famous affirmation in the *Shema* that "The LORD is our God, the LORD alone" (Deut 6:4) amounts to a "practical" monotheism:

> *Yhwh is our Elohim, Yhwh alone.* He [the Deuteronomist] was not concerned with abstract theological formulations. He stated that there was only one God who was interested in Israel. God demonstrated that by divine care in the past. This God demands their undivided loyalty in the present. Yhwh is the one and only God for their future. The people were bound to Yhwh by means of a legal contract, called the covenant. It defined the shape of their loyalty and specified how they would remain in God's good graces.[7]

Although the Jewish Scriptures generally admit the existence of other deities, if monotheism is redefined as a theology in which one supreme power rules over all other beings, then the ancient Israelite authors were monotheistic (i.e., they revered only YHWH).[8] This attitude is found even in the Christian Testament: "Indeed, even though there may be so-called

---

6. Flynn, "Yahweh, YHWH," 614.

7. Bandstra, *Reading the Old Testament*.

8. See Sommer, "Monotheism in the Hebrew Bible."

gods in heaven or on earth—as in fact there are many gods and many lords— yet for us there is one God, the Father, from whom are all things and for whom we exist, and one Lord, Jesus Christ, through whom are all things and through whom we exist" (1 Cor 8:5–6).

It is only in the biblical books written after the return from exile (538 BCE) that assertions of "pure" monotheism—that there is only one God and no other—start to appear. This is especially pronounced in Deutero-canonical books like Baruch (Letter of Jeremiah), which repeatedly asserts that the gods of Babylon are merely powerless idols made of wood and stone: "They can neither curse nor bless kings; they cannot show signs in the heavens for the nations, or shine like the sun or give light like the moon. The wild animals are better than they are, for they can flee to shelter and help themselves. So we have no evidence whatever that they are gods; therefore do not fear them" (Bar 6:66–69; see also Wisd 23:23–14:31). This form of monotheism finds expression in the Deutero-Pauline writings, which speak of "one God and Father of all, who is above all and through all and in all" (Eph 4:6), "there is one God; there is also one mediator between God and humankind, Christ Jesus, himself human, who gave himself a ransom for all" (1 Tim 2:5–6a). However, as Mark S. Smith has argued, some of the attributes of the ancient Canaanite deities El, Baal and Asherah, were assimilated into the one God of Israel, YHWH, who is conceived as creator, king, warrior, father, nurturer and mother in both Testaments.[9] Laurel Schneider reminds us that such human and approachable deities, appearing as local-warrior-king-protector, were merged into the more cosmic and abstract source of all things, a single God because, "the assault of more than a half millennium of war, exile, and colonization, [created] the conditions that made *exclusive* monotheism both intelligible and persuasive, particularly when what was at stake was cultural survival."[10] This does not mean to imply that the construction of monotheism was seamlessly monolithic or always consistent. The opposite claim could be made. Even the most exclusive form of monotheism that influenced the later period of the Second Temple period (20–70 CE) shows three distinctively different types of monotheism as Mach claims:[11] (1) there is only one (Jewish) God and no other; (2) the Jewish God is the same as the One of Greek philosophy; (3) the deities of the Gentiles are in fact demons. It is also true that the develop-

9. Smith, *Early History of God*, 182–99.

10. Schneider, *Beyond Monotheism*, 33–38.

11. Mach, "Concepts of Jewish Monotheism," 22–25.

ment of Jewish Christian monotheism is not strictly to be understood to maintain a religious identity but inseparably be linked with the survival of cultural and political identity amidst the Roman colonial occupation. It is important, then, to remember that we do not lose sight of the complicated relationships and issues that are tangled with theological matters when we study God in the Bible.

After all this talk of monotheism and divine multiplicity, it may be surprising to some readers that there has been no mention of the Trinity. This is because the Trinity is a post-biblical doctrine; that is, as Karen Kilby puts it,

> The technical language of the doctrine of the Trinity is not bibli-cal, and while the NT contains a number of threefold formulae for God (arguably 1 Cor. 6:11 and 12:4–6; Gal. 3:11–14; Heb. 10:29; 1 Pet. 1:21 and most crucially Matt. 28:19) and some deliberately threefold patterning, the question of how God can be both three and one was not for the NT a locus of extended struggle or ex-tended reflection.[12]

For the purposes of this book, it is sufficient to note that Trinitarian thought began with the fact that early Christians worshipped Jesus Christ as divine, while maintaining the Jewish belief in one God. Trinitarian doc-trine was expressed in a definitive form in the Nicene Creed (325 CE), and its affirmation of belief in one God, comprised of the Father, the Son, and the Holy Spirit. Kilby observes that the theologians of the twentieth and twenty-first centuries have subjected the doctrine of the Trinity to exten-sive analysis, but that this has not resulted in consensus or clarity: "All sides are at one in affirming it is crucially important for Christian theology to be properly Trinitarian, but cannot seem to agree on what this means."[13] Perhaps the approach of apophatic theology, where the mystery of the di-vine nature takes precedence over the presumption of knowing (cataphatic theology), is the best approach in the quest for understanding.[14]

---

12. Kilby, "Trinity," *Cambridge Dictionary of Christian Theology*, Kindle Edition, loc. 26543. It should be noted that the "crucial" Trinitarian formula of Matt 28:19 is regarded by many scholars as a late interpolation into the text of Matthew.

13. Ibid. loc. 26628.

14. MacFarland, "Apophatic Theology," *Cambridge Dictionary of Christian Theology*, loc. 2082.

Satan in the Bible

Obviously, God, YHWH Elohim, figures prominently in the Jewish Scriptures. For many Christians, it is surprising to find out that his "opposite," Satan, is nearly absent—even from passages that are popularly believed to feature Satan as a character. For example, in Genesis 3, the serpent in the Garden of Eden is not identified as Satan; he is merely a crafty, talking snake. The classic text for the legend of the rebellion of Satan ("Lucifer") and his angelic hordes, Isa 14:3–21, is actually a prophetic taunt-song, triumphing over the defeat of a Babylonian king ("you will take up this taunt against the king of Babylon," v. 4) who, like other ancient near eastern monarchs, regards himself as a god (vv. 12–14), but who will be defeated, and cast down into Sheol like all other living beings (vv. 15–21). It was not until more than a thousand years after the career of Isaiah that the designation "Day Star" (v. 12; Hebrew: *hayleel*) was translated into Latin as "Lucifer" ("Light-Bearer"). The notion that Satan/Lucifer was an archangel who rebelled against God, and that the angels who followed him became demons, is Christian and post-biblical; it was not known by the writers of the Christian Testament.

While the idea of Satan was a post-biblical phenomenon, early Christian theologians speculated on the figure and its significance. In the theology of Origen of Alexandria (third century CE), Satan appears in his cosmology as the first soul to fall from the precreated state. This fallen soul had been counted among the stars. "Even Satan was once light," he writes, "before he went astray and fell to this place."[15] This fall is depicted like a process of being cooled. Satan's passion for life, devotion and love seem to have lost their intensity. Origen was a theologian who did not believe in predestination but instead believed that no one is doomed, not even Satan. He believed that should Satan, the first fallen soul, seek to ascend back to the contemplation of God, he might possibly re-enter the constellation of God's cosmos. In the same way a human soul may fall into the domain of the demonic but may be redeemed, returned back to the divine state. Fiona Thompson, an Origen scholar, captures his theology this way: "For Origen, the incarnation destroys the whole conspiracy of demons, and through the soteriological grace it mediates, demonic power became ultimately ineffectual for those who had turned toward God."[16] God's union with humanity

---

15. Thompson, "Demonology," 85.
16. Ibid., 86.

is stronger than human will, a will which may, due to Satan's influence, seek to detach from God.

In Hebrew, the term translated as "Satan" is *haSatan*, "the adversary." To put this in the form of a verb we might say Satan is "someone who opposes." The sense of this verb is mostly used in the Jewish Scriptures in a secular sense (Gen 50:15, Ps 38:21; 1 Sam 29:4; 1 Kgs 5:18). The meaning of Satan took a religious tone only in postexilic writings such as the book of Job.[17] In Job 1–2, the Satan appears as a member of the divine council, one of the *bene Elohim* whose function is to tempt and accuse humankind (1:6; 2:1). The Satan famously wagers that the righteous Job will turn against God if his wealth, family and health are taken from him. God takes the challenge and allows the adversary to afflict the innocent Job, who ultimately passes the test, and has his fortunes restored (42:7–17). The Satan figure only appears in the first two chapters of Job, and it is very clear that he is subordinate to YHWH; Job's afflictions are ultimately from God, not Satan. In this depiction Satan is not an enemy of God but one in service of God, playing a God-given role, the role of accusing humankind. One of the morals of the story is expressed by Job himself: "Shall we receive good at the hand of God, and shall we not receive evil?" (2:10). Both good and evil come from God; Satan is not the powerful and primordial enemy of God, but his servant.

The other two Jewish scriptural references to Satan as a character are found in Zech 3:1–5 and 1 Chr 21:1, both post-exilic writings. In Zechariah, as in Job, the Satan functions as the prosecutor in a trial before God, in this case, of the high priest Joshua, who is defended by "the angel of YHWH" and is cleared of the charges brought against him. Only in 1 Chr 21:1 does the term "Satan" (not "*the* satan") seem to function as a proper name: "Satan stood up against Israel, and incited David to number Israel." Here, the Chronicler clears up the problem created by his source (2 Sam 24), in which it is YHWH who incites David to take a census of Israel and Judah, and action that, strangely, incurs God's anger against the kingdom in the form of a plague that kills 70,000 (24:1, 15). By attributing the census to Satan rather than God, the Chronicler alleviates the problem of David's obedience to a divine command that leads to disaster.

Adam Porter notes that,

> By the time of the Christian Testament, Jews had come to understand Satan as a more independent and evil entity, opposed

17. Betz et al., *Religion Past and Present*, 6.

to God, rather than obeying God (Rom 16:20, Rev 17:7–9, Rev 20:7–10). Through time, people's understanding of Satan's characteristics and power continued to shift and develop. In the English-speaking world, most modern conceptions of Satan are based on John Milton's *Paradise Lost* (1667) more than on biblical sources. . . . the image of Satan shifted over time, moving from obnoxious but obedient servant of God to being evil and opposed to God.[18]

Porter is correct that Milton's epic poem, where Satan, "revolting from God, and drawing to his side many legions of Angels, was, by the command of God, driven out of Heaven, with all his crew, into the great Deep" (*Paradise Lost*, Book 1, The Argument), is overwhelmingly influential on western Christian demonology. However, this is a scenario never found in the Bible.

The Christian Testament references to Satan (also called the "Devil," from the Greek *diabolos*), demons (*daimonia*) and unclean spirits (*pneumata akathartos*) have more in common with early Jewish apocalyptic writings than they do with the later Christian Lucifer legend. Early Jewish writings posit supernatural adversaries as a way to explain the existence of evil in the world, and, especially, Israel's misfortunes: "In these texts an individual—whether it is Belial (1QH, 2 Cor 6:14–15), Melchiresa (11QMelch), Mastema (*Jub.* 10:7–9), or Satan (Job 1–2, Zech 3, Matt 4:1–11)—stands in opposition to God's plan, and his chosen people or agents."[19] The Christian Testament does not recognize any difference in content between Satan and Devil. But the earlier writings including the Gospel of Mark and Pauline letters use the term "Satan," while the later writings such as the Gospel of John, Johannine letters, and the Revelations tend to speak of the "devil,"[20] a term that means "accuser" or "backbiter" in Greek (*diabolos*). The Christian Testament's Satan/Devil is a more hostile figure than the Adversary of Job, Zechariah and 1 Chronicles, but, as Henry Ansgar Kelly explains,

> Satan is not a likeable character in the Christian Testament, and he is scheduled for unceremonious retirement from his official position of Governor of the World . . . The most extreme forecast of his retirement is set forth in terms of a great battle in Heaven and of the punishment in store for the future; but at the same time it is also explained that Satan, up until this time, retained

18. Porter, "Satan."
19. Sullivan, "Demons," 95.
20. Betz et al., *Religion Past and Present*, 6.

his position as heavenly Prosecutor, and that he has now been removed from it . . . [21]

That is, while Satan's prosecutorial role is intensified in the Christian Testament writings, to the point that his activities become extreme and dangerous, he is still a member of the heavenly court, a tester and accuser who tries even Jesus (Mark 1:12–13; Matt 4:1–11; Luke 4:1–13).

In the Christian Testament, demons/unclean spirits function independently of Satan; even in the famous exorcism story where Jesus asks "how can Satan cast out Satan" (Mark 3:23), the ruler of the demons is identified as Beelzebul (3:22), not Satan; here, as Kelly suggests, *satanas* should be translated not as a proper name ("Satan") but in its Hebrew meaning of "adversary": "Jesus is saying in effect that a satan, that is, an adversary, is not likely to act against a fellow adversary."[22] Both ancient Jews and Greeks regarded the *daimonia* who possessed people and caused illnesses and seizures as restless spirits of the dead (see especially Mark 5:1–20).[23] In Jewish apocalyptic speculation, these harmful spirits were popularly connected to the strange story in Gen 6:1–4, where the *bene Elohim* ("sons of God" or "sons of gods") mate with the daughters of humans, giving rise to a generation of giants (*Nephilim*), "the heroes that were of old, warriors of renown" (6:4). While this legend is told in Genesis without any negative value judgement on the behavior of the divine beings or their offspring, in intertestamental times, the "sons of God" were interpreted as rebellious angels, the Watchers, who in their lust for human women taught the human race all kinds of godless arts, including magic. Their offspring, the giants, were violent and greedy, consuming everything in their path, including human beings. In this mythology, God sends the flood to purge the earth of the Nephilim. However, the spirits of the Nephilim live on as demons, while the angelic Watchers are chained in the underworld until the final judgement. The myth of the Watchers appears in its most complete form in 1 *Enoch*, but it is alluded to in other early Jewish writings (e.g., Wisd 14:6; Jdt 16:7; Sir 16:7; Bar 3:25–28; 3 *Macc* 2:4; *Jub* 4:15; 5:1; 7:21–25; *Damascus Document* 2:18), as well as in the Christian Testament (2 Pet 2:4; Jude 6).[24]

Although Satan, and the demons, are portrayed in the Christian Testament as entities hostile to humanity, the notion that they constitute

21. Kelly, *Satan: A Biography*, 327.
22. Ibid., 83.
23. See Bolt, *Jesus' Defeat of Death*.
24. See Wink, *Naming the Powers*, 24–25.

an army of fallen angels locked in primal conflict with the forces of good
("the war between good and evil") owes more to Zoroastrian doctrine,[25]
which, as discussed in chapter 5, exerted an influence on early Jewish and
Christian apocalyptic thinking, and to post-biblical Christian speculation
inspired by the radical reinterpretation and conflation of biblical passages
like Isa 14:3–21, Luke 10:18 and Rev 12:4.[26]

The following table summarizes the differences between the bibli-
cal/Jewish/Christian Testament demonology and post-biblical Christian
developments:

Jewish (biblical)	Christian (post-biblical)
The Satan ("Adversary") is an angel of God who tests humanity	*Satan/the Devil is identified with Lucifer, a fallen angel*
Demons are the offspring of "giants" (Nephilim) who drowned in the flood	*Demons are angels who "fell" along with Lucifer*
Satan inhabits the air; demons are associated with the dead	*Both Satan and the demons are associated with Hades/Hell*
The Watchers are chained in the underworld (Tartarus)	

As mentioned earlier, these apocalyptic writings were influenced by
such dualistic religions as Zoroastrianism, but their dualism is less radical. More often than not, there is no separation of supernatural beings into
good and evil. Theologian Catherine Keller makes a strong case in this regard. She examines the book of Revelation in relation to Genesis to show
how the last book of the Bible darkly mirrors the first, not in a linear sense,
but in a spatial and non-dualistic sense. She writes,

> Revelation 12 narratively reconfigures Genesis's mythology of
> creation-mother of life (*Hava*, Eve), snake, and fall—as the de-
> feat of the rebellious angels in heaven . . . The text promotes the
> snake back up from garden-variety creep to cosmic Evil worthy
> to oppose the Good. Apocalypse [in Revelation] does not casu-
> ally *reverse* Genesis. The 'fall' of the first creation narrative is *re-
> played*, taken into spiral, in order to solve it—to end it. Not that
> the serpent-dragon-figured slithering around so many neolithic

25. See Kelly, *Satan*, 328.
26. Ibid., 191–215.

pots, slicing through earth and water . . . had represented "good." It seems to have vitalized a spatiality "beyond good and evil," beyond the binary construct which depends—for good and ill—upon heroic monotheism.[27]

However, the image of slithering dragon and snake as evil continues to feature very strongly in popular culture, especially in films.

Two things need to be clarified here in the discussion of Satan in relation to God. Satan and other "demonic" beings are not completely independent of God. Even the theologian Augustine of Hippo who developed the concept of Original Sin (see chapter 2) claimed that "Evil is a turning away from immutable goods and a turning towards changeable goods."[28] In this sense evil is not the opposite of goodness, but its absence. At least in his youthful theological development, Augustine had a less dualistic notion of good and evil and a more positive notion of the free choice of human will. In fact, Satan/demons were often understood by early Christians as "gods of strangers/others" in polytheistic religious traditions.[29] These traditions assume a hierarchy of gods. Even in the monotheistic religious traditions such a hierarchy exists. Medieval Christians, for example, imagined a hierarchy that started from the highest God, to Christ, and descended to the lowest anti-gods.[30] But as the monotheistic religious traditions became more dualistic in worldview, Satan/the Devil became popularly regarded as the evil opposite of God, imagined as an independent power.

In dualistic views of the world, there are often negative social consequences for weaker or minority groups within society. In the case of Christianity, for example, women as the "opposite" of men were sometimes linked to "Satanic" power in a way that justified controlling and oppressing them. The persecution of women as witches in the early modern period is a prime example. Unfortunately, even today this kind of dualism is at work in certain Christian churches. In less obvious ways, the God/Satan dualism is not far from the psyche of most modern Christians. Even Pope Francis in a recent homily spoke of the existence of Satan in the twenty-first century:

> We too are tempted, we too are the target of attacks by the devil because the spirit of Evil does not want our holiness, he does not want our Christian witness, he does not want us to be disciples of

27. Keller, *Apocalypse Now and Then*, 69.

28. Augustine, *On Free Choice of the Will*, 82–83.

29. Betz et al. *Religion Past and Present*, 8.

30. Ibid., 8.

Christ. And what does the Spirit of Evil do, through his temptations, to distance us from the path of Jesus? The temptation of the devil has three characteristics and we need to learn about them in order not to fall into the trap. What does Satan do to distance us from the path of Jesus? Firstly, his temptation begins gradually but grows and is always growing. Secondly, it grows and infects another person, it spreads to another and seeks to be part of the community. And in the end, in order to calm the soul, it justifies itself. It grows, it spreads and it justifies itself.[31]

The Pope's understanding of Satan in this homily is very closely related to temptation. He sees temptation as the work of Satan, who has the pervasive power to seduce people to sin and do harmful acts. It is difficult to separate temptation from the discussion of sin which is the key theme of chapter 2. At the same time, it is almost an impossible task to divide sin from the idea of Satan.

The biblical doctrine of Satan is neither simple nor clear. The Bible speaks about Satan in various ways. However, it is clear that the association of Satan with the notion of evil is linked to a dualistic worldview. If we do not approach the diverse biblical references to Satan with a preconceived dualism, we notice that the figure of Satan is ambiguous and the work of Satan is complex: he is a tempter and a adversary, but also a tester and a catalyst, an integral part of the divine unfolding. Within a less dualistic frame of interpretation, human beings appear as beings created in God's image, capable of and fully responsible for both good and evil.[32]

To conclude, what does the Bible say about God and Satan? It says many things. In the case of God, God has many names and yet God cannot be named with a single name. Even the prevalent monotheistic God was a later development which did not completely ignore the pluralistic views of God in the Bible. In the case of Satan, the Bible does not say much. Unlike the strong portrayal of Satan in popular culture, Satan in the Bible is insignificant and unimportant.

---

31. See http://www.news.va/en/news/pope-francis-satan-exists-in-the-21st-century.
32. Craigo-Snell and Monroe, *Living Christianity*, 75.

God and Satan in the Movies

Watch: *Spiderman II* (2004)

Discussion Questions

Before the viewing

What kinds of teachings have you heard about God and Satan?

Does it surprise you that Satan is not an important figure in the Jewish Scriptures?

Where does the idea that the Bible is about "the battle between good and evil" come from?

After the viewing

In the movie, who is the God figure(s), and who is the Satan figure(s)?

What about Spiderman reminds you of the Bible?

Would you describe the movie as apocalyptic in any way?

Discussion Notes

The authors viewed this movie together with a student group sponsored by the Catholic campus ministry, in collaboration with the university's ecumenical chaplaincy. At the beginning of the evening, one of the students asked why we had chosen *Spiderman II*, as opposed to the many other Spiderman movies. The answer was that it is the most theologically profound one. Although the answer was a bit flippant, there is some truth to it. This particular film contains several of the themes of the chapters in this book, in addition to God and Satan: Sin and Salvation, Christ and Antichrist, Suffering and Sacrifice, even Creation and Apocalypse. Although the viewers saw all these themes in the movie during the post-movie discussion, a common response from students and campus ministers alike was that when they'd seen the movie before, that had not noticed the biblical elements.

Figure 1: Mary Ann Beavis, Spiderman, and HyeRan Kim-Cragg

After the viewing, the first student to respond to the question of how the movie related to the theme of God and Satan described himself as not very religious; however, he quickly saw that Spiderman represented God, and the supervillain Dr. Otto Octavius ("Dr. Octopus") represented Satan. This does not mean that the filmmakers meant Spiderman to "be" God, or Doc Oc to "be" Satan, but that the two figures, representing the forces of good and evil, are subtly aligned in the viewer's mind with these biblical cultural archetypes.

As noted in chapter 2 ("Sin and Salvation"), American superheroes are often portrayed not only as on the side of God, but as Christ figures. *Spiderman II* does a particularly good job of subtly aligning Spiderman/ Peter Parker with Christ figure motifs. In this movie, Peter Parker conforms particularly to the "suffering servant" aspect of Christ (Mark 10:45; Isa 53:1–12), a poor, nearly-homeless young man trying to eke out a living as a pizza delivery boy and freelance photographer for an editor who has no respect for him, and who hates Spiderman. As Peter, he is unfortunate and accident-prone; his beloved Mary Jane has grown up to be a famous actress, who becomes engaged to the handsome astronaut son of Peter's nasty editor. Although as Spiderman, Peter faithfully fulfills his mission as savior of New York City, neither the superhero nor the ordinary man get much credit for what they do for others, except from the "little people" who admire him—children, the shy daughter of his mean landlord, astonished onlookers. Mary Jane, who can't understand why Peter is so aloof, calls him a mystery, and is having difficulty imagining a romantic relationship with him, though she is in love. Due to his broken promises (e.g., to show up at the theater), she is uncertain that he is in love with her to the point that she is ready to give up on their friendship.

In the midst of all his troubles, Peter begins to lose faith in his superheroic mission, and starts to lose his powers. Viewers familiar with the Gospel of Mark will recognize the themes of the secret messiah,[33] the relationship between faith and miracles (Mark 2:5; 4:40; 5:34; 10:52; 11:22), and the suffering of the Human One (Mark 8:31–33; 9:12; 10:33) echoed throughout the movie. *Spiderman II* even features a recognition scene (Mark 8:27–30), where Mary Jane finally realizes that the lowly Peter is in fact the famous superhero, the Mary Magdalene to Peter's Jesus. Peter's best friend, Harry Osborn, the son of another Satan figure, Norman Osborn (aka the Green Goblin), plays the Judas figure to Spiderman's Christ.

Spiderman's nemesis in this film, Dr. Octavius, is a brilliant scientist whose technological marvel backfires on him, making him a diabolical eight-limbed monster (Dr. Octopus) with four electronic arms melded directly into his nervous system. The movie portrays Octavius very much in terms of the Lucifer myth; he is a fallen genius who initially wants to do good, but who is perverted by his pride and rashness. His artificial arms are serpentine, inciting him to evil deeds by whispering in his ear (Figure 2).

Figure 2: Dr. Octopus (Alfred Molina), *Spiderman II]*

33. See Beavis, *Mark*, 80.

With Dr. Octopus loose in the city, Peter Parker must, in good apocalyptic fashion, regain faith in his mission as Spiderman to engage in battle with the supervillain. It is only after Peter is impelled to save the terrified passengers of a runaway train put in motion by the supervillain that he realizes that his destiny is to be a superhero, even if this involves suffering and sacrifice, including giving up an unambitious desire to simply live an ordinary life. This aspect of Spiderman's identity is telegraphed to the viewers by the cruciform pose struck by Peter/Spiderman at the front of the train (Figure 3). After he has successfully stopped the train, he passes out inside a railway car, and is revived by the grateful passengers, who, although he is unmasked in the struggle, promise that they'll never reveal his identity: the death and resurrection of Spiderman is achieved in part through the communal support of the ordinary people.

Figure 3: Peter Parker/Spiderman in Cruciform Pose, *Spiderman II*

In a poignant scene shortly before Peter recommits to his mission as Spiderman, his Aunt May makes a speech that one of the member of our discussion group described as like that of a prophet:

Too few characters out there, flying around like that . . . saving old girls like me.

And Lord knows, kids like Henry need a hero.

Courageous, self-sacrificing people setting examples for all of us.

Everybody loves a hero.

People line up for them. Cheer them. Scream their names.

And years later, they'll tell how they stood in the rain for hours just to get a glimpse of the one who taught them to hold on a second longer.

I believe there's a hero in all of us that keeps us honest, gives us strength, makes us noble, and finally allows us to die with pride. Even though sometimes we have to be steady and give up the thing we want the most. Even our dreams.[34]

In their own ways, both Peter and Dr. Octavius exercise their free will by the end of the movie; Peter, to embrace his identity as Spiderman, and Dr. Octavius, to resist the evil promptings of his invention and cooperate to save the city from destruction.

Other Resources

Kelly, Henry Ansgar. *Satan: A Biography*. Cambridge, UK: Cambridge University Press, 2006.
MacLean, Catherine Faith, and John H. Young. *Preaching the Big Questions: Doctrine Isn't Dusty*. Toronto: United Church Publishing House, 2015.
Schneider, Laurel C. *Beyond Monotheism: A Theology of Multiplicity*. New York: Routledge, 2011.

34. "Spider-Man 2 Script—Dialogue Transcript," http://www.script-o-rama.com/movie_scripts/s/spider-man-2-script-transcript.html.

7

Christ and Antichrist

WHAT DOES IT MEAN to call Jesus "Christ"? This chapter distinguishes between Jewish scriptural and early Jewish conceptions of Messiah, and the radical Christian reconceptualization of the term as applying specifically to Jesus. Next, we will turn to the subject of Christ's "opposite number," the Antichrist, portrayed in popular culture, and all-too-often in Christianity, as a satanic emissary of evil who figures dramatically in end-time scenarios. We will see that although the term "antichrist" is found in the Bible, it does not appear in the Book of Revelation; nor does it refer to the kind of character featured in apocalyptic horror movies. We will argue that Antichrist discourse often occurs in the context of the fear of others when others are viewed as a threat to Christianity. We will also examine the Antichrist rhetoric used in the practice of labeling others. The chapter will then briefly investigate the origins of the Antichrist legend, in contrast with the biblical meaning of the term, and offer an alternative interpretation of the Antichrist through the visions of Hildegard of Bingen. To conclude, we will discuss concepts of Christ and Antichrist in popular culture, with special reference to the movie *Agora* (dir. Alejandro Aménabar, 2012).

Messiah, Christ, Jesus

The designation "Jesus Christ," or simply "Christ," is often used to identify Jesus of Nazareth, as if Jesus was his first name, and Christ his surname. Jesus (Joshua, Jeshua) is, in fact, a proper name, shared with several biblical figures—notably, Moses's successor, Joshua, after whom the biblical book of that title is named. However, the term Christ is not a personal name but a title, in Greek *christos*. The Greek word translates the Hebrew *mashiach*, "anointed." In English, the Hebrew term is rendered as Messiah, so to refer to Jesus as "Christ" (or, as is more usual in Greek, *ho christos*, "the Christ") is to identify him as Messiah.

Christians often assume that Jewish messianic expectation was unified and widespread in Jesus' time, and are sometimes puzzled as to why more of Jesus' contemporaries did not recognize him as messiah. In fact, as James Charlesworth has observed, the question "Why did Jews not recognise Jesus was the Messiah?" is based on the misunderstanding that first-century Jews had a uniform and consistent understanding of the term based on the witness of the Jewish Scriptures.[1] However, the Jewish Scriptures use the term *mashiach* in different ways. In its most commonplace sense, the object of an anointing could be either a person or an object: "People were variously anointed for either cosmetic (Ruth 3:3; cf. Luke 7:46) or medicinal purposes (Isa 1:6; Luke 10:34; cf. John 9:6, 11) or as part of the embalming process (Mark 16:1; cf. Matt 26:12)."[2] More symbolically, anointing could set apart, in the sense of consecrate to honor or venerate, an object or person to God: "The anointing of a stone pillar signified that the place where it was erected was sacred (Gen 28:16–18). Similarly, the tabernacle and its furnishings and implements were anointed with oil to set them apart from common, profane uses to a holy and sacred function (Lev 8:10; Num 7:1)."[3] Aaron and subsequent high priests of Israel were anointed to signify their status as consecrated to divine service (Exod 29:7; Lev 8:12; 21:10). In the Pentateuch, the priests of Israel are the first and foremost of God's "messiahs," anointed ones.

Other categories of biblical persons described as "anointed" in a special way were prophets and kings. In the case of prophets, the anointing was not necessarily a physical pouring of oil, but a metaphorical empowerment for a divinely appointed task (e.g., Isa 61:1): "The spirit of the Lord God is upon me, because the Lord has anointed me; he has sent me to bring good news to the oppressed, to bind up the broken-hearted, to proclaim liberty to the captives, and release to the prisoners" (cf. Ps 105:5; 1 Chr 16:22).[4] When in Luke 4:18–19, Jesus quotes this Isaiah passage in a synagogue ser-

---

1. Charlesworth, "From Messianology to Christology," 13.

2. Cargal, "Anoint," 65.

3. Ibid., 66.

4. The only biblical reference to the literal anointing of a prophet is in 1 Kgs 19:16, with reference to the anointing of Elisha.

mon, he both invokes the "anointed" (*echrisen*) status of the prophet, but also applies it to himself in another sense—as an anointed king (*mashaich, christos*) of Israel (cf. Luke 19:38; 23:23, 38; Acts 17:7). Unlike the metaphorically anointed prophets, kings of Israel were literally anointed with oil as part of their enthronement ceremony (e.g., 1 Sam 10:1; 16:13; 2 Sam 2:4; 5:3; 1 Kgs 1:39). In its application to royalty, the "anointed" was not a future, supernatural redeemer figure, but the historical, human king of Israel/Judah. However, the notion that a descendant of David, an anointed king, would always occupy the throne of Israel, is often expressed in the Jewish Scriptures: "Great triumphs he gives to his king, and shows steadfast love to his anointed, to David and his descendants for ever" (Ps 18:50; 132:16–18; 2 Sam 23:1–7; 7:13). When applied to the Davidic king, the term *mashiach* refers to a royal, military figure, a man who, like other men, will one day die, and be succeeded by members of his dynasty, adopted sons of God:

> When your days are fulfilled and you lie down with your ancestors, I will raise up your offspring after you, who shall come forth from your body, and I will establish his kingdom. He shall build a house for my name, and I will establish the throne of his kingdom for ever. I will be a father to him, and he shall be a son to me. When he commits iniquity, I will punish him with a rod such as mortals use, with blows inflicted by human beings. But I will not take my steadfast love from him, as I took it from Saul, whom I put away from before you. Your house and your kingdom shall be made sure for ever before me; your throne shall be established for ever. (1 Sam 7:12–16)

The eternal covenant with the Davidic line was a guarantee of national sovereignty for Israel; a promise that was not fulfilled historically in the light of the Babylonian exile (586–538 BCE), after which the Davidic monarchy was not restored.

It is in the so-called "intertestamental" period, between the return from exile and the emergence of early Christianity, similar to the emergence of the concept of afterlife discussed in chapter 5, that messianic beliefs began to take shape in early Judaism. One of the Dead Sea Scrolls famously refers to a "messiah of Israel" and a "messiah of Aaron," kingly and priestly figures who would reign in the age to come (1 QS 9:11; cf. Zech 4:14).[5] Other Jewish writings of this era (e.g., 1 *Enoch*, 4 *Ezra*, 2 *Baruch*, *Psalms of Solomon*) develop the messianic idea in different directions, but

5. See Wolters, "Messiah in the Qumran Documents," 78.

with a profile that boils down to "an eschatological [end-time] ruler, chosen by God to act decisively on behalf of the righteous of God's people Israel."[6] Messianic elements shared by more than one, but not all, of these documents include: "Davidic lineage, pre-existence, effects of his disclosure or coming; warrior activity; the interpretation of certain biblical texts (esp. Psalm 2; Daniel 7; and Isaiah 11); and other designations that apply from the narrative contexts."[7] There was no universally accepted "core tradition" about the messiah (or messiahs) that all Jews subscribed to, but a variously expressed hope that God would intervene to restore the world to rights, and Israel to native rule under a duly appointed descendant of David. However, it should be noted that messianic attributes could also be applied to non-Davidic, and even non-Jewish, rulers: Cyrus of Persia (Isa 45:1) and, later, the Roman Emperor Vespasian, identified by the Jewish historian Josephus (first century CE) as the ruler whose nation would take over the world, mistakenly believed by the Jews to be one of them, but actually, a Roman (*Jewish War* 312–13).

In view of the latitude of early Jewish messianic beliefs, it is not surprising that one of the titles ascribed to Jesus of Nazareth by his followers was Messiah/Christ (*christos, mashiach*). Perhaps significantly, the Jesus of the Synoptic Gospels (Matthew, Mark, and Luke) is portrayed as rather reticent about accepting, or perhaps publicly proclaiming, the title (Mark 8:27–30; Matt 16:13–20; Luke 4:41; 22:67). However, as evidenced by the hundreds of references to Jesus as Christ in the Christian Testament, for early Christians, the title Christ/Messiah very quickly applied *only* to Jesus, so that the title became tantamount to a name: Jesus Christ, as opposed to Jesus *the* Christ. Thus, in Christian belief, Jesus takes on many of the Jewish messianic attributes listed above, and the term Christ becomes merged with all of the other titles applied to Jesus in the Christian Testament: Savior, Redeemer, Son of Man, Son of God, Logos, Lord, King of the Jews, Son of David, Servant, High Priest, etc. The meaning of the term Christ in Christianity thus took on a specificity, and a range of connotations, not attached to Messiah in the Jewish tradition, and the one and only Christ became Jesus.

6. Stuckenbruck, "Messianic Ideas," 112.

7. Ibid., 112.

Antichrist

Unlike the term Christ, which has its origins in the Jewish Scriptures and early Jewish tradition, the Antichrist figure of Christian apocalyptic mostly emerges in the post-biblical era. Surprisingly, no figure called the Antichrist is mentioned in the Book of Revelation, although subsequent generations of Christians often read the Antichrist into the Book of Revelation.[8] The only Christian Testament usages of the term appear in 1–2 John:

> Children, it is the last hour! As you have heard that antichrist is coming, so now many antichrists have come. From this we know that it is the last hour. (1 John 2:18)

> Who is the liar but the one who denies that Jesus is the Christ? This is the antichrist, the one who denies the Father and the Son. (1 John 2:22)

> . . . and every spirit that does not confess Jesus is not from God. And this is the spirit of the antichrist, of which you have heard that it is coming; and now it is already in the world. (1 John 4:3)

> Many deceivers have gone out into the world, those who do not confess that Jesus Christ has come in the flesh; any such person is the deceiver and the antichrist! (2 John 1:7)

Although these references place *antichristos* ("against-Christ-person") in the end times ("the last hour"), antichrist is not a single figure ("many antichrists have come"), but anyone who denies that Jesus is the Christ/ Messiah, and particularly that he was a real human being (2 John 1:7). Here, an "antichrist" seems to be anyone who preaches a doctrine of Christ that differs from that taught in the Johannine letters.

What this suggests is that the Johannine concept of antichrist is neither used to identify a singular person nor a single group. It is rather associated with those spreading a false teaching. To be labeled antichrist means that one has been teaching what is contrary to the core Christian faith—Jesus as the anointed one, the incarnational one, Savior of the world who "has come in the flesh" (1 John 4:2). Here one may note the emphasis of the author of the Gospel of John on the incarnational nature of Jesus as the Christ, the One who became flesh in the same way that other human beings

8. Theologian David Jensen begins his chapter on Antichrist with the story of a group of church members who just finished a Bible study of the Book of Revelation. They jumped from Revelation to Antichrist. See his *Living Hope*, 94.

are flesh. Jensen speculates that antichrist might have been the teaching of early Gnostics who denied the bodily nature of Christ.[9]

In post-biblical times, Christians began to merge these references to "antichrist" with other "against Christ" figures of the Christian Testament, especially in apocalyptic contexts: the Beast (*thērion*) of Revelation whose number is six hundred and sixty-six (Rev 13:18); the "false christs" (*pseudochristoi*) of the Gospel apocalypses (Mark 13:22; Matt 24:24); and the "lawless one . . . the one destined for destruction" of 2 Thess 2:3–12. However, while Christian speculation on the Antichrist has biblical DNA, consensus about this mysterious figure seems to have taken several centuries to develop. In the fourth century, John Chrysostom warned against undue interest in the Antichrist, dismissing this kind of conjecture as childish fables and gossip: "And have you not often heard, when you were children, persons talking much even about the name of Antichrist, and about his bending the knee? For the devil scatters these things in our minds, while yet tender, that the doctrine may grow up with us, and that he may be able to deceive us."[10] Augustine of Hippo, writing in the early fifth century, remarked of 2 Thess 2:1–12, "No one can doubt that Paul is here speaking of the Antichrist, telling us that the day of judgment (which he calls the day of the Lord) will not come without the prior coming of a figure whom he calls the Apostate, meaning, of course, an apostate from the Lord God" (*City of God* 20.19.2).[11] Around 409 CE, St. Jerome expressed the by-then commonplace notion that the Antichrist would be a sort of "evil twin" of Christ: "Just as in Christ the fullness of divinity existed corporally, so all the powers, signs and prodigies will be in Antichrist, but all of them will be false."[12]

This early version of the legend of the Antichrist as an end-time figure who would be an evil parody of the true Christ has been transmitted and reinterpreted throughout the centuries, and speculations have abounded as to whom the Antichrist will be. As David MacLachlan observes:

> The concept and symbols of the antichrist appear often through history as a way of denouncing one's enemies or opponents both inside and outside of Christianity. Various individuals and nations

9. Jensen, *Living Hope*, 97.

10. *Homily on 2 Thessalonians* 1. http://www.newadvent.org/fathers/23051.htm.

11. See Gorday, *Ancient Christian Commentary on Scripture, New Testament IX*, 111.

12. *Letter to Algasia* 121.11, 59, cited in Hughes, *Constructing Antichrist*, 77.

have been assigned this status from the Pope in the time of the Reformation to Hitler in the last century.[13]

MacLaughlan sagely warns that due to the many and varied suggestions as to "his" identity, we should be aware that the Antichrist symbol is highly subject to manipulation and misrepresentation.[14]

MacLaughlan's warning further points out the potential danger of Antichrist rhetoric to lead to violence. Thus we must critically investigate the contexts behind the emergence of Antichrist discourse. One of these contexts is the fear of others. In the case of the first letter of John, this fear of the other may include the fear of the human body associated with early Gnostics—or, conversely, fear of new and challenging doctrines. Detaching a certain aspect of our own physical being and denying it as if it does not belong to us is indeed a process of othering. The denial of the body can lead to all kinds of violence against oneself and others who one associates with the dangers of the body. In this dualistic world view, women and nature have for centuries been associated with the body, thus regarded as dangerous, by men.[15] The burning of women as witches in Europe and the exploitation of nature throughout European colonialism all over the world in the last few centuries are salient examples that clearly demonstrate the violent consequences of the fear of the body. It also illustrates the disastrous consequences of defining those who disagree with us, including the Gnostics, as heretical and dangerous—even if they question our cherished beliefs.

While it is painful to note how historic Christian ideologies of dualism, "us versus them," have perpetuated such violence, it is even more painful to acknowledge how Christianity has manipulated and misrepresented other groups fueling the "fear" of them as "the Other." These so-called others who are different from Christians come to be understood as a threat to Christianity. This sense of fear creates an urge among Christians to defend and protect themselves from this threat. This perceived need for protection is then used to justify discrimination and exclusion. The way of such defense and protection can go as far as xenocide, an attempt to wipe out the existence of the others. Xenocide emerges from xenophobia, fear of others. The fear of others in extreme cases results in the violence of killing, which can be so easily and so often found in the long history of Christianity.[16]

13. MacLachlan, "Antichrist," 23.

14. Ibid., 23.

15. Kim-Cragg, "A Christian Feminist Theological Reflection," 170–76.

16. Brock and Parker, *Saving Paradise*.

Another context for the Antichrist discourse is found in the debate about what is right teaching and what is wrong teaching in Christianity. The label "Antichrist" is applied to those who are seen to be propagating the faith incorrectly. One great example of this labeling discourse is found in the thought of John Calvin. As a Reformer who was deeply concerned with the abuses in the Roman Catholic Church, he used the label "Antichrist" in referring to the pope. "By making their pontiff universal they declare him to be Antichrist," Calvin wrote.[17] David Jensen notes that Calvin was not only guilty of anti-Catholic bias but also mistaken biblical interpretation when he equated Antichrist with the "lawless one" of 2 Thessalonians (2:3).[18] It is unclear whether Calvin was the first Reformer who labelled the pope as Antichrist, but it is very clear that such labeling was nothing new or uncommon.

Christians in the Reformed traditions will likely have heard such accusations regarding the pope and the Catholic Church. They began in the Reformation era and continue into the twenty-first century. One recent example occurred during the Pope's visit to Korea in 2014. About 10,000 fundamentalist Protestants organised a demonstration, calling Catholicism blasphemous and denouncing the Pope.[19] Earlier, these same Christians had called the World Council of Churches (WCC) the Antichrist during its General Assembly in Busan, Korea, in 2013. One of the leaders of this group, which consists of seventy-one churches in South Korea, made a public speech outlining why the WCC must bear the Antichrist label: "Religious pluralism is heresy, denying the authority of the Bible, and is an Antichrist scheme aimed at rooting out Christianity." Here religious pluralism includes acknowledging not only different gods, but also embracing communism, homosexuality and other lifestyles.[20]

This context of labeling a certain group as Antichrist is related to the first context of the fear of the other. Those we perceive as the "enemy" or as "bad" are easily othered. But what affects both of these contexts is the balance of power between those who are labeling and those who are being labeled. In many cases, those who do the labeling have more power than

---

17. Calvin, *Institutes of Christian Religion*, 4.7.21.

18. Jensen, *Living Hope*, 99.

19. A public protest against Pope Francis when he visited Korea. See http://time.com/3106784/south-korean-protestants-rally-against-pope-francis-visit/.

20. See http://ivarfjeld.com/2013/11/04/thousand-protest-against-wcc-in-south-korea/.

the ones being labeled, since labeling is an exercise of exerting social power over others in order to oppress them. Jews, sexual minorities and racial minorities have been given the Antichrist label by White heterosexual supremacists. In doing so the White heterosexual supremacists are giving voice to the abuse of power that is sanctioned and justified in society. The crimes perpetrated by Hitler's Nazism were the logical conclusion of this form of labeling.

In short, the use of the label of Antichrist has existed throughout the history of Christianity, though it has very little biblical precedent other than as a word signifying false teaching about the Christian faith. Indeed David Jensen has argued that the way the term as used in Christian discourse is "antithetical to the kingdom that Jesus proclaimed."[21]

A refreshing alternative to the kind of apocalyptic speculation associated with the notion of Antichrist is found in the work of one of the most influential women in the church of her time, the medieval abbess Hildegard of Bingen (1098–1179).[22] One of her most famous visions is her bizarre and disturbing account of the birth of the Antichrist (see Figure 1):

> And I saw again the figure of a woman whom I had previously seen in front of the altar that stands before the eyes of God; she stood in the same place, but now I saw her from the waist down. And from her waist to the place that denotes the female, she had various scaly blemishes; and in that latter place was a black and monstrous head. It had fiery eyes, and ears like an ass's, and nostrils and mouth like a lion's; it opened wide its jowls and terribly clashed its horrible iron-colored teeth. And from this head down to her knees, the figure was white and red, as if bruised by many beatings; and from her knees to her tendons where they joined her heels, which appeared white, she was covered with blood. And behold! That monstrous head moved from its place with such a great shock that the figure of the woman was shaken all through her limbs. And a great mass of excrement adhered to the head; and it raised itself up upon a mountain and tried to ascend the height of heaven (*Scivias*, Book 3, Vision 11).[23]

21. Jensen, *Living Hope*, 96.

22. E.g., Flanagan, *Hildegard of Bingen*; Newman, *Hildegard of Bingen*; Newman, *Sister of Wisdom*.

23. Translation in Elledge, "Contextualizing Hildegard of Bingen's Violent and Apocalyptic Imagery." An image of Hildegard's painting of the birth of the Antichrist may be viewed at: http://www.pbs.org/wgbh/pages/frontline/shows/apocalypse/explanation/legend.html.

As Elledge admits, Hildegard's vision is both violent and apocalyptic,[24] and modern readers might regard it with confusion and distaste. However, Hildegard's vision should not be read as literally referring to the birth of a demonic being, but in the context of the church politics of her times: "The age into which Hildegard was born was a turbulent, disorderly age, a time of petty wars, and fierce struggles, of unruly secular leaders and undisciplined Church officials . . . in short, of bloody conflict between Church and State . . . The struggles between the Empire and Church continued throughout Hildegard's lifetime."[25] For Hildegard, the woman giving birth symbolizes the church, and her bizarre offspring is church corruption: "The Church herself is corrupt, especially 'at the place that denotes the female,' and as excrement covered the head of Evil as it came out of her body. Even though this image suggests that all hope is lost and the recovery of the Church is now impossible, Hildegard left room for hope and the anticipation of reform: *Ecclesia*'s shoes are white, which indicates a time of goodness and spiritual reform."[26] While the color coding of "white" as good and "black" as evil is problematic from a contemporary race-critical perspective, Hildegard's vision expresses her critique of the evils of "clerical abuse, secular corruption, heresy, simony, and spiritual decline."[27] Rather than being an expression of apocalyptic determinism, Hildegard's vision holds hope for future church renewal, while critiquing the reality of church corruption. Her unique interpretation of the Antichrist (against-Christ) as issuing from the personified church is a lens through which we can see a glimpse of both her turbulent medieval society, and the similarly tempestuous world—and church—of our own times.

24. Elledge, "Hildegard of Bingen," 3.

25. Baird and Ehrman, *Letters of Hildegard of Bingen*, 1:10–11.

26. Elledge, "Hildegard of Bingen," 45; see also Emmerson, "Representation of Antichrist," 95–110.

27. Elledge, "Hildegard of Bingen," 46.

Christ and Antichrist in Popular Culture

Watch: *Agora* (2012)

Discussion Questions

Before the viewing

What does the term "Christ" mean to you?

What are your preconceptions about "the Antichrist"?

After the viewing

Which characters in the movie represent Christ?

Which characters in the movie could be described as Antichrist (against Christ)?

Discussion

Due to the dominance of the term Christ as a designation for Jesus, the notion of Jesus Christ encapsulates much more than Jesus of Nazareth, the Jewish prophet from Galilee. Rather, Christ in western culture is the perfect human being, the embodiment of what it is to be a good person: to be "Christ-like" is to do what Jesus Christ, the ideal person, would do. More-over, as discussed in chapter 2, as the consummate savior figure, Christ is the archetype of the American superhero, a savior who will ultimately figure in the Last Judgement and consign Satan and his minions to eternal destruction (Rev 20:10).

The popular film genre of apocalyptic horror makes extensive use of the Antichrist legend, as opposed to the biblical concept of antichrist(s), developing it in ever-more sensational directions. For example, in the classic Antichrist film *The Omen* (dir. Richard Donner, 1976; dir. John Moore, 2006), the Antichrist is Damien Thorn, supposedly the son of an American diplomat, but really the offspring of Satan and a female jackal. In *Lost Souls* (dir. Janusz Kaminski, 2000), Satan chooses to possess a psychiatric patient on his thirty-third birthday; the traditional age of Jesus when he was cruci-fied. In *The Prophecy V: Forsaken* (dir. Joel Soisson, 2005), a mysterious scripture called the Lexicon keeps rewriting itself, leaving the identity of the Antichrist for the movie's sequel, which, fortunately, was never made. In *End of Days* (dir. Peter Hyams, 1999), the lead character Jericho Cane (played by Arnold Schwartzenegger) prevents the Antichrist from being conceived at the turn of the millennium. In these films, Christ, if portrayed at all, is an afterthought compared to the Antichrist, who is temporarily thwarted by a human character who is a "stand-in" for Christ.[28]

In addition to these "secular" retellings of the Antichrist legend, there is also a tradition of Christian-produced apocalyptic horror movies, some of which include *The Omega Code* (dir. Robert Macarelli, 1999), *Megiddo: The Omega Code II* (dir. Brian Trenchard-Smith, 2002), and the *Left Behind* series.[29] From a biblical standpoint, these Christian apocalyptic movies, ostensibly intended to promote scriptural teaching about the end-times, are as grounded in the Antichrist legend as the secular productions. While their portrayals of gleefully wicked and conniving Antichrists may be en-tertaining, they are no more biblical than the *Omen* movies' portrayal of Damien, and less edifying than Hildegard's critique of the church through the Antichrist symbol. It is important to remember that in the Bible, Christ is many orders of magnitude more important than "Antichrist."

28. An exception to this rule is *The Omen III*, where Damien is undone by his mis-reading of the invented scripture the *Book of Hebron* (see Beavis, "Angels Carrying Sav-age Weapons.")

29. *Left Behind* (dir. Vic Sarin, 2000), *Left Behind II: Tribulation Force* (dir. Bill Corco-ran, 2002), *Left Behind: World at War* (dir. Craig R. Baxley, 2005). A remake of the initial film (dir. Vic Armstrong, 2014) is also available. For a list of Christian-produced end-time movies, see http://www.imdb.com/list/ls000738847/.

Figure 1: Michael York as the Antichrist in *Megiddo: The Omega Code II*

For this chapter, rather than watching an apocalyptic horror movie, our church group viewed the historical drama *Agora* (2012), which portrays the conflict between the pagan philosopher, Hypatia of Alexandria (d. 415 CE) and Egyptian Christians, in the time of the Bishop Cyril (376–444 CE). This particular film was suggested by a visiting student from South Korea who was shocked by the idea that not only had early Christians been persecuted by pagans, but that Christians had persecuted pagans! The film tells the story of a historical woman, Hypatia, a renowned teacher of philosophy, mathematics and astronomy, who was blamed by the Christians of Alexandria for a feud between the bishop and the pagan governor of the city, Orestes. She was abducted and gruesomely murdered by a Christian mob, an act that fuelled public resentment against Christians:

> dragging her from her carriage, they took her to the church called Caesareum, where they completely stripped her, and then murdered her with tiles. After tearing her body in pieces, they took her mangled limbs to a place called Cinaron, and there burnt them. This affair brought not the least opprobrium, not only upon Cyril, but also upon the whole Alexandrian church.[30]

As the Christian historian Socrates Scholasticus remarked shortly after her death, "surely nothing can be farther from the spirit of Christianity than the allowance of massacres, fights, and transactions of that sort."[31]

30. Socrates Scholasticus, *The Life of Hypatia*, from his *Ecclesiastical History* (http://www.cosmopolis.com/alexandria/hypatia-bio-socrates.html).

31. Ibid.

The "othering" of the dignified and virtuous pagan Hypatia as a sort of "antichrist" by the Christian zealots in turn led them to act in a very anti-Christ-like way.

While it is difficult to find much that is Christ-like in the behavior of the Christian characters in the film, one exception is the fictional figure of Davus, a slave in the household of Hypatia's father who is in love with the beautiful philosopher. Eventually, he joins the Christians, and he is eventually freed by Hypatia after he repents of trying to rape her. It is in his repentance of his violent ways, and his embrace of the example of charity modeled by some of the monks, where the influence of Christ is most apparent. In the end, it is the Christian Davus who does his best to save the pagan Hypatia from her execution at the hands of the fanatical crowd. Painfully and ironically, he decides to kill her himself in order to preserve her dignified life from inhumane insanity.

Figure 2: Rachel Weisz as Hypatia, *Agora*

Other Resources

The Antichrist. The History Channel, 2005.

From Jesus to Christ: The First Christians. PBS Frontline, 1998.

Fuller, Robert C. *Naming the Antichrist: The History of an American Obsession*. New York: Oxford University Press, 1996.

Jensen, David H. *Living Hope: The Future and Christian Faith*. Louisville: Westminster John Knox, 2010.

McGinn, Bernard. *Antichrist: Two Thousand Years of the Human Fascination with Evil*. San Francisco: HarperSanFrancisco, 1994.

8

Gender and God

WHEN THE QUESTION OF gender-inclusive language in bible translation is raised, Christians will often be comfortable with language that includes women ("men and women," "brothers and sisters"), but balk at applying feminine language to the divine. "God is neither male nor female," some will object. Others will insist (rather paradoxically) that the scriptures portray God in overwhelmingly masculine terms: as Lord, Father, Warrior, King. Surely, they assert, these titles must mean that God is masculine in some significant way. As our students in religious studies and seminary sometimes put it, Jesus called God "Father," so God must be male! Since in Christian doctrine, the Son is part of the Holy Trinity along with the Father, surely this must mean that maleness is somehow intrinsic to divine identity. At the same time, women students, especially, are often intrigued by the notion of female Christ figures and other feminine representations of the divine. As one young woman student answered when I asked her why she had chosen to make a presentation on the movie *Dead Man Walking* (dir. Tim Robbins, 1995), she read that it featured a female Christ figure, so she was in!

The notion of divine maleness is reinforced in traditional Christian hymnody and art. The visual image of God as an elderly patriarch enthroned in the heavens is imprinted on the western Christian mind (think of Michelangelo's *Creation of Adam*), reinforced by traditional hymns like:

> The Lord is King! lift up thy voice,
>
> O earth; and all ye heavens, rejoice!

From world to world the joy shall ring,

The Lord omnipotent is King.[1]

For Christians, the impact of this kind of imagery may be to imply that men are more "like God" than women, reinforcing cultural norms of male dominance and female subordination.

It is undeniable that God is often portrayed in masculine terms in the Bible. This is an outcome of the patriarchal societies in which the scriptures were written. However, in recent decades feminist theologians and biblical scholars have excavated a wealth of female images of the divine in the Bible, both Jewish Scriptures and Christian Testament, and in early Christian literature. Attention to the language of gender and God began in part as a growing numbers of women were entering ordained ministry in the 1960s and 1970s. Questions were raised regarding the normative use of male gender pronouns. With more female leadership the church began to pay attention to how language honors or marginalizes people.[2] This chapter will introduce some of the insights of feminist theology and exegesis, and relate them to the film *Babette's Feast* (dir. Gabriel Axel, 1987), in which the mysterious woman Babette is the God-figure.

Mother-God in the Jewish Scriptures

Far from being marginal to the biblical tradition, expressions of the female divine are grounded in Gen 1:27: "So God created humankind in his image, in the image of God he created them, male and female he created them." Although the translation alternates singular and plural pronouns for God ("Let *us* make humankind according to *our* image," Gen 1:26; "*he* created them," Gen 1:27), the verse refers to the creation of *adam* ("humankind," "humanity") as male and female, in the image of God. The Hebrew word for God used here is the plural *Elohim*, indicative of divine fullness, both beyond and inclusive of gender diversity. As discussed in chapter 6, all language referring to the divine is metaphorical, since God "as-God-is" is unknowable to limited human beings. God is not literally male or female, mother or father, warrior or peacemaker. That is, God can only be understood by analogy, by comparison to things in human experience. In Gen 1:27, God is implicitly compared to human beings, male and female.

---

1. Conder, "The Lord is King, Lift Up Thy Voice" (1824).
2. Duck, *Worship for the Whole People of God*, 101.

Although all language referring to the divine is metaphorical, it is impossible in English not to use third-person singular personal pronoun without gender.[3] People using languages like English, therefore, have an extra challenge. Some languages (such as Korean) do not use gendered pronouns, but this does not get around the problem of a male dominant culture, a culture that pervades language in other ways. Some scholars and liturgists try to avoid the male pronoun and invent alternative ways of referring to God, men and women. For example, Elisabeth Schüssler Fiorenza writes wo/men whenever she refers humanity. This fractured way of writing is to show that wo/men are not the same but also undermines the use of "man/men" to represent humanity. Similarly spellings like G*d or the*logy are intentionally used to problematize the gendered deity and its study.[4] The archaic spelling Godde has sometimes be used for the same reason.[5] *The Inclusive Bible*, when the reference to God is descriptive, uses "Most High," or "Sovereign One," in place of "Lord." When "Lord" is used in the context of invoking or praising God, it uses *Adonai* (a biblical Hebrew title of respect) in the Jewish Scriptures; "Rabbi" or "Teacher" in the Christian Testament when addressing Jesus' public ministry. *The Inclusive Bible* uses *Abba* or "Loving God" for "Father" where it expresses an intimate and familial relationship.[6] These translation strategies destabilize conventional ways of referring to the divine in masculine terms while remaining faithful to the terminology of the Bible.

For Christians, the metaphor of God as Father is a familiar one, due to the frequent use of this title in the Gospels (e.g., Matt 6:9; Mark 8:38; Luke 2:49; John 1:18). To call God "Father" is to compare God to a human parent on earth (e.g., benevolent, protective, caring); it does not mean that God is a big patriarch up in heaven. Actually, God is not often explicitly compared to a father in the Jewish Scriptures (e.g., Deut 32:6; Isa 63:16; 64:8; Mal 2:10). In fact, as Virginia Ramey Mollenkott has shown, maternal God-language is more common.[7] For example, in Hosea 11:3–4, God speaks in the guise of a mother who taught the people of the tribe of Ephraim to walk: "I was like to them like those who lift infants to their cheeks. I bent down to them and fed them." God speaks as a mother soothing her child in Isa 66:13: "As a

---

3. Baron, *Grammar and Gender*, 99.

4. Schüssler Fiorenza, "Between Movement and Academy," 3–17.

5. E.g., Gateley, *A Warm, Moist Salty God*, iii.

6. Dearborn, "Preface," *The Inclusive Bible*, vi.

7. Mollenkott, *The Divine Feminine*.

mother comforts her child, so I will comfort you; you shall be comforted in Jerusalem." The Psalmist addresses God in maternal terms: "like a weaned child with its mother; my soul is like the weaned child that is within me" (131:2). The God of the Jewish Scriptures endures labor (Isa 42:12), gives birth (Deut 32:18), and nurses her young (Isa 49:15). Like a mother bear, God is fiercely protective of her young (Hos 13:8); like a mother eagle, she hovers over her chicks (Deut 32:11–12). In Ps 22:9–10, God is portrayed as a midwife: "Yet it was you who took me from the womb; you kept me safe on my mother's breast. On you I was cast from my birth, and since my mother bore me you have been my God." Psalm 123:2 compares God to the mistress of a household supervising her staff: "As the eyes of servants look to the hand of their master, as the eyes of a maid to the hand of her mistress, so our eyes look to the Lord our God, until he has mercy upon us."

In the Jewish Scriptures, the most striking and pervasive imagery of the female divine appears in the Wisdom literature, especially the Book of Proverbs and the Deutero-canonical books of Wisdom and Sirach. In Hebrew, the term for divine wisdom is feminine (*Hochmah, Sophia*), making divine Sophia ripe for female personification as a wise, strong and confident woman:

> Wisdom has built her house, she has hewn her seven pillars. She has slaughtered her animals, she has mixed her wine, she has also set her table.
>
> She has sent out her servant-girls, she calls from the highest places in the town,
>
> "You that are simple, turn in here!" To those without sense she says,
>
> "'Come, eat of my bread and drink of the wine I have mixed.
>
> Lay aside immaturity, and live, and walk in the way of insight."
> (Prov 9:1–5)

Johnson has uncovered the myriad ways in which Lady Wisdom figures in these scriptures. She is a singular manifestation of the divine image (Wisd 7:25–26); a pre-existent mediator of creation (Prov 8:22–31; Wisd 7:22; 8:6), who orders and sustains creation and good governance (Wisd 8:1; Prov 8:15); a redeemer figure whose deeds are shown throughout history (Wis10:1–19:17); an all-pervasive spirit who holds the cosmos together (Wisd 7:22–23) and inspires friends of God and prophets (Wisd 7:27); one who is with human beings through difficulties (Wisd 10:17–18) and imparts the divine gift of life (Prov 8:35; Wisd 8:35); who enlightens, nourishes, teaches, and guides (Prov 9:5); judges wrongdoing (Prov 1:20–33) and overcomes evil (Wisd 7:29–30); one who abides with Israel (Sir 24:8, 10–12) and embodies Torah (Sir 24:23; Bar 3:27).[8] Sirach 24:9–10 portrays Lady Wisdom as priest: "In the holy tent I [Wisdom] ministered before him, and so I was established in Zion. Thus in the beloved city he gave me a resting place, and in Jerusalem was my domain." As Johnson observes: "Wisdom in the scriptures of Israel is simply God: reaching out to the world, forming the beloved community, forever drawing near and passing by. . . . She personifies divine reality; in fact, she *is* a most intense expression of divine presence and activity in the world."[9] These expressions of God as mother, midwife, and Lady Wisdom are no more or less metaphorical than images of the divine as father, king or warrior, but the female metaphors have been obscured by many centuries of male-centered theology and culture.

Christ-Sophia in the Christian Testament

The first-century Jewish teacher Jesus tapped into the tradition of the divine feminine in the scriptures of Israel when he taught in parables. In Matt 23:37 (Luke 13:34), he portrays God as a mother hen, longing to gather her chicks protectively under her wings. Two parables borrow from the sphere of women's work, depicting a woman searching for a lost coin, a *drachma* (amounting to two days' wages for a female laborer), as a comparison to God's care for a "lost" sinner (Luke 15:8–10). The so-called "Parable of the Leaven" compares the spread of the reign of God to "yeast that a woman took and mixed in with three measures of flour until it was all leavened" (Matt 13:33; Luke 13:20–21); here, God is the woman kneading the leaven through the dough. The famous poem "Bakerwoman God" by Alla Renee Bozarth elaborates eloquently on this familiar image of the female divine:

> Bakerwoman God,
>
> I am your living bread.
>
> Strong, brown Bakerwoman God,
>
> I am your low, soft, and being-shaped loaf.[10]

8. Johnson, "Wisdom was Made Flesh," 99–102.

9. Ibid., 102.

10. For complete poem, see http://www.poemhunter.com/poem/bakerwoman-god/.

The Christian Testament also develops the Wisdom theology of the Jewish Scriptures. The Pauline writings call Jesus the power of God and the Wisdom (*Sophia*) of God (1 Cor 1:22–24); the mediator of creation (1 Cor 8:6); the image of the invisible God (Col 1:15); the firstborn of creation (Col 1:15). Luke portrays Jesus as a child of Sophia who justifies her and is rejected (7:35; see also *1 Enoch* 4:1–2); Matthew portrays him as an embodiment of Sophia who speaks her words and performs her deeds (11:28–30; see also Sir 6:23–31), and who is rejected in Jerusalem (Matt 23:37–39). Jesus speaks with the voice of Wisdom in the invitation: "Take my yoke upon you, and learn from me; for I am gentle and humble in heart, and you will find rest for your souls. For my yoke is easy, and my burden is light" (Matt 11:28–29). Compare this with the instruction of Jesus Sirach:

> keep her [Wisdom's] ways with all your might. Search out and seek, and she will become known to you; and when you get hold of her, do not let her go. For at last you will find the rest she gives, and she will be changed into joy for you. Then her fetters will become for you a strong protection, and her collar a glorious robe. Her yoke is a golden ornament, and her bonds are a cord of blue. (Sir 6:26–30)

Johnson describes the Gospel of John as "suffused with wisdom themes. Seeking and finding, feeding and nourishing, revealing and enlightening, giving life, making people friends of God, shining as light in the darkness, being the way, the truth, and the life: these are but some of the ways Jesus embodies *Sophia's* roles and is interpreted as Wisdom herself."[11] The Letter to the Hebrews draws extensively on the tradition of divine Woman Wisdom: "Like Sophia, Christ, the 'word' of God, is a mediator of creation (Heb 1:2; Wisd 7:22—8:1), enthroned with God (Heb 1:3; 12:2; Wisd 9:4, 10), a savior and leader of the people of God (Heb 7:25; 12:2; Wisd 10:1–11:14). . . . Jesus in Hebrews . . . leads the faithful from the earthly Sinai to the heavenly Mount Zion/Jerusalem (Heb 12:18–24)."[12]

The earliest Christians also understood the Holy Spirit in feminine terms, especially those who spoke and wrote in Syriac, an ancient semitic language related to the Aramaic spoken by Jesus and his disciples. In both languages, the word for spirit (*ruach, ruha*) is gendered as feminine; as with *Hochmah/Sophia*, this encourages female personification. For example, the *Acts of Thomas* (third century) calls the Spirit "compassionate Mother" and

11. Johnson, "Wisdom Was Made Flesh," 104.

12. Beavis and Kim-Cragg, *Hebrews*, xxxviii.

"hidden Mother" (§27, §50). The Christian Persian sage Aphraphat (fourth century) interpreted Gen 2:24 in spiritual terms:

> Who is it who leaves father and mother to take a wife? The meaning is as follows: as long as a man has not taken a wife, he loves and reveres God his Father and the Holy Spirit his Mother, and he has no other love. But when a man takes a wife, then he leaves his (true) Father and his Mother.[13]

Sebastian Brock concludes that "among early Christian writers, Greek and Latin as well as Syriac, one can find scattered pieces of evidence which may suggest that there was once a fairly widespread tradition which associated the Holy Spirit with the image of mother."[14]

Toward Expansive Language of Gender and God

Finding the most apt word for naming God is no small task. But it is one of the most critical tasks for people of faith who worship God as well as for people of no faith who live in a culture that still speaks about God. This critical task begins with an intentional effort to move beyond our own favorite images of God. It is no longer an option to simply follow dominant cultural norms that reinforce certain images of God. What is needed, instead, is a serious attempt to expand the language of God beyond using certain gender and human centered references. Unlike the hymn introduced above at the beginning of this chapter, the hymn, "Bring Many Names," written by Brian Wren is a good example of such attempt since he uses both less typical images of parenthood, while expanding the images of God. Interestingly, Wren articulates mother God as "strong" and father God as "warm and caring," contesting a conventional notion of father as strong and mother as caring. Wren also describes God as "old, aching and grey" as well as God as "young and growing," eager to move us for justice. Such humane earthly descriptions of God, however, do not misses the point that God is "far beyond our seeing closer yet than breathing."

This hymn affirms the unknowablity of God. Yet it also affirms the intimacy of God, close to our very being, by seeing God as a communal and

---

13. Quoted by Brock, "The Holy Spirit as Feminine." See also Kateusz, *Finding Holy Spirit Mother.*

14. Ibid.

relational being.[15] The Bible in both Jewish Scriptures and Christian Testament affirm divine mystery (see chapter 6). In order to appreciate the mysterious dimension of God fully, we must be comfortable with ambiguity.

Continuing the theme of ambiguity, it is worth noting that in recent decades many have challenged the assumption that gender is a binary reality. What is being suggested today is an openness to gender ambiguity and gender-fluid multiplicity.[16] Once gender dualism is destabilized, one can even realize that "gender is always relative to the constructed relations in which it is determined," as Judith Butler claims.[17] Let us unpack her claim here. A woman (singular gender) must be referred to with reference to her relationships as, for example, a daughter, a sister, an aunt, a mother, a wife, a grandmother within her one immediate family. Within a blended and extended family, the signifiers of her identity would multiply. Once she moves into the wider society, she becomes even more plural, taking multiple roles as a teacher, a student, a pastor, a parishioner, a volunteer, a citizen, an immigrant, a visitor, a host, to name just a few. Imagine this on a global scale: how much more complicated and expansive a singular gender identity would become once it had been multiply located. It turns out that seemingly contradictory identities can co-exist and operate concurrently. One is a citizen of one country yet a visitor to another country; one is a teacher of a particular subject, and at the same time, a student of another subject. That is how identity works; it shifts and changes as one's life shifts and changes. Gender as a particular identity does the same. That is why it is necessary to understand gender as an open, multiple, and ambiguous reality rather than a fixed, singular and binary entity. Again Butler is helpful: "Gender is a complexity whose totality is permanently deferred, never fully what it is at any given juncture in time. . . . it will be an open assemblage that permits of multiple convergences and divergences without obedience to a normative telos of definitonal closure."[18]

Another aspect of expanding the language of God beyond the gendered God is to pay attention to symbols and their roles. In the past fifty years, especially since Vatican II, the appreciation of symbols has shifted. Once dismissed as an inferior form of communication, symbols are now recognized as capable of expressing the meaning of life in significant and

15. Catherine M. LaCugna, *God for Us*.

16. Butler, *Gender Trouble*; Coyote and Spoon, *Gender Failure*.

17. Butler, *Gender Trouble*, 10.

18. Ibid., 16.

important ways. In the Catholic Church tradition in which the Eucharist is believed to be the "*real* presence" of Christ, a Protestant's claim that Christ is only present symbolically sounds superficial, if not heretical. This Pre-Vatican II modernist view presupposes that a symbol is something that stands for something else, something less real than itself. There is an assumption that in this view of the symbol, "one *can* grasp reality, and consequently, that representations of reality can be severed from what they represent."[19] Sacramental theologian Susan A. Ross challenges this assumption by arguing, "Such an attitude presupposes that the conceptual is superior to the representational, . . . and theologically, that the doctrinal is superior to the symbolic."[20] Thanks to the recent work of postmodern thinkers, feminist scholars and others, attitudes that downplay the symbolic have been shown to have misled us. Now we know that reality outside language is illusion. As David Tracy explains, our claim to sure knowledge is questionable once we realize that our knowledge is bound to the history of plurality and ambiguity: "There is no such thing as an unambiguous tradition."[21] The only thing that is sure, then, ironically speaking, is ambiguity. Therefore, ambiguity is to be recognized, celebrated, and enjoyed. It is not to be denied, confused, or avoided. This does not mean, however, that attention to ambiguity is always positive. In fact, to note a reality as a condition of ambiguity is to acknowledge "its ambiguity as both oppressive and liberating."[22] In short, there is nothing neutral or naïve about gender ambiguity. It is always politically and socially conditioned; one must be cautious of both its edges.

Symbols and symbolic expressions are crucial in our effort to affirm and fully embrace ambiguity along with its threatening and yet comforting graciousness. Symbolic meanings are conveyed through diverse media including but not limited to visual art, poetry, dance, and music. The very purpose of symbolic expression lies in conveying the ambiguity of life, both its ordinariness and its extraordinariness. Furthermore, depending on the viewers and the readers of these symbols, various meanings can emerge, which then enhance and deepen our understanding of life, including religious life. Most of all, expanding the symbolic language of God with regards to gender helps us face unpredictable realities and appreciate both the

19. Ross, *Extravagant Affections*, 139.

20. Ibid.

21. Tracy, *Plurality and Ambiguity*, 36.

22. Ross, *Extravagant Affections*, 86.

ugliness and the beauty of life, by trusting God as a being who is both near to us and yet beyond our ability to fully understand.

The Feast of Divine Wisdom in Film

Watch: *Babette's Feast* (1986)

Discussion Questions

Before the viewing

Are there any qualities of God that can't be applied to women?

When considering the role of a Christ-figure, does the gender of the individual have any significance?

After the viewing

Is the old pastor a Christ figure or a false idol for the villagers?

Which character or characters represent God/Christ in the movie?

Discussion Notes

Critically engaging popular culture with the help of religious symbols can lead to a better understanding of both our culture and our lives. This is one of the main reasons why we, the authors, intentionally choose a thematically relevant film to discuss it in each chapter of this book. But it is even more important for younger generations who are conscious of gender issues to engage films that portray God in ways that move "beyond God the Father."[23] Joyce Ann Mercer did research on adolescent girls who are searching for religious meanings in their lives. She found that their questions about faith were closely connected to their questions around sexuality,

---

23. Mary Daly wrote the book, *Beyond God the Father* in 1974, which challenged the conventional image of God in Christian theology.

gender roles, and their own gender identity. As discussed in chapter 9 on Purity and Sex, young people's identity around gender is critical. This identity can be vulnerable to injury if it is not carefully explored. Mercer notes, especially regarding gender roles associated with parents, that the girls in her study who referred to God as Father intimately related that image of God to their own fathers. Typically the girls in her study fell into two groups: some opted for calling God as Father as a way of dealing with the gap between their actual human fathers and the wished-for, namely, idealized Father. Others opted out of the use of the image of God the Father as a way of leaving behind a painful relationship with their human fathers. In either case, the research demonstrates that one should be cautious about automatically using "Father" when referring to God.[24] Furthermore, there is a danger in switching to the Mother image when addressing God. That is, it may be equally limiting and unhelpful to overemphasize the maternal image of God since it can reinforce the gender binary, as if all women's experiences including mothering are benevolent and positive, while paternal male experiences are malevolent and negative. Not all women are mothers (or even want to be mothers); likewise, not all men are fathers. One must guard against the glorification of the distinctly female, or male, aspects of humanity and divinity.[25] Rather, we must take into consideration the complexity of human experiences.

Given the patriarchal and male-centered sexist culture in which we live, however, films that overcome male-dominant views and instead imagine other paradigms can be helpful in giving us a perspective from which to better judge the dominant reality. The movie *Babette's Feast* is one such example. Set in nineteenth-century Denmark, it opens on a stormy night when two elderly sisters living in an isolated fishing village are visited by a desperate war refugee from France, a woman named Babette. Babette is weak, exhausted and vulnerable; she begs the sisters to employ her so that she will be able to survive. Although they can only offer her room and board, the sisters compassionately take the mysterious stranger in as a servant and cook.

The two sisters are the daughters of a Puritan minister who had a loyal following of disciples during his lifetime; by the time Babette appears, the little community of his aged followers meets regularly in the sisters' home. However, in their later years, the disciples have become quarrelsome, and

24. Mercer, *Girl Talk, God Talk*, 116–19.
25. Flax, *Thinking Fragments*, 179.

despite their professed faith, they are anxious about the fate of their souls after death. Babette not only serves the sisters, but the elderly followers, who appreciate the way she prepares their frugal meals of bread and fish. As the years pass, the faithful servant Babette makes everything better for the sisters and the disciples, who recognize her as a blessing to them.

One day, much to her surprise, and the sisters' concern, Babette receives word that she has won the lottery back in France. Her one wish to spend the windfall is for the sisters to allow her to prepare a proper French meal for themselves and their friends in honor of the one hundredth anniversary of their father's birth. They reluctantly agree that she should return to France to buy the ingredients, fearful that she will never return; they are even more afraid that enjoying a lavish meal will endanger their Calvinist souls.

Babette does return as promised, and the banquet she prepares exceeds anything the sisters and their friends had ever experienced. Not only are the flavors of the abundant foods and wines a feast for the senses, but a foretaste of the end-time banquet in the kingdom of God, where "steadfast love and faithfulness will meet; righteousness and peace will kiss each other" (Ps 85:10)—a verse quoted several times throughout the film. The disciples, mellowed by the delicious food and drink, relax and forgive each other for their petty differences. At the end of the evening, they sing a beautiful hymn, anticipating the heavenly realm:

> The time for us to rest approaches . . .
>
> The sand in our hourglass will soon run out
>
> The day is conquered by the night
>
> The glories of the world are ending
>
> So brief their day, so swift their flight
>
> God, let thy brightness ever shine
>
> Admit us to Thy mercy divine.

In this film, the God-figure is the woman Babette, who, like Lady Wisdom, prepares a banquet for the simple, who eat her food and drink her wine (Prov 9:1–6); Sophia-like, she brings them wisdom, faith and understanding. She represents God similarly to the character of Naomi in the Book of Ruth. As Mollenkott explains, for the Moabite Ruth, the person who embodies *Shaddai*, the God of Israel, is her Judean mother-in-law Naomi: "In other words, Ruth converts . . . and gives her life-long faith to a God she has seen chiefly in the image of an older woman, because of her love for that woman and her utter dedication to that woman."[26] Like Naomi, Babette is a widow, a stranger, a refugee: "the God who is imaged by Naomi is a God identified with powerlessness, emptiness, nonentity."[27] It is probably not accidental that the divine name invoked by Naomi, Shaddai (1:20–21), means "the God with Breasts,"[28] so that "Naomi for all her limitations remained for Ruth the image-bearer of the undivided One God who births and breastfeeds the universe."[29] The movement of Ruth and Naomi from barrenness to fertility, from emptiness to satisfaction in Bethlehem, the "House of Bread," parallels the journey of the sisters and their friends from stinginess and fear to generosity and faith.

Figure 1: Stéphane Audran in *Babette's Feast*

26. Mollenkott, *Divine Feminine*, 57.

27. Ibid.

28. Ibid., 57, citing Cross, *Canaanite Myth and Hebrew Epic*, 54–55.

29. Mollenkott, *Divine Feminine*, 58.

Other Resources

Duck, Ruth. *Gender and the Name of God: The Trinitarian Baptismal Formula.* Cleveland: Pilgrim, 1991.

Johnson, Elizabeth A. *She Who Is: The Mystery of God in Feminist Theological Discourse.* New York: Crossroad, 1992.

Mollenkott, Virginia Ramey. *The Divine Feminine: The Biblical Imagery of God as Female.* New York: Crossroad, 1983.

9

Purity and Sex

IN CONSERVATIVE CHRISTIAN CIRCLES, both Catholic and Protestant, "purity" has become identified with sexual abstinence for adolescents, especially girls, whose virginity is supposed to be closely guarded by their fathers, and encouraged by attendance at "Purity Balls" and by the purchase of "Pure Fashion."[1] The premium placed on female virginity is commonly attributed to the Bible; as one of the girls interviewed in the documentary *The Virgin Daughters* remarks, "it's one of the Ten Commandments." When questioned as to which commandment, the girl's mother helpfully explains that it is the seventh commandment against adultery (Exod 20:14). She further explains that pre-marital sex counts as adultery because a girl who engages in such relationships is cheating on her future husband.

This ingenious, and, to the advocates of the purity movement, persuasive argument is required at least partially because the Bible seldom associates purity and virginity. A truly "biblical" understanding of virginity needs to take into account the meaning and regulation of sexuality in ancient Israel, and the reframing of these scriptural mores in the early church. This chapter will discuss what the Bible actually says about sexuality and purity. It will also discuss the gendered cultural norms of honor and shame, which, much more than biblical purity legislation, relate to the way that women, men and sex are understood in the Bible. The movie feature for this chapter, *The Virgin Suicides* (Sofia Coppola, 1999), has been chosen to illustrate the negative consequences, especially for young girls, of the reduction of a woman's worth "to her ability—or her refusal—to be sexual."[2]

1. See the documentary *The Virgin Daughters* (dir. Jane Treays, 2008); http://top-documentaryfilms.com/virgin-daughters/; see also Valenti, *The Purity Myth*.

2. Valenti, *Purity Myth*, 10.

Biblical Sexual Norms

In general, the Bible presupposes that marriage, the family, sex and pro-creation are good. As the *Oxford Companion to the Bible* observes, "The paradigmatic biblical statement on sexuality and sexual behavior is found in Gen 1:26–28, the creation of human beings in God's image as male and female with the duty to 'be fruitful and multiply.'"[3] However, attitudes and practices respective to sex and marriage reflected in the Bible are very different from what the phrase "family values" may evoke today (e.g., nuclear family, monogamy, romantic love, marital faithfulness). The biblical stories were written thousands of years ago, and they reflect the sexual values of their times. For example, in ancient Israel:

> All sexual behavior that did not produce legitimate Israelite off-spring to the holy community was, in varying degrees, censured or controlled, and there was a concomitant double standard with regard to sexual behaviour . . . Homosexuality, bestiality, contraception, and masturbation were all prohibited, directly or by inference.[4]

What the practices mentioned above have in common is that they do not produce offspring—they are not conducive to "being fruitful and multiplying."

The "double standard" mentioned in the quotation, much as it does today, allowed greater sexual latitude for men than for women. Premarital virginity was required of females, but not of males. A woman who voluntarily had sex before marriage was subject to the death penalty (Deut 22:13–21), whereas there is no such stipulation for males. This is not because virginity (*bethulim*) was valued for its own sake as a state of moral or physical purity, but in order to ensure that a child born to a young bride was her husband's, and not some other man's (i.e., to enforce the husband's paternal rights over his children). As Peggy L. Day explains, "The patrilineal system of reckoning descent and the concomitant transfer of property was premised on controlling female sexuality so that paternity could be reliably be determined."[5]

Endogamy (i.e., marriage within Israel, and preferably marriage within the clan) was preferred. First-cousin marriage was the ideal (e.g., Isaac and

---

3. *Oxford Companion to the Bible*, "Sex," 690.

4. Ibid., 690–91.

5. Day, "Virgin," 1358.

Rebekah, Jacob and Rachel/Leah, Tobias and Sarah). According to Genesis, the ancestors of Israel, Abraham and Sarah, shared the same father—they were half-siblings (Gen 20:12)—although later, Torah forbids marriage between half-brothers and sisters (Lev 18:11). These customs were designed to keep the "holy community" of Israel intact; exogamy or "out-marriage," as exemplified by King Solomon and his many foreign wives and concubines, was perceived by the authors of the Bible as a threat to the integrity of Israel, and an affront to God: "The Lord had said to the Israelites, 'You shall not enter into marriage with them, neither shall they with you; for they will surely incline your heart to follow their gods;' Solomon clung to these in love" (1 Kgs 11:2).

As the example of Solomon illustrates, polygyny, the custom of one man having several wives and concubines, was taken for granted in ancient Israel, although it may have been prevalent mainly with the wealthy due to the affluence required to support multiple wives and concubines. However, there are very few references to polygyny in post-exilic Judaism. It comes as a surprise to many undergraduate students that there is no biblical law against prostitution, although Israelite priests are specifically forbidden to marry prostitutes (Lev 21:7), and daughters of priests are forbidden from engaging in prostitution on pain of death (Lev 21:9). Generally, prostitution (for women) was tolerated, but not respectable.

Men could divorce their wives, but there is no provision in Torah for women to divorce their husbands (Deut 24:1–4). In the case of divorce, the children would likely remain in the father's household. Adultery was considered to be a crime against a husband. A wife could commit adultery by sleeping with another man, and a man could commit adultery by sleeping with another man's wife, but a married man could have sex with as many unmarried women as he liked and not be considered an adulterer. The penalty for adultery (for either a man or a woman) was death by stoning (Lev 20:10). As with the premium on female premarital virginity, the concern with adultery was not the betrayal of the spousal relationship, but the fear that a woman who slept with a man other than her husband might become pregnant with the other man's child, thus undermining the patrilineal inheritance system. The concern is with paternal bloodlines and economic inheritance, not with chastity as an end in itself.

In biblical law, marriage is a contractual arrangement between two families, not a "sacrament" as the Catholic Church teaches. It is much less an equal relationship between two willing parties. A wife could not inherit her husband's estate (although provision for a widow could probably be written into the marriage contract). Normally, only sons inherited their father's wealth, with preference given to the firstborn. Daughters could only inherit if there were no sons (Num 27:1–11). A woman whose husband died without fathering any heirs was obligated to marry her brother-in-law in order to bear an heir for her deceased husband (levirate marriage), although the man could be released from this requirement through a ceremony, considered to be humiliating, called *chalitzah* ("removal") (Deut 25:5–10).

The actual biblical laws and customs with respect to sexuality, then, are a far cry from what contemporary Christians regard as family values, at least as represented in the Jewish Scriptures. In general, the tendency of Jewish legal interpretation throughout the centuries has been to soften or set aside the legislation that is most disadvantageous to women or incompatible with later social conditions, e.g., the levirate law was suspended in the early centuries CE; polygamy was "officially" discontinued in the eleventh century CE (although it had not been widely practiced for many centuries). This tendency partially accounts for the markedly different teachings with regard to marriage and sexuality reflected in the Christian Testament.

While the Christian Testament writers were heavily influenced by scriptural norms, and by developments in early Judaism, they were also affected by Greco-Roman philosophical attitudes to sexuality, which tended to devalue the body, marriage, procreation and sexuality. The Jewish Book of Wisdom (Wisdom of Solomon) illustrates the influence of this kind of thinking as early as the first century BCE in a philosophically-inspired teaching that challenges the ancient command to "be fruitful and multiply:" "For blessed is the barren woman who is undefiled, who has not entered into a sinful union; she will have fruit when God examines souls. Blessed also is the eunuch whose hands have done no lawless deed, and who has not devised wicked things against the Lord; for special favor will be shown him for his faithfulness, and a place of great delight in the temple of the Lord" (Wisd 3:13–14). Here, childlessness with virtue is preferred to fruitfulness with sin; although there is no assertion that childbearing in itself is sinful, there is a subtle alignment of moral virtue with physical barrenness: "For there are eunuchs who have been so from birth, and there are eunuchs who have been made eunuchs by others, and there are eunuchs who have made themselves eunuchs for the sake of the kingdom of heaven. Let anyone accept this who can" (Matt 19:12). This tendency to devalue marriage and procreation was likely compounded by the belief of some early Christians that the end of the world was imminent: "Woe to those who are pregnant and to those who are nursing infants in those days!" (Mark 13:17; Matt 24:19; Luke 21:23). The Gospels contain quite a number of sayings, attributed to Jesus, that are critical of the traditional family (e.g., Matt 8:21–22; 10:34–37; 19:10–12; Luke 8:19–21; 11:27–28). For Jesus and the early church, the "true family" was the family of believers, not the biological family. Paul regarded marriage as a compromise of the spiritual life, but preferable to being consumed by lust (1 Cor 7:1, 7–9).

Compared to the Jewish scriptures, the Christian Testament writings tend to apply sexual ethics even-handedly between the sexes, e.g., adultery and extra-marital sex are forbidden for both men and women (Rom 1:26–27; 1 Tim 1:10; 1 Cor 6:9); divorce is forbidden (or allowed) for both sexes (Mark 10:2–9; cf. Matt 5:32; 19:9; 1 Cor 7:10–16); both male and female homosexuality are mentioned (Rom 1:26–27). The later letters of the Christian Testament, however, portray the patriarchal household typical of the Greco-Roman world, where men ruled over wives, children and slaves, except that male *as well as* female chastity before and after marriage was required (Eph 5:22–25; 1 Tim 2:15; 4:1–4; 5:14; Heb 13:4). Slavery is presupposed as a social reality throughout the Christian Testament, and slaves, like wives and children, are exhorted to be subject to their masters, husbands and fathers (Eph 6:5–8), although the male head of the household is instructed to be loving and patient with wives and children (who are supposed to be obedient), and to "stop threatening" their slaves (Eph 6:9).

Purity and Impurity, Honor and Shame

In the Bible, the terms "virgin" and "pure" or "undefiled" seldom occur together. Torah stipulates that a priest must avoid ritual defilement by marrying only a virgin, as opposed to other kinds of women (widows, divorcees, prostitutes), including a "woman who has been defiled" (Lev 21:14). The kind of "defilement" referred to here is not specified; possibly, it refers to a woman who has been divorced, remarried, divorced or widowed by the second husband, and remarried to the first husband (Deut 24:1–4). A priest is allowed to "defile himself," i.e., incur corpse impurity, by tending to his deceased "virgin sister" who has no husband to perform these duties for her (Lev 21:3). The Deutero-canonical Book of Judith speaks of the rape of a virgin as a sort of "defilement" (Jdt 9:2). Revelation 14:4 refers to "the one hundred forty-four thousand who have been redeemed from the earth" as "these who have not defiled themselves with women, for they are virgins" (14:4). Here, the virginity of the men seems to be related to their proximity to the heavenly sanctuary, where they sing before the throne of the Lamb (14:3). Possibly, there is a military reference: "These 'virgins' are the ritually pure soldiers around the military Lamb-Lion" (see Deut 20; 23:9–10; 1 Sam 21:5; 2 Sam 11:11).[6] With the possible exception of the Judith reference,[7] virginity and purity (or impurity) are mentioned in the context of the fitness of individuals, usually priests, to function ritually in holy places: the tabernacle, the temple, the heavenly throne room.

The scarcity of biblical references to *virginal* purity is due to the fact that purity laws (Leviticus 17–26) do not pertain primarily to sex, but to bodily states that render persons, especially priests, ritually fit or unfit to engage in acts of worship, especially in the context of offering sacrifices in the temple. Ritual impurity could be incurred through disease, contact with a corpse, bodily discharges (including, but not confined to, menstruation), and sexual activity (which involves bodily discharges for both men and women). Objects as well as people could be considered impure in this sense, illustrating the non-moral nature of ritual impurity: to be impure was not sinful, and did not necessarily imply dirtiness. Good actions (e.g., caring for the dead, giving birth, having sex with one's spouse) would inevitably incur impurity, which could be dealt with by appropriate rituals and the passage of time. Both men and women in the course of their lives incurred ritual impurity through the discharge of bodily fluids, including menstruation for women and semen for men (Leviticus 15). Contrary to the impression given by some Christian scholarship that Jewish women were particularly hampered by menstrual impurity, the rules regarding male discharges are as or more extensive than those pertaining to women. In Jesus' time, there were no prohibitions against menstruating (or haemorrhaging) women appearing in public, or any idea that impurity could be transferred simply by touching someone. As Amy-Jill Levine notes with respect to the Gospel story of the hemorrhaging woman who touches Jesus' garment and is healed (Mark 5:25–34; Matt 9:20–22; Luke 8:43–48): "There is no reason why the woman would not be in public; there is no reason why she should not seek Jesus' help. . . . Jesus abrogates no Laws . . . for there is

6. Ford, *Revelation*, 234.

7. Here, the reference to defilement may refer to the virgin being rendered unfit to marry a priest (Lev 21:14).

no Law forbidding the woman to touch him or him to touch her."[8] Even on the understanding that ritual purity could be transmitted from a menstruating woman to another person, this would not be a problem unless the person was about to visit the holy precincts of temple. Insofar as the biblical purity legislation maintained the special status of the holy nation of Israel, it encompassed sexual behavior along with other human activities, but the regulation of sexual behavior was not its main focus, nor was it applicable to most people most of the time.

An ancient cultural category more directly relevant to biblical notions about sex is the dichotomy between honor and shame. In Judith 9:2, mentioned above, there is a reference to the heroine's ancestor Simeon who took revenge on the men of Shechem for the rape of the virgin Dinah (Genesis 34): "O Lord, the God of my ancestor Simeon, remember how you armed Simeon with a sword to take revenge on those foreigners who seized Dinah, who was a virgin, tore off her clothes, and defiled her; they stripped her naked and shamed her; they raped her and disgraced her, even though you had forbidden this." Here, the virgin is shamed/disgraced by the rape, and it is up to her brother to exact revenge, thus restoring the family honor. As Bruce J. Malina and Jerome H. Neyrey point out, in the ancient Mediterranean world, including Israel, honor and shame were "pivotal values."[9] These values were gender-based: men, associated with honor, were aligned with the public sphere, assertiveness, authority, and even aggression; women, associated with shame, belonged to the home. For women, shame was particularly related to sexual behavior; women who were modest and circumspect with regard to sex were guardians of the family (male, public) honor, but women whose sexual behavior violated cultural expectations brought shame upon themselves and their families, especially the men. The shaming of a woman, like Dinah, could provoke aggression on the part of male family members to restore the family honor. Malina and Neyrey show how gender-based honor frequently underlies the narrative of Luke-Acts, e.g.: the pregnant Elizabeth "hides herself" at home, where she greets her young relative, the pregnant Mary (Luke 1:24, 40–43); Jesus' appearance in the women's quarters of Peter's home to heal his mother-in-law's illness needs to be carefully explained (Luke 4:38–39); the parable of the lost sheep focuses on the activities of the shepherd, outdoors, while the parable of the lost coin focuses on the indoor search of the woman (Luke 15:3–7, 8–10);

8. Levine, *Misunderstood Jew*, 174.

9. Malina and Neyrey, "Honor and Shame in Luke-Acts," 25–66.

the "woman of the city" who anoints Jesus' feet is a "sinner," assumed to be shameless (Luke 7:36–39);[10] in Acts 1:13, the widowed Mary, unprotected by a male relative, is "in a most precarious situation. But Luke defends the honor of Jesus by guarding the shame of Mary by locating her in a new family, an honorable household, the church."[11] Paul's much-interpreted discussion of women's head-covering (1 Cor 11:2–16) uses the language of honor and shame to recommend that women should wear veils, even in the quasi-familial yet public setting of the church: "Any man who prays or prophesies with something on his head disgraces his head, but any woman who prays or prophesies with her head unveiled disgraces her head—it is one and the same thing as having her head shaved. For if a woman will not veil herself, then she should cut off her hair; but if it is disgraceful for a woman to have her hair cut off or to be shaved, she should wear a veil" (vv. 4–6). Paul's seemingly tortured logic here rests on the premise that the honor of the church rests on properly modest female behavior; women should not risk bringing shame on the assembled believers by appearing to be immodest. Men, on the other hand, were free to show themselves in public with heads uncovered; to act otherwise (like properly shame-full women) would bring dishonor on the church. As John J. Pilch puts it: "Honor and shame are thus external controls on human behavior that depend upon the opinions of others."[12] Within this framework, it is understandable why the conduct of women, whether married, widows or virgins, and their potential to bring shame upon the Christian community, is a matter of some consternation in early Christian writings (e.g., 1 Cor 14:34–36; Col 3:18; Eph 5:22–23; 1 Tim 2:8–15; 5:2, 9–15; Titus 2:4; 1 Pet 3:1–6). The concern is not with "purity," but with women's particular responsibility in the Mediterranean ("biblical") world for upholding the public honor of the church through their modesty and discretion. "Shameful" behavior is interpreted not in terms of guilt and sin, but in terms of public perception of disgrace, as the Pauline references to the need for proper conduct towards "outsiders" illustrate (1 Cor 14:16, 23, 24; Col 4:5; 1 Thess 4:12; 1 Tim 3:7).

10. Ibid., 62–63.

11. Ibid., 63. See also John 29: 26–27.

12. Pilch, "Honor and Shame."

Virginity and Celibacy

There is no evidence in the Bible that virginity (read as never engaging in sexual intercourse) or celibacy (read as remaining unmarried) was valued as an end in itself. However, in the post-biblical church, Mary, Jesus and Paul came to be traditionally regarded as lifelong virgins, and Paul's teaching that celibacy was preferable to marriage in view of the urgency of evangelization (1 Cor 7:38) "was foundational for Jerome's contention that virginity is superior to marriage (*Jov. 7*),"[13] to the point that virginity was seen as a mark of superior virtue.

The most prominent and symbolic figure of virginity in the Christian (especially the Roman Catholic) tradition is Mary, the mother of Jesus. Among the four doctrinal teachings about Mary, the foremost doctrine is *Semper Virgo*, the teaching that Mary became pregnant and gave birth to Jesus, while she continued in her virginity until she died.[14] While the virginity of Mary at the birth of Jesus is suggested by the accounts in the Matthew and Luke, with regards to Mary's virginity following the birth of Jesus, there are clear references to brothers and sisters of Jesus (Matt 1:25; 13:34; Mark 6:6; John 7:33). Even so, the claim that Mary was forever a virgin prevailed in the later years of the early church and persists in many Christian communities to this day. However, it must be noted that such a doctrine became institutionalized between the fourth and seventh centuries, four to seven hundred years after Jesus' death.[15] What's more, the doctrine was vigorously debated and faced fierce opposition, similarly to original sin, as discussed in chapter 2. Early Christian theologians such as Tertullian and Origen refused to believe that Mary was a virgin because that would imply that Jesus was not fully human.[16] The major rationale behind the claim that Mary remained a virgin derives from the view of the body and of sexuality as things that are impure and dirty, thus to be denied. In order for Jesus to save us, he must be sinless, and the one who bore him, thus, must also be sinless. Since sexual intercourse, a necessary process for having a baby, was at that time in church

---

13. McFarland, "Virginity," *Cambridge Dictionary of Christian Theology*, Kindle Edition, loc. 27195.

14. Engelsman, *Feminine Dimension of the Divine*, 128. The other three doctrines are *Theotokos* (the Mother of God), Immaculate Conception, and Assumption (being taken up into heaven).

15. Harvey, *Handbook of Theological Terms*, 56.

16. Boff, *Maternal Face of God*, 147.

history regarded as sinful, the story of the virginity of the mother of Jesus had to be elaborated to show how she could be free from this sinful act.

The discussion around Mary's virginity is closely related to the discussion around Eve, traditionally represented as the original sinner (see chapter 2). But this logic has the danger of fueling a misogynist view (hatred of women), since the body is often culturally associated with women. If the body is to be denied, so the logic goes, then women must be also be denied or downgraded. Many feminist theologians around the world have challenged this view and provided alternative interpretations of the virginity of Mary since the 1970s.[17]

Theologian Kwok Pui-lan has investigated the development of celibacy in the context of the Crusades. Kwok shows how the declaration at the First Lateran Council (1139) that the marriage of clergy was invalid was in part the result of a need to recruit men for the Crusades. Warfare, and the long treacherous journey to Jerusalem, required many sacrifices including abstinence from sexual relationships. "During the Crusades," she writes, "the physical journey to recover the Holy Land was tied to the spiritual journey to reform in order to prepare for the eternal journey from earth to heaven."[18] In order to justify this war, the physicality and sexuality of the warriors and their religious leaders had to be erased. The demand for the celibacy of clergy was deemed necessary despite a movement toward a strong affirmation of clerical marriage on the part of some others. The Crusades were turned into a purely asexual spiritual journey. The priests and bishops who constantly had to preach about this necessary and holy war so as to send the male laity out as soldiers to do battle had to prove themselves holy by abstaining from sexual relations. In this so-called rescue mission, these soldiers' abstinence, like the priests', was marked as a holy act. Furthermore, Rosemary Radford Ruether argues that the intricate matrix of the three Cs, namely celibacy, the Crusades, and clergy, resulted in reinforcing the church in maintaining a hierarchical and dualistic order between male and female, clergy and laity, celibate and married in the Middle Ages: "The celibate male clergy . . . was sharply distinguished from

17. E.g., Ruether, *Religion and Sexism*; Han, "Mariology as a Base for Feminist Liberation Theology," 234–40; Park, *Korean Nation and Tasks for Feminist Theology*; Katoppo, *Compassionate and Free*.

18. Kwok, *Postcolonial Imagination*, 13.

the married laity. Their celibacy made priests innately superior to married lay people, whose sexual relations were tarred by the suspicion of sin."[19]

Abuses of clerical power, compounded by such problematic church teachings, contributed to the Protestant Reformation. McFarland notes that the Christian exaltation of virginity "was sharply contested by Protestants from the period of the Reformation onwards. While fully endorsing traditional beliefs regarding virginity prior to marriage and acknowledging perpetual virginity as a legitimate (though rare) calling, the Reformers viewed consigning large numbers of boys and girls to lives of virginity through monastic oblation as contrary to God's intention for the majority of human beings and correspondingly natural."[20] The post-Vatican II Catholic church affirms both marriage and celibacy as legitimate Christian lifestyles.

Purity and Sex at the Movies

Watch: *The Virgin Suicides* (1999)

Discussion Questions

Before the viewing

Have you heard of the practice of holding Purity Balls for young Christian girls?

Is there a sexual double standard for Christian men and women, especially youth?

After the viewing

Does the sexual behavior of the various sisters relate to their moral worth? To their value as human beings?

How are Christian values with respect to sexuality represented in the movie?

19. Ruether, *Christianity and the Making of the Modern Family*, 58.
20. McFarland, "Virginity," loc. 27195.

Discussion Notes (with Jessie Vitic)

The movie *The Virgin Suicides* is about five angelic-looking Catholic sisters whose parents, an overbearing mother and an ineffectual father, over-protectively guard them from the outside world in order to protect their virginal purity. Despite, or because of, their parent's preoccupation with their physical chastity, all five girls commit suicide within a little more than a year. We watched this movie together with a group of students invited by the university's Ecumenical Chaplaincy. Later, one of the students, Jessie Vitic, liked it so much that she decided to write her term paper for Dr. Beavis's Bible and Film class on it. With her permission, some of her insights about the biblical themes and echoes in the movie are quoted in this section.

As Vitic observes, significantly, "the girls are younger than eighteen—the age of adulthood—but older than twelve—the average age of puberty—so they embody womanhood, but still represent youth."[21] The youngest sister, Cecilia dies first, on her second suicide attempt: "The latter four sisters all died in one night, over a year after Cecilia's first attempt: Bonnie hanged herself in the basement, Mary put her head in the oven, Therese overdosed on sleeping pills, and Lux suffocated from car exhaust."[22] Obviously, the ostensibly upright Catholic Lisbon family is dysfunctional behind closed doors, as symbolized by the leaky ceilings of their house: "The Lisbon family's situation at home is demonstrated just before the homecoming dance, when the father takes a photo of the girls. Lux is distracted by the fact that the ceiling is leaking. Again, when the boys find Bonnie hanging in the basement, water is leaking heavily from above. These two situations indicate an unmistakable reality: even if the family's mansion looks nice on the outside, the girls reside in a 'broken' home. Regardless of going to church, the sisters live in a dystopia of some form."[23]

The girls' parents play the kinds of stereotypical roles association with Christian family values: "The father, Ronald Lisbon, is a math teacher at the local school. While the mother's occupation is not explicitly stated, the audience assumes she is a stay-at-home mom."[24] However, the mother is

21. Vitic, "*The Virgin Suicides*: A Biblical Film Analysis" (student paper, RLST 365.3, March 15, 2016), 2.

22. Ibid., 2.

23. Ibid., 3.

24. Ibid., 6.

the domineering one, and the father is relatively passive. Vitic perceptively observes that the only math lecture Mr. Lisbon gives in the movie is about the laws of intersection and union:

> Intersection commonly refers to a point where two lines come in contact, while union involves the full joining or merging of two things. The Bible speaks about two main types of union: union between a man and woman (Gen 2:24) versus union with Christ (Rom 6:5; 1 Cor 6:17; Phil 2:1–2). Union between a man and woman means to become "one" through marriage and sex. Though Mr. and Mrs. Lisbon are married and have obviously had sex, their relationship is disconnected. In their house, they are two people (lines) merely passing by each other, one acting more as a parent to their spouse than a wife. . . . Though the Lisbons are religious, they are not seen going to church once and never speak of Christ in the home apart from prayer at supper time; there is no personal bond established with God. In contrast with these classes of union—marriage and Christ—intersection may represent the superficial connection achieved by the Lisbons.[25]

Another symbol for the unhealthy family in the movie is the elm tree: "Five elm trees of the neighbourhood represent the sisters' lives, each of which receives a 'notice of removal' (death notice) before being cut down. Cecilia's identity is transferred to the family's elm tree when she imprints her hand into the knot that is freshly coated with white paste. The tree is cut down after Cecilia dies."[26] The deaths of the trees reflect on the state of the sisters: "The girls are inwardly dead even though they are physically living. Each tree is notably cut down by a group of people, suggesting that the daughters were killed more so at the hands of another than by themselves. In the Bible, Jesus makes a fig tree wither when he sees it doesn't bear fruit (Matt 21:18–22). The elm trees in this movie are alternatively bearing fungus. What is this fungus? Is it sin? Mental illness? Lack of faith? The Lisbon girls are not properly raised and cared for, which withers their spirits."[27]

As depicted in the movie, the virginity of girls before marriage is still viewed by many Christians as a hard and fast rule, an expectation of high Christian virtue. The movie well portrays how such an expectation is forced and imposed upon young women to the point that any breach carries major consequences. Parents with these views believe that the control of their

25. Ibid., 7.
26. Ibid., 10.
27. Ibid., 10–11.

daughters is required by their faith. When that control is lost and the rules are broken, severe punishment is called for. The movie shows this view carried out to the logical extreme of violence and death, both physical and spiritual. Sex educator and Christian ethics professor Kate Ott's advice is salient here: "Faith that is forced is not really faith . . . . Raising kids is not like assembling furniture or hooking up a new computer with one-size-fits-all directions that, when followed correctly, result in a working product."[28] In fact, the parents in *The Virgin Suicides* could not understand what happened to their daughters, completely convinced that they had raised their daughters so decently and so faithfully. The movie ends without any resolution. Instead of offering the answer to why and what exactly happened, it begs other questions such as, "What is the role of faith and theology in understanding sexuality?"; "Why were these parents so afraid of their daughters' interactions with men?"; and "How are the expectations of purity and virginity played out in the lives of young people, especially young women?"

Figure 1: Scene from *The Virgin Suicides*

The conclusion of this chapter will attempt to respond to these questions. In response to the first we would like to affirm that Christian notions of purity and sex are closely connected to the theological ideas of *agapē* and *eros*, two ways of viewing love. In fact, there are many terms that can be translated as love in the Jewish and Christian Scriptures. Catherine Keller spells this out: the Bible refers to love in the original languages of Hebrew and Greek, as well as in Latin, as "*ahabah, eros, philia, agape,*

28. Ott, *Sex + Faith*, 17, 8.

caritas, cupiditas," translated as "love of friend, and of foe, of neighbor, and of stranger, sexual and spiritual, human and divine, intimate and political, self-sacrificial, self-transforming, or selfish, passionate and dispassionate, celibate, marital, and extra, mystical, and mundane, hetero-, homo-, hetairic, or queer."[29] Despite the diversity of understandings of love in scripture, Christian theological traditions have privileged *agapē* ("spiritual love") over *eros* ("erotic love"), downplaying (to the point of denying) bodily and sexual love. When the body is viewed as impure and tainted, sexuality that involves a body is consequently impure and tainted. However, we know that sexuality is not identical to sexual intercourse. While sexuality involves the body, it involves senses and emotions as integral to experience. These dimensions are seen as enhancing human relationships. Sexuality is a complex part of who we are. Furthermore, it can be affirmed that these are aspects of the human that were created in God's image and thus, ultimately, should be seen as a gift from God.

Jessie Vitic notes that in the film, three kinds of love are depicted. First, there is "discipline, punishment, and supposed protection," as depicted by the very religious Mrs. Lisbon, who claims: "None of my daughters lacked for any love. *There was plenty of love in our house.* I never understood why [they died]."[30] Trip Fontaine, the boy who is initially infatuated with Lux and then abandons her after they've had sex, personifies pursuit: "Trip's definition of love seems to be sexual experience as a reward for diligent pursuit."[31] The neighborhood boys through whose eyes the story is told claim to love the girls, but in fact: "The audience sees continuously that these boys are obsessed—something they interpret as love—and act more like stalkers than detectives. . . . Biblically, this behaviour is not in agreement with the love God describes between any kind of person, whether a man and a woman or two neighbours."[32] None of these ways of "loving" the girls shows much interest in them as multidimensional human beings; rather, they are identified with their sexuality in different ways.

Like the rigid and repressive character of Mrs. Lisbon, our dualistic Christian traditions and teachings have continued to paint sexuality as sinful and dirty, discouraging young (and older) people from engaging in sexual relationships. This has led to unhelpful consequences. Preaching the

29. Keller, "Afterword: A Theology of Eros," 366.
30. Vitic, "Biblical Film Analysis," 11.
31. Ibid., 12.
32. Ibid., 13.

danger of sexual relationships and imposing the expectation of virginity before marriage (especially for girls) can, as the film illustrates, bring negative and unhealthy results. Research findings show that "abstinence-only-until-marriage education and pledges do not prevent teens from engaging in sexual intercourse prior to marriage. . . . Those teens in the study who broke the pledge were one-third less likely to use contraception than teens who had not pledged."[33] Other research shows that this kind of education promotes gender stereotypes and leads youth to define abstinence as avoiding vaginal intercourse. Thus, many teens believe that any other kind of sexual behavior is okay.[34] What these research findings point out is a need for a holistic sex education that values the human body and human sexuality. A renewed theological understanding of sexuality is desperately needed in order to deliver us from the false and distorted association of purity and virginity. Since each person's sexuality is valued as good, we must honor and care for it rather than denying it or punishing ourselves for experiencing it. Since sexuality encompasses relationships, it must be fostered within relationships of mutual respect and responsibility.

Other Resources

Easy A (dir. Will Gluck, 2010).

Kivel, Paul. *Living in the Shadow of the Cross: Understanding and Resisting the Power and Privilege of Christian Hegemony*. Gabriola Island, BC: New Society, 2013.

Mercer, Joyce Ann. *Girltalk/GodTalk: Why Faith Matters to Teenage Girls—and Their Parents*. San Francisco: John Wiley & Sons, 2008.

Valenti, Jessica. *The Purity Myth: How America's Obsession with Virginity is Hurting Young Women*. Berkeley: Seal, 2009.

The Virgin Daughters (dir. Jane Treays, 2008). http://topdocumentaryfilms.com/virgin-daughters/.

Whitehead, James D., and Evelyn Eaton Whitehead. *Holy Eros: Recovering the Passion of God*. Maryknoll: Orbis, 2009.

33. Bearman and Brückner, "Promising the Future," 859–912, cited in Ott, *Sex + Faith*, 128.

34. Remez, "Oral Sex among Adolescents," 128.

10

Suffering and Sacrifice

IN THE CHRISTIAN MIND, the twin themes of suffering and sacrifice are intertwined. Jesus' death on the cross is interpreted as the ultimate sacrifice, and his suffering on the cross is seen as essential to salvation. As the old Fanny Crosby hymn goes,

> Tell of the cross where they nailed Him
>
> Writhing in anguish and pain
>
> Tell of the grave where they laid Him
>
> Tell how He liveth again
>
> Love in that story so tender
>
> Clearer than ever I see
>
> Stay let me weep while you whisper
>
> Love paid the ransom for me.[1]

The association of suffering, sacrifice and the cross are deeply rooted in the Christian tradition, but the biblical meanings of these terms are poorly understood by modern-day Christians. In this chapter, we will show that in the Bible, sacrifice is not associated with suffering—or even necessarily with sin. Further, we will demonstrate that Jesus' death on the cross was not a sacrifice in the biblical sense. Finally, we will suggest some alternatives to the theology of atonement that the sacrificial interpretation of the crucifixion entails, using the movie *Chocolat* (dir. Lasse Hallström, 2000) as a basis of discussion.

---

1. Crosby, "Tell Me the Story of Jesus" (1880).

Sacrifice in the Jewish Scriptures

Sacrificial rituals were not unique to ancient Israel; other Ancient Near Eastern and Mediterranean peoples had their own priesthoods, temples and sacrificial regimes: "Sacrifice was 'mainstream' religion in the ancient world."[2] The practice of offering animals and agricultural produce to God is presupposed throughout the Bible. The Book of Leviticus gives lengthy and detailed instructions regarding the procedures to be followed by the Israelite priests in making such sacrifices: burnt offerings, grain offerings, offerings of well-being, sin offerings, and restitution offerings (Leviticus 1–7). In the English language, the term "sacrifice" is used to cover all of these rituals, but each has a specific name in Hebrew: *'olah, minhah, zevah shelamim, hatta't, 'asham*.[3] The more general Hebrew term that captures the sense of all these practices is *qorbān*, meaning "something brought forward, offering."[4] These offerings were made in the temple (or tabernacle), by a priest, for various purposes—as a gift to God, in thanksgiving and celebration, for ritual purification, or in restitution for sins. None of these ritual practices had the negative connotation of the English term "sacrifice," which is often associated with loss, suffering, and even death. They do reflect the meaning of the Latin term, *sacrificare*, from which the English word is derived, which has the sense of "to make sacred."

While most of these offerings required the death of animals, death was not the point; nor was the suffering of the animals. As Gilders points out, "The killing of the animals is a means to an end. Killing the animal makes its flesh and blood available for special use."[5] The purpose of these sacrificial rituals was to maintain, repair and celebrate the relationship between the people of Israel and their God. In contrast to the negative connotations of the English word "sacrifice," the Hebrew *quōrbanim* are portrayed positively, unless they are offered unworthily, or as a substitute for upright conduct (e.g., Pss 54:6; 66:15; 51:16–19; 40:6). Isaiah's prophecy of the restoration of Israel captures the celebratory mood of sacrifice:

> all who keep the sabbath, and do not profane it,
> and hold fast my covenant—
>
> these I will bring to my holy mountain,

2. See Gilders, "Sacrifice in Ancient Israel."
3. Ibid., 2.
4. Ibid., 1.
5. Ibid., 2.

and make them joyful in my house of prayer;

their burnt-offerings and their sacrifices

will be accepted on my altar;

for my house shall be called a house of prayer

for all peoples (Isa 56:6b–7).

As mentioned above, not all of the Israelite sacrifices were associated with sin; only the *hatta't* and the *'asham* dealt with "forms of disruption in the relationship between human beings and God."[6] The principal sacrifice offered to cleanse Israel from its sins on an annual basis was the Day of Atonement (*Yom Kippur*), described in detail in Leviticus 16. As Barry Bandstra summarizes the ritual:

> On the Day of Atonement, the high priest—here, Aaron—offers a bull as a purification offering. Then he takes two goats. He slaughters one of them, collects its blood, and sprinkles it on the mercy seat, a term designating the lid of the ark of the covenant. After exiting the tabernacle, he places his hands on the head of the other goat, thereby transferring the sins of the people to this animal. Called the goat for Azazel in Hebrew (where *azazel* may designate the underworld), this goat has come to be called the "scapegoat." It was sent way into the wilderness to disappear, symbolically taking with it the sins of the people.[7]

This ritual was performed only once a year, by the high priest, who alone was allowed to enter into the holiest part of the temple/tabernacle (the Holy of Holies). There was no idea that the sacrificial animals died in place of the people of Israel, i.e., there was no belief in substitutionary atonement. Rather, the blood of the animals was seen as purifying, as was the transfer of the nation's sins to the scapegoat. Since the destruction of the Second Temple in 70 CE, the festival has been transformed from a priestly ritual into a day of communal prayer, repentance and fasting (cf. Lev 16:29, 31): "This shall be an everlasting statute for you, to make atonement for the people of Israel once in the year for all their sins" (Lev 16:34a).

---

6. Ibid., 2.

7. Bandstra, *Reading the Old Testament*, 158.

Cross and Sacrifice

In the time of Jesus and the earliest Christians, the temple in Jerusalem was very much in operation, and the sacrifices stipulated in Leviticus were offered regularly by priests. In the Gospels, the incident known as "the cleansing of the temple" (Mark 11:15–18; Matt 21:12–13; Luke 19:45–46; John 2:14–16) illustrates Jesus' respect for the *beit Hamikdash*, the "holy house" where the daily rituals took place; the Book of Acts portrays the disciples spending time together in the temple, as well as in their homes (2:46). The Gospel of John portrays Jesus as in Jerusalem for Jewish festivals (2:23; 4:45; 5:1; 6:4; 7:2, 10; 10:22; 13:1); those specifically named are Passover (2:23; 6:4; 13:1), the Feast of Booths (7:2), and the Dedication (Chanukkah; 10:22). The "festival of the Jews" mentioned in John 5:1 likely refers to the Feast of Weeks (Pentecost). Three of these—Passover, Pentecost, and Booths—were pilgrimage festivals, in which Jewish men were obligated to travel to Jerusalem to present offerings of livestock and agricultural produce (Exod 34:18–23; Deut 16:1–17). It is likely that, as suggested by John, Jesus regularly participated in these festivals and their concomitant sacrifices, like other pious Jewish men.

In Christian doctrine, the crucifixion has long been interpreted in sacrificial terms, to the point that, for many Christians, the statement that the death of Jesus was not a sacrifice seems nonsensical. In view of the discussion above, however, it is clear that no-one actually observing the crucifixion would have mistaken it for a sacrificial ritual undertaken by a priest in a temple. Nor would they have viewed it as a joyous occasion of celebration, of "making sacred." Rather, crucifixion was a particularly painful, violent and shameful form of execution suffered by many ancient men, women and children, including Jesus. Unlike sacrifice, the point of crucifixion was death, suffering and fear—a decidedly unholy trio. The etymological meaning of crucifixion is derived from the Latin words *crucis* and *figere*, meaning "to fasten to a cross." The cross was used as the Roman Empire's tool of torture, as a killing tool to sentence a person to death for crimes (real and imagined) against a person, property or the state. It was not only a killing tool but also a medium of torture, an inhumane way to kill a person. To fix a human body to the stake with nails caused unbearable pain and prolonged suffering. The fact that Jesus died on a cross means that he died with cruelty and horror.

In view of the horrific and cruel reality of crucifixion, the earliest generations of disciples struggled to find ways of explaining the death of Jesus, and their overwhelming sense of finding meaning in its aftermath, in scripturally comprehensible terms. Since sacrificial rituals were very much part of the experience of the Jewish disciples, it was natural for some of them to interpret the crucifixion as a kind of metaphorical sacrifice, analogous to the offering of the Passover lamb (John 1:29, 36; 19:14, 31), or of the sacrificial goat on the Day of Atonement (Rom 3:25; Heb 2:17). Since crucifixion was a form of execution that entailed great suffering on the part of the victim, it is not surprising that the equation of suffering and sacrifice became part and parcel of the sacrificial interpretation of the cross, although this is not an association made anywhere in the Christian Testament. The Letter to the Hebrews, which develops the doctrine of the atoning death of Christ as both high priest and sacrifice in its most definitive scriptural form (Heb 9:23–28), also refers to the suffering of Jesus "in the days of his flesh" (Heb 5:7–10; 12:2), but never associates his suffering with sacrifice. True to the celebratory mood of Jewish sacrificial rituals, Hebrews portrays the sprinkling of Jesus' blood in the heavenly Holy of Holies in festive terms:

> But you have come to Mount Zion and to the city of the living God, the heavenly Jerusalem, and innumerable angels in festal gathering, and to the assembly of the firstborn who are enrolled in heaven and to God the judge of all, and to the spirits of the righteous made perfect, and to Jesus, the mediator of a new covenant, and to the sprinkled blood that speaks a better word than the blood of Abel (Heb 12:22–24).

In addition to the Day of Atonement imagery associated with the crucifixion, the sacrifice of the Passover lamb was also invoked in connection with the death of Jesus, especially in the Gospel of John. The Passover sacrifice, however, was not atoning (making amends for one's crime or sin), but apotropaic (turning away), with the power to avert evil or misfortune: the blood of the slaughtered lamb was applied to the doorposts of the Israelites' houses so that their firstborn would be saved from death (Exod 12:1–14; cf. John 1:29, 36; Rev 5:6). As Jesper Tang Nielsen observes, in John:

> Both the preserving of Jesus' bones and the mentioning of hyssop and blood recall elements of the Passover ritual: hyssop and blood have to do with preventing death, and the fact that Jesus' bones are not broken has to do with the protection of Israel. This leads to the conclusion that the Passover lamb traditions are utilized in the crucifixion scene in order to present the crucifixion as a protection against death.[8]

8. Nielsen, "The Lamb of God," 253.

The early Christian writers also used non-sacrificial metaphors to explain the saving significance of the death of Jesus: in terms of redemption, i.e., a ransom paid to buy the freedom of a slave or prisoner (e.g., Mark 10:45); or as scapegoating—bearing away the sins of others, like the second goat on the Day of Atonement (cf. John 1:29). As Rausch observes:

> The early Church Fathers described both goats as prefiguring Christ's sacrifice. Cyril of Alexandria and Theodoret identified the goats as representing Christ in both his natures: his human nature dying in the flesh as the Son of Man and the scapegoat seen as the Son of God escaping death through resurrection. Christ-as-scapegoat carries away the sins of the world.[9]

The death of Jesus is also interpreted in terms of martyrdom, where a righteous person is willing to suffer, and even die, to uphold the Law. As Alan F. Segal explains, the model of Jesus as suffering martyr fits his death in a more literal way than the sacrifice, redemption or scapegoat metaphors:

> Jesus died as a martyr, trying to protect and fulfill and protect the teaching of the Jewish law, especially as he had preached repentance and understanding for sinners. In the eyes of his followers, his martyrdom was seen as a symbol of the beginning of the promised recompense for the righteous' suffering, the apocalyptic consummation.[10]

In early Jewish writings, martyrdom is interpreted as an atoning act with salvific effects for Israel (4 Macc 17:22; 6:28–29; 2 Macc 7:37–38). Moreover, as with Jesus, the suffering and death of the Jewish martyrs was associated with resurrection (2 Macc 7:8, 11, 14, 22, 29): "Resurrection is exactly the reward that apocalypticism promises for martyrs, but resurrection does not come until the end is nigh."[11] Thus, Christians have long believed that the resurrection of Jesus is the firstfruits of the end times (1 Cor 15:22–24).

Over time, the sacrificial metaphor for the crucifixion, along with its association with suffering, has become reified—the metaphor has been confused with the "real thing." In addition, the concept of crucifixion-as-sacrifice has been collapsed together with other metaphors: redemption, scapegoating, martyrdom. What all these metaphors have in common is

---

9. Rausch, Jr., "Scapegoat," 471.

10. Segal, *Life after Death*, 395.

11. Ibid., 393.

their focus on the death of Jesus, and the understandable concern of the earliest Christians to understand why their companion, teacher and leader had died in such a shocking and shameful way; as Paul puts it, a stumbling block to Jews, and foolishness to Greeks (1 Cor 1:23).

The idea that the death of Jesus was a sacrifice is expressed by countless hymns, sermons, and even in popular culture. The contemporary worship song "Behold the Lamb" expresses this theology as traditionally as eighteenth- and nineteenth-century hymns:

> Behold the Lamb who bears our sins away,
> Slain for us—and we remember
> The promise made that all who come in faith
> Find forgiveness at the cross.
> So we share in this bread of life,
> And we drink of His sacrifice
> As a sign of our bonds of peace. . . .
> As we share in His suffering
> We proclaim Christ will come again!
> And we'll join in the feast of heaven
> Around the table of the King
> ("Behold the Lamb," Gettymusic.com)

> What can wash away my sin?
> Nothing but the blood of Jesus
> What can make me whole again?
> Nothing but the blood of Jesus"
> (Robert Lowry, nineteenth century)

> And can it be that I should gain
> An int'rest in the Savior's blood?
> Died He for me, who caused His pain?
> For me, who Him to death pursued?
> Amazing love! how can it be
> That Thou, my God, shouldst die for me?
> Amazing love! how can it be
> That Thou, my God, shouldst die for me?
> (Charles Wesley, eighteenth century)

Of course, there is nothing wrong with the liturgical expression of traditional doctrines. The challenge for us who carry this liturgical tradition is that certain images, especially the blood of Jesus, conjure up triumphant emotions that may lead to the glorification of violence. The opposite reaction is also possible. Because it is too grotesque and gruesome to face the violence associated with the blood of Jesus, some may avoid the issue, unable to confront violence even in order to stop it. Whichever way we look at his death, overemphasizing the blood of Jesus as sacrifice and atonement can push people to extremes of either condoning or concealing violence.

The Passion of the Christ, a much-debated and controversial movie, as discussed in chapter 2, is worth further discussing here because it clearly demonstrates the difficulty with the sacrificial metaphor, and because it is alive and well in popular media culture. This movie is the highest grossing R-rated film in United States history, the highest grossing religious film, and the highest grossing non-English-language film of all time. What the R-rating indicates is its high level of violence. The film, however, was a major commercial hit, grossing in excess of $600 million during its theatrical release. The equivalent of almost one-third of the entire population of the United States watched this movie within two months of its release. The fact that the movie was released on February 25, 2004, Ash Wednesday, is a signal that it was directly targeting Christians. It targeted both regular church goers and so-called Easter/Christmas Christians. The numbers show that Christians of all stripes rushed to the theaters. People seemed to regard watching this movie has a kind of worship experience, as if watching a movie could replace the act of repentance, the traditional Ash Wednesday ritual observance. One may question if its success was due to its detailed graphic violence since violence sells and what connection people made between that violence and their Christian faith.

The other big controversy with *The Passion of Christ* was its anti-Semitic content. A group of Catholic and Jewish scholars thoroughly reviewed the film and concluded that Mel Gibson, a cowriter and director, added many scenes that had no basis in the Gospels. These scenes depict Jews as malevolent, sadistic, and satanic. These scholars addressed their concerns to Gibson. Mary Boys, a member of that group recalls that Gibson reacted to this critique strongly by expressing his contempt for the teachings of Vatican II regarding the special bond between Jews and Christians.[12] Fur-

12. See the Declaration on the Relation of the Church to Non-Christian Religions, *Nostra Aetate*, Proclaimed By His Holiness Pope Paul VI on October 28, 1965. See

thermore, Gibson portrayed himself as a victim, claiming he was being persecuted by a group that had perverted the Gospel. He masterfully used his celebrity and publicity so as to paint the group of scholars who challenged this movie's violence and anti-Semitism as "dupes of the Jews," "forces of Satan," an "arrogant gang of so-called scholars," and even as "antichrist."[13]

The controversy over *The Passion of Christ* teaches us many things. It clearly shows how influential movies can be. It also lays bare some of the challenges facing those who would critically engage popular culture as scholars and people of faith. While the group failed to stop the movie from being released to the public, it nonetheless made an impact. As a result of their action the subtitles for the dialogue no longer used the phrase "curse of Jews." Most importantly, the public, including the newspapers and religious groups, were engaged. It did not go unnoticed.

Ultimately, the problem with associating the crucifixion with sacrifice and atonement in our own theology and popular culture is that it is overly connected with death and suffering. Many people of faith (and those who are critical of religions) have found this a very problematic aspect of Christianity. It is definitely a factor that dismays, if not disgusts, many people. Christian Eberhart expresses this negative response when reflecting on the scriptures that describe the ritual sacrifice in Judaism, a ritual which laid an important template for how Christians understand Jesus' crucifixion: "Some today think that the very center of Israelite/Judean worship was occupied by an institution bent on the ritual annihilation of life, suggesting that Levitical priests should be considered 'butchers.'"[14] Does religion glorify the butcher business? If we rid ourselves of ritual sacrifice as a metaphor for the crucifixion are we throwing the baby out with the bathwater? While a few Christians have totally abandoned the sacrifice and atonement motif to the point that they no longer see a need for the person of Jesus as a sacrificial and savior figure, we suggest that this is like tossing the baby, since Christianity without Jesus ceases to be Christian. What is needed, then, is a nuanced and well informed biblical and theological understanding of sacrifice and atonement. It is often the lack of biblical knowledge that leads to misinformation and distortion of certain theological concepts and meanings. Is it possible to anchor Christian faith as expressed in the Bible, as a journey toward new life, resurrection from

---

http://www.vatican.va/archive/hist_councils/ii_vatican_council/documents/vat-ii_decl_19651028_nostra-aetate_en.html.

13. Boys and Lee, *Christians and Jews in Dialogue*, 58.

14. Eberhart, *Sacrifice of Jesus*, 5.

the dead, a symbol of hope and of the resilience of life, despite the threat and the horror of violence in the real world? Can we envision the crucifixion not as a symbol of death but as a locus of resurrection? Our final section below is one such attempt to behold that vision.

Beyond Atoning Sacrifice

The doctrine of vicarious (or substitutionary) atonement, which interprets the death of Jesus as a sacrifice that atones for the sins of humanity, has been part of Christian doctrine for many centuries, although it has been articulated in many different ways.[15] The point to be noted here is that these Christian theological interpretations may use the biblical language of atonement and sacrifice, but have little to do with the sacrificial rituals of ancient Israel in the Bible, none of which see the sacrificial victim as dying "instead of" the people.

As mentioned above, the early Christian fixation on the meaning of the death of Jesus is understandable in view of the traumatic impact of his execution on his disciples. However, even in the Christian Testament, there is an important body of scripture that does not focus on the cross, but that interprets the resurrection as the locus of salvation. This is Luke-Acts, a two-volume set that takes up about a third of the Christian Testament canon. As Mark Alan Powell notes, "Luke finds the basis for salvation to be manifest in Jesus' life and in his resurrection/exaltation."[16] In the Lukan writings, the crucifixion is not denied, but it is not given any soteriological significance. For example, in Peter's speech in the temple, he summarizes the arrest and execution of Jesus without explicitly mentioning the crucifixion:

> The God of Abraham, the God of Isaac, and the God of Jacob, the God of our ancestors has glorified his servant Jesus, whom you handed over and rejected in the presence of Pilate, though he had decided to release him. But you rejected the Holy and Righteous One and asked to have a murderer given to you, and you killed the Author of life, whom God raised from the dead. To this we are witnesses. And by faith in his name, his name itself has made this man strong, whom you see and know; and the faith that is through Jesus has given him this perfect health in the presence of all of you (Acts 3:13–16).

15. See McCormack, "Atonement," 43–45.
16. Powell, "Salvation in Luke-Acts," 8.

The healing of a lame man that precedes the speech is connected with the resurrection (3:1–9), and the salvific power of faith in the name of Jesus. There is no emphasis on suffering, sacrifice, or atonement. Throughout Luke-Acts: "Jesus is Messiah and Lord on earth during his life (Luke 2:11), and he is officially installed as Messiah and Lord in heaven by virtue of his resurrection and exaltation (Acts 2:36). As such, he has the right to bestow salvation on whomever he chooses."[17]

In fact, paintings of the corpse of Jesus did not appear in churches for a thousand years. Rita Nakashima Brock and Rebecca Ann Parker uncovered many surprises in their review of art books and in their journey to the Mediterranean regions where Christianity originally spread. Expecting to find the dead body of Jesus painted, etched and woven into ancient church images, what they discovered instead was a multitude of images of "the incarnate, risen Christ, the child of baptism, the healer of the sick, the teacher of his friends, and the one who defeated death and transfigured the world with the Spirit of Life."[18] The meaning of paradise depicted in this art is not the afterlife but a dimension of the life in this world, "the best that life could be."[19] As discussed in chapter 5, paradise, like heaven for early Christians, was a place of salvation within this world. The central image of Christian churches until the tenth century was paradise. It was not the death of Jesus, his suffering and sacrifice. "It took Jesus a thousand years to die,"[20] or one may say, Jesus died again in the tenth century. Somehow Christianity made a drastic turn from life to death at the turn of the first millennium. It is, then, natural to ask why and how such shift occurred.

One possible explanation is given by Brock and Parker. They retrace the origin of this shift to the imperial regime of King Charles the Great, known as the Charlemagne (742–814). Before his reign, the Old Saxons accepted a form of Christianity that embraced pagan religious traditions. Christian priests celebrated rituals and feasts that came from pagan cultures. Their hybrid and fluid Christian practices viewed this world as something good and delightful. They felt called by God to enjoy the world rather than feeling the need to call on God to be rescued from it. However, this changed when Charlemagne forcefully and violently banned certain pagan practices. These were rituals that often happened in the forest, at places of

17. Ibid., 9.
18. Brock and Parker, *Saving Paradise*, xi.
19. Ibid., xvii.
20. Ibid., ix.

ritual gathering and around sacred trees. Not only did this regime behead those who resisted this change but also deforested Europe in an attempt to be rid of these pagan influences.[21] Theologically speaking, what was happening around that time was the establishment of a theological orthodoxy which was understood as a correction of or rescue from the previous practices, by separating Christians from pagan religious traditions. It became a crime to transgress this boundary. Those who opposed and resisted were heavily punished. The focus of preaching on sin and punishment for sinful pagan traditions followed. Gradually, after two hundred years of conflict and suppression, fearful and horrific images of death became more prominent in the psyche of Saxon-Christians. They began to hew "an image of the tortured and dead body of Christ hanging from the tree."[22] The Gero Cross (965–970), the oldest depiction of the dead Christ, was in fact carved from the once sacred oak tree of Saxon Christianity's spirituality of life! (See Figure 1.) The following centuries, right up to the height of the medieval era, gave rise to more and more gruesome images of the dead body of Christ, images of Christ's blood spurting from his side and filling a chalice. In the fourteenth century, the image of Christ dying *in* a chalice was created.[23]

21. Brown, *Rise of Western Christendom,* 124–25, cited in Brock and Parker, *Saving Paradise,* 230.

22. Brock and Parker, *Saving Paradise,* 232.

23. Ibid., 236.

Figure 1: Gero Cross, Cologne Cathedral, Germany.
Oak sculpture, life size (source: Wikimedia Commons)

Death, however, did not defeat life. Some Saxons resisted and produced counter narratives. These Saxon Christians wrote an epic, called the
Heiland (the healer), a mid-ninth-century Gospel story of resistance in the
German vernacular. To write in German instead of Latin was itself an act
of resistance. *Heiland* is written in ways that people could sing and chant.
In this epic, Jesus is depicted as "the Best of healers," and peasants are represented as a people who work together with the noble high class members
of society against the hatred of the enemy.[24] The journey of the Christ child
fleeing from death for the sake of life conjures up the image of paradise
in this life: "They (the family of Jesus) flee by night to Egyptland, to the

24. Ibid., 242.

green meadows by the best earth, where a river flows, the fairest of streams, northward to the sea—the mighty Nile."[25]

The resilience of the Saxons' faith had not completely disappeared. This trait survived and continues to this day to evoke the imagination and inspire new generations of Christians who see that the centrality of the Christian message lies in the life and the resurrection of Christ. We can even find such an idea expressed in our twenty-first-century movie.

Suffering and Sacrifice at the Movies

Watch: *Chocolat* (2000)

Discussion Questions

Before the viewing

Why do you think that the English word "sacrifice" has the implications of suffering and deprivation?

If the crucifixion was not literally a sacrifice, how else can it be understood theologically by contemporary Christians?

After the viewing

How would you describe the religious identity of Vianne? Is her spirituality incompatible with Christianity?

What do you think of the priest's suggestion that it is better to focus on Jesus' humanity than his divinity?

Discussion Notes

We watched *Chocolat* with a small group of feminist Christian women shortly after Easter. The timing was good, since the story is framed by the beginning of Lent and Easter Sunday. In parabolic form, film portrays the

25. Ibid., 243.

over-emphasis of many forms of Christianity on the twin themes of suffering and sacrifice to the detriment of the Gospel themes of resurrection and life.

The story is set in a small, conservative French village in the 1950s. When a young woman and her daughter arrive there and set up a chocolate-shop at the beginning of the Catholic season of Lent, the pious people of the town are outraged. The mayor of the village, especially, is scandalized by the newcomer Vianne ("Life"), who not only concocts extravagant chocolate delicacies during a time of prayer and fasting, but who is not, by her own admission, a Christian. The friction between the followers of the self-denying mayor and the socially marginal friends of Vianne escalates to a dangerous crescendo that is finally resolved on Easter Sunday, when the youthful parish priest delivers a homily that emphasizes the humane, life-affirming themes of the Gospel:

> I'm not sure what the theme of my homily today ought to be. Do I want to speak of the miracle . . . of our Lord's divine transformation? Not really, no. I don't want to talk about His divinity. I'd rather talk about His humanity. I mean, you know, how he lived his life here on Earth. His kindness. His tolerance. Listen, here's what I think. I think we can't go around . . . measuring our goodness by what we don't do. By what we deny ourselves . . . what we resist and who we exclude. I think we've got to measure goodness . . . by what we embrace . . . what we create . . . and who we include.[26]

The film ends with an Easter fertility festival celebrated by all the townspeople, Christian and pagan alike.

The film's blending of Christian and pagan motifs is reminiscent of the Saxon Christian *Heiland*, with its themes of healing, reconciliation and paradise, and the early Christian emphasis on life in this world as the best that life can be: "The *Heiland's* Eucharist is a sign of the birth of Christ, of the incarnate Word, and of the life-creating power of his teaching. It uses the Saxon runes and their magical power . . . to identify the Eucharist as a holy image, embodying the shining light of the divine presence. . . . For the poet of the *Heiland*, Jesus' crucifixion had no healing power. Those who did not love him in life would not be changed by his death."[27]

The movie's emphasis on fullness of life does not only lead to the conversion of the austere mayor and the villagers who follow his example. As

---

26. *Chocolat* Script—Dialogue Transcript, http://www.script-o-rama.com/movie_scripts/c/chocolat-script-transcript-johnny-depp.html.

27. Brock and Parker, *Saving Paradise*, 248.

the women in our discussion group observed, Vianne, too, learns that she has been compromising her daughter's, and her own, happiness by restlessly travelling from town to town, following the example of her own mother, so that in the end, when "The Wind spoke to Vianne . . . of towns yet to be visited, friends in need, yet to be discovered, battles yet to be fought," she left it to be followed "by someone else. . . next time. And so it was, the North Wind grew weary . . . and went on its way."[28] Vianne and her daughter are freed to settle down, find love, and live life to the fullest with their neighbors.

Figure 2: Scene from *Chocolat*, with Johnny Depp and Juliette Binoche

Other Resources

Beavis, Mary Ann, and HyeRan Kim-Cragg. *Hebrews*. Wisdom Commentaries. Collegeville, MN: Liturgical, 2015.

Eberhart, Christian. *The Sacrifice of Jesus: Understanding Atonement Biblically*. Minneapolis: Fortress, 2010.

The Passion of the Christ (dir. Mel Gibson, 2004).

28. *Chocolat* Script—Dialogue Transcript, http://www.script-o-rama.com/movie_scripts/c/chocolat-script-transcript-johnny-depp.html.

Bibliography

Augustine. *On Free Choice of the Will.* Translated by A. S. Benjamin and L. H. Hackstaff. Indianapolis: Bobbs-Merrill, 1964.

Augustine. *The City of God Against the Pagans.* Translated by Philip Levine. Cambridge, MA: LCL, 1966.

Ayres, Jennifer. "Learning on the Ground: Ecology, Engagement, and Embodiment." *Teaching Theology & Religion* 17.3 (2014) 203–17.

Baird, Joseph L., and Radd K. Ehrman, eds. *The Letters of Hildegard of Bingen* Volume 1. Oxford: Oxford University Press, 1994.

Baker-Fletcher, Karen. *Sisters of Dust, Sisters of Spirit: Womanist Wordings on God and Creation.* Minneapolis: Augsburg, 1998.

Bandstra, Barry. *Reading the Old Testament: Introduction to the Old Testament,* 4th ed. Belmont, CA: Wadsworth, 2000. Online: http://barrybandstra.com/rtot4/rtot4-08-ch5.html#section1.

Baron, Dennis. *Grammar and Gender.* New Haven, CT: Yale University Press, 1986.

Bearman, Peter S. and Hannah Brückner. "Promising the Future: Virginity Pledges as They Affect Transition to First Intercourse." *The American Journal of Sociology* 106 (2001) 859–912.

Beavis, Mary Ann, and HyeRan Kim-Cragg. *Hebrews: Wisdom Commentary,* Vol. 54. Collegeville: Liturgical, 2015.

Beavis, Mary Ann. "'Angels Carrying Savage Weapons': Uses of the Bible in Horror Films," *Journal of Religion and Popular Culture* 7.2 (2003). Online: https://www.unomaha.edu/jrf/Vol7No2/angels.htm.

———. "Jesus of Montreal." In *Bible and Cinema: Fifty Key Films,* edited by Adele Reinhartz, 145–49. New York: Routledge, 2013.

———. *Mark.* Paideia Commentaries. Grand Rapids: Baker Academic, 2011.

———. "The New Covenant and Judaism." *The Bible Today* 22 (1984) 24–30.

Bergant, Dianne. *Genesis: In the Beginning.* Collegeville, MN: Liturgical, 2013.

Bernard, McGinn. *Antichrist: Two Thousand Years of the Human Fascination with Evil.* San Francisco: HarperSanFrancisco, 1994.

Betz, Hans Dieter, et al., eds. *Religion Past and Present: Encyclopedia of Theology and Religion.* Vol. 4. Boston: Brill, 2008.

Biale, David. "The God with Breasts: El Shaddai in the Bible." *History of Religions* 21.3 (1982) 240–256.

Black, Kathy. *A Healing Homiletic: Preaching and Disability.* Nashville: Abingdon, 1994.

Boff, Leonardo. *The Maternal Face of God: The Feminine and its Religious Expressions.* San Francisco: Harper & Row, 1987.

Bolt, Peter G. *Jesus' Defeat of Death: Persuading Mark's Early Readers.* Cambridge: Cambridge University Press, 2003.

Boys, Mary C., and Sara S. Lee. *Biblical Interpretation in Religious Education.* Birmingham: Religious Education, 1980.

———. *Christians and Jews in Dialogue: Learning in the Presence of the Other.* Woodstock, VT: Skylight Paths, 2006.

———. *Has God Only One Blessing? Judaism as a Source of Christian Self-Understanding.* New York: Paulist, 2000.

Brock, Sebastian. "The Holy Spirit as Feminine in Early Syriac Literature," http://www.womenpriests.org/theology/brock.asp.

Brock, Rita Nakashima, and Rebecca Ann Parker. *Proverbs of Ashes: Violence, Redemptive Suffering, and the Search for What Saves Us.* Boston: Beacon, 2001.

———. *Saving Paradise: How Christianity Traded Love of This World for Crucifixion and Empire.* Boston: Beacon, 2008.

Brown, Peter. *The Rise of Western Christendom: Triumph and Diversity AD 200–1000.* Malden: Blackwell, 2003.

Butler, Judith. *Gender Trouble: Feminism and the Subversion of Identity.* New York: Routledge, 1990.

Calvin, John. *Institutes of Christian Religion.* Translated by Henry Beveridge. Grand Rapids: Eerdmans, 1953.

Carbine, Rosemary. "Erotic Education: Elaborating a Feminist and Faith-Based Pedagogy for Experiential Learning in Religious Studies." *Teaching Theology & Religion* 13.4 (2010) 320–88.

Cargal, Timothy B. "Anoint." In *Eerdmans Dictionary of the Bible*, edited by David Noel Freedman, Allen C. Myers, and Astrid B. Beck, 65. Grand Rapids: Eerdmans, 2000.

Charlesworth, James. "From Messianology to Christology: Problems and Prospects." In *The Messiah: Developments in Earliest Judaism and Christianity*, edited by James Charlesworth, 3–35. Minneapolis: Augsburg Fortress, 2009.

Chazan, Robert. *In the Year 1092: The First Crusade and the Jews.* Philadelphia: Jewish Publications Society, 1996.

———. *Medieval Stereotypes and Modern Antisemitism.* Berkeley: University of California Press, 1997.

Colijn, Brenda B. *Images of Salvation in the New Testament.* London: InterVarsity, 2010.

Conzelmann, Hans. *The Theology of St. Luke.* Translated by Geoffrey Buswell. London: Faber and Faber, 1960.

Coyote, Ivan E., and Rae Spoon. *Gender Failure.* Vancouver: Arsenal Pulp, 2014.

Craigo-Snell, Shannon, and Shawnthea Monroe. *Living Theology: A Pastoral Theology for Today.* Minneapolis: Fortress, 2009.

Cross, Frank. *Canaanite Myth and Hebrew Epic.* Cambridge: Harvard University Press, 1997.

Crossan, Dominic John. *The Historical Jesus: The Life of a Mediterranean Jewish Peasant.* New York: Harper, 1991.

Dalton, Russell, W. *Video, Kids, and Christian Education: How to Use Video in your Christian Education Program*. Minneapolis: Fortress, 2001.

Daly, Mary. *Beyond God the Father: Toward a Philosophy of Women's Liberation*. New York: Beacon, 1974.

Davies, Alan. "Antisemitism: An Enduring Problem in Western Society." In *Bearing Faithful Witness: United Church-Jewish Relations Today*. Toronto, 2003. Online: http://www.united church.ca/files/partners/relations/witness.pdf.

Day, Peggy L. "Virgin." In *Eerdmans Dictionary of the Bible*, edited by Noel David Freeman, Allen C. Myers, and Astrid B. Beck, 1358. Grand Rapids: Eerdmans, 2000.

Dearborn, Joe. "Preface." In *The Inclusive Bible: The First Egalitarian Translation*, v–vii. New York: Rowman and Littlefield, 2007.

deSilva, David. *Introducing the Apocrypha: Message, Context and Significance*. Grand Rapids: Baker Academic, 2004.

Duck, Ruth. *Gender and the Name of God: The Trinitarian Baptismal Formula*. Cleveland: Pilgrim, 1991.

———. *Worship for the Whole People of God: Vital Worship for the 21st Century*. Louisville: Westminster John Knox, 2013.

Eberhart, Christian A, *The Sacrifice of Jesus: Understanding Atonement Biblically*. Minneapolis: Fortress, 2010.

Edwards, Katie B. *Admen and Eve: The Bible in Contemporary Advertising*. Sheffield, UK: Sheffield Phoenix, 2014.

Ehrman, Bart. *After the New Testament: A Reader in Early Christianity*. Oxford: Oxford University Press, 1998.

Eisenbaum, Pamela. *Paul Was Not a Christian: The Original Message of a Misunderstood Apostle*. San Francisco: HarperOne, 2008.

Emmerson, Richard K. "The Representation of Antichrist in Hidegard of Bingen's Scivias: Image, Word, Commentary, and Visionary Experience." *Gesta* 41.2 (2002) 95–110.

Engelsman, Joan Chamberlain. *The Feminine Dimension of the Divine*. Asheville, NC: Chiron, 1992.

Farley, Edward. *The Fragility of Knowledge: Theological Education in the Church and University*. Minneapolis: Fortress, 1988.

———. *Theologia: The Fragmentation and Unity of Theological Education*. Minneapolis: Augsburg, 1994.

Flanagan, Sabina. *Hildegard of Bingen, 1098-1179: A Visionary Life*. London: Routledge, 1998.

Flax, Jane. *Thinking Fragments: Psychoanalysis, Feminism, and Postmodernism in the Contemporary West*. Berkeley: University of California Press, 1990.

Flynn, Shawn W. "Yahweh, YHWH." *Dictionary of the Bible and Western Culture*, edited by Mary Ann Beavis and Michael J. Gilmour, 614. Sheffield: Phoenix, 2012.

Ford, Massyngberde Josephine. *Revelation*. Anchor Bible 38. Garden City, NY: Doubleday, 1975.

Fredriksen, Paula. *Jesus of Nazareth, King of the Jews*. New York: Vintage, 2000.

———. "Why Should a 'Law-Free' Mission Mean a 'Law-Free' Apostle?" *Journal of Biblical Literature* 134.3 (2015) 637–50.

Gale, Aaron M. "Matthew." *Jewish Annotated New Testament*, edited by Amy-Jill Levine and Mark Zvi Brettler, 1–55. Oxford: Oxford University Press, 2011.

Gateley, Edwina. *A Warm, Moist Salty God: Women Journeying Towards Wisdom*. Trabuco Canyon, CA: Source Books, 1993.

Gilders, William K. "Sacrifice in Ancient Israel." *Teaching the Bible: An e-newsletter for Public School Teachers by Society of Biblical Literature*. Online: http://www.sbl-site. org/assets/pdfs/TBv2i5_Gilders2.pdf.

Gorday, Peter, ed. *Ancient Christian Commentary on Scripture, New Testament IX*. Downers Grove, IL: InterVarsity, 2000.

Gottwald, Norman K. *The Hebrew Bible—A Socio-literary Introduction*. Minneapolis: Fortress, 1985.

Gudmundsdóttir, Armfriður, "The Passion of the Christ." *Bible and Cinema: Fifty Key Films,* edited by Adele Reinhartz, 202–5. London: Routledge, 2013.

Halperin, David. "Is There a History of Sexuality?" *History and Theory* 28.3 (1989) 257–74.

Han, Kuk Yum. "Mariology as a Base for Feminist Liberation Theology." In *Asian Women Doing Theology*, edited by Asian Women's Resource Centre for Culture and Theology (AWRC) 234–40. Hong Kong: AWRC, 1989.

Harrington, Daniel S.J. *Invitation to the Apocrypha*. Grand Rapids: Eerdmans, 1999.

Harvey, Van A. *A Handbook of Theological Terms*. New York: MacMillan, 1964.

Heyward, Carter. *Saving Jesus: From Those Who Are Right: Rethinking What it Means to be Christian*. Minneapolis: Fortress, 1999.

Horsley, Richard A. *Jesus and the Spiral of Violence: Popular Jewish Resistance in Roman Palestine*. San Francisco: Harper & Row, 1987.

Jensen, David. *Living Hope: The Future and Christian Faith*. Louisville, KY: Westminster John Knox, 2010.

Johnson, Elizabeth A. *She Who Is: the Mystery of God in Feminist Theological Discourse*. New York: Crossroad, 1992.

———. "Wisdom was Made Flesh and Pitched Her Tent Among Us." In *Reconstructing the Christ Symbol: Essays in Feminist Christology,* edited by Maryann Stevens, 95–117. Eugene, OR: Wipf & Stock, 1993.

Kateusz, Ally. *Finding Holy Spirit Mother*. Kansas City, MO: Divine Balance, 2008.

Katoppo, Marianne. *Compassionate and Free: An Asian Women's Theology*. Maryknoll: Orbis, 1980.

Keck, Leander E. "Death and Afterlife in the New Testament." In *Death and Afterlife: Perspectives of World Religions,* edited by Hiroshi Obayashi, 83–93. Westport, CT: Greenwood, 1992.

Keller, Catherine. "Afterword: A Theology of Eros, After Transfiguring Passion." In *Toward a Theology of Eros: Transfiguring Passion at the Limits of Discipline,* edited by Virginia Burrus and Catherine Keller, 366–74. New York: Fordham University Press, 2006.

———. *Apocalypse Now and Then: A Feminist Guide to The End of the World*. Boston: Beacon, 1996.

———. "The Flesh of God: A Metaphor in the Wild." In *Theology That Matters: Ecology, Economy, and God,* edited by Kathleen Ray Darby, 91–108. Minneapolis: Fortress, 2006.

Kelly, Henry Ansgar. *Satan: A Biography*. Cambridge: Cambridge University Press, 2006.

Kienicki, Leon, and Geoffrey Wigoder, eds. *A Dictionary of the Jewish-Christian Dialogue*. New York: Paulist, 1995.

Kim-Cragg, HyeRan. "A Christian Feminist Theological Reflection on Economy of Life." *The Ecumenical Review* 67.2 (2015) 170–76.

———. *Story and Song: A Postcolonial Interplay between Religious Education and Worship*. New York: Peter Lang, 2012.

Kivel, Paul. *Living in the Shadow of the Cross: Understanding and Resisting the Power and Privilege of Christian Hegemony.* Gabriola Island, BC: New Society, 2013.

Koslovic, Anton Karl. "The Structural Characteristics of the Cinematic Christ Figure." *Journal of Religion and Popular Culture* 8 (2004). Online: http://dspace2.flinders.edu.au/xmlui/bitstream/handle/2328/14295/2004054629.pdf?sequence=1.

Kugel, James L. *The Bible As It Was.* Cambridge, MA: Harvard University Press, 1999.

Kushner, Harold. *When Bad Things Happen to Good People.* New York: First Anchor Book, 2004.

Kwok, Pui-lan. *Postcolonial Imagination and Feminist Theology.* Louisville: Westminster John Knox, 2005.

———. "Roundtable Discussion: Anti-Judaism and Postcolonial Biblical Interpretation." *Journal of Feminist Studies in Religion* 20.1 (2004) 91–132.

LaCugna, Catherine M. *God for Us: The Trinity and Christian Life.* San Francisco: Harper & Row, 1991.

Levenson, Jon. *The Death and Resurrection of the Beloved Son.* New Haven: Yale University Press, 1993.

Levine, Amy-Jill. "The Disease of Postcolonial New Testament Studies and the Hermeneutics of Healing." *Journal of Feminist Studies in Religion* 20.1 (2004) 91–132.

———. "Lilies of the Field and Wandering Jews: Biblical Scholarship, Women's Roles, and Social Location." In *Transformative Encounters: Jesus and Women Re-viewed*, edited by Rosa Ingrid Kitzberger, 329–52. Leiden, Netherlands: Brill, 2000.

———. *The Misunderstood Jew: The Church and the Scandal of the Jewish Jesus.* San Francisco: HarperOne, 2006.

Levine, Amy-Jill, and Marc Zvi Brettler, eds. *The Jewish Annotated New Testament.* Oxford: Oxford University Press, 2011.

Lewis, John Shelton, and Robert Jewett. *The Myth of the American Superhero.* Grand Rapids: Eerdmans, 2002.

Lorber, Judith. *Paradoxes of Gender.* New Haven: Yale University Press, 1994.

MacLachlan, David. "Antichrist." In *Dictionary of the Bible and Western Culture*, edited by Mary Ann Beavis and Michael Gilmour, 23. Sheffield: Phoenix, 2012.

MacLean, Catherine Faith and John H. Young. *Preaching the Big Questions: Doctrine Isn't Dusty.* Toronto: United Church Publishing House, 2015.

Malarkey, Alex, and Kevin Malarkey. *The Boy Who Came Back from Heaven: A Remarkable Account of Miracles, Angels, and Life Beyond This World.* Carol Stream, IL: Tyndale, 2010.

Malina, Bruce J., and Jerome H. Neyrey. "Honor and Shame in Luke-Acts: Pivotal Values in the Ancient Mediterranean World." In *The Social World of Luke-Acts*, edited by Jerome H. Neyrey, 25–65. Peabody, MA: Hendrickson, 1991.

Matsuoka, Fumitaka, *Out of Silence: Emerging Themes in Asian American Churches.* Cleveland: United Church Press, 1995.

Mazis, Glen A. "Ecospirituality and the Blurred Boundaries of Humans, Animals, and Machines." In *Ecospirit: Religions and Philosophies for the Earth*, edited by Laurel Kearns and Catherine Keller, 125–55. New York: Fordham University Press, 2007.

McCormack, Lindley Bruce. "Atonement." In *Cambridge Dictionary of Christian Theology*, edited by Ian A. McFarland, David A.S. Fergusson, Karen Kilby, and R. Iaian Torrance, 43–45. Cambridge: Cambridge University Press, 2014.

McFague, Sallie. "Epilogue: Human Dignity and the Integrity of Creation." In *Theology That Matters: Ecology, Economy, and God,* edited by Kathleen Ray Darby, 199–212. Minneapolis: Fortress, 2006.

———. *Life Abundant: Rethinking Theology and Economy for a Planet in Peril.* Minneapolis: Fortress, 2001.

McFarland, Ian A. "Virginity." *Cambridge Dictionary of Christian Theology,* Kindle Edition, loc. 27195.

Mercer, Joyce Ann. *Girl Talk, God Talk: Why Faith Matters to Teenage Girls—And Their Parents.* San Francisco: Jossey-Bass, 2008.

———. "Virtual Sex, Actual Infidelity?" In *City of Desires—A Place for God: Practical Theological Perspectives,* edited by Ruard R. Ganzevoort, Rein Brouwer, and Bonnie McLemore, 71–80. Berlin: LIT, 2013.

Metzger, Bruce, and Michael David Coogan, ed. "Sex." In *Oxford Companion to the Bible,* 690–91. Oxford: Oxford University Press, 1993.

Mollenkott, Virginia Ramey. *The Divine Feminine: The Biblical Imagery of God as Female.* New York: Crossroad, 1983.

Moltmann, Jürgen. *Theology of Joy.* London: SCM, 1973.

Moreman, Christopher. *Beyond the Threshold: Afterlife Beliefs in World Religions.* Lanham, MD: Rowman & Littlefield, 2008.

Nelson, James B. *Body Theology.* Louisville: Westminster John Knox, 1992.

Newman, Barbara, ed. *Hildegard of Bingen: Voice of the Living Light.* Berkeley: University of California Press, 1998.

———. *Hildegard of Bingen: Woman of Her Age.* New York: Doubleday, 2001.

———. *Sister of Wisdom: St. Hildegard's Theology of the Feminine.* Berkeley: University of California Press, 1998.

Nielsen, Jesper Tang. "The Lamb of God: The Cognitive Structure of a Johannine Metaphor." In *Imagery in the Gospel of John: Forms, Themes, and Theology of Johannine Figurative Language,* edited by Jörg Frey Jan G. van der Watt and Ruben Zimmerman, 217–56. Tübingen: Mohr Siebeck, 2006.

Nietzsche, Friedrich. *Thus Spoke Zarathustra* [1883]. Translated and Edited by Walter Kaufmann in *The Portable Nietzsche.* New York: Viking, 1954.

Orr, David W. *Ecological Literacy: Education and the Transition to a Postmodern World.* Albany: SUNY Press, 1991.

Ott, Kate. *Sex + Faith: Talking with Your Child from Birth to Adolescence.* Louisville: Westminster John Knox, 2013.

Pagels, Elaine. *Adam, Eve, and the Serpent.* New York: Vintage, 1988.

Park, SoonKyung. *Korean Nation and Tasks for Feminist Theology.* Seoul: Korean Christian Literature Society, 1983.

Pearson, Patricia. *Opening Heaven's Door: Investigating Stories of Life, Death, and What Comes After.* Toronto: Random House Canada, 2014.

Perrin, Andrew B. "Sheol." In *Dictionary of the Bible and Western Culture,* edited by Mary Ann Beavis and Michael J. Gilmour, 488–89. Sheffield: Phoenix, 2012.

Pilch, John J. "Honor and Shame." *Oxford Bibliographies.* Online: http://www.oxfordbibliographies.com/view/document/obo-9780195393361/obo-9780195393361-0077.xml.

Plaskow, Judith. "Anti-Judaism in Feminist Christian Interpretation." In *Searching the Scriptures Volume 1: A Feminist Introduction,* edited by Elisabeth Schüssler Fiorenza, 119–24. New York: Crossroad, 1995.

———. "Blaming Jews for the Birth of Patriarchy." In *Nice Jewish Girls: A Lesbian Anthology*, edited by Evelyn Torton Beck, 45–51. Boston: Beacon, 1982.

Porter, Adam, "Satan." *Bible Odyssey*. Online: http://www.bibleodyssey.org/en/tools/ask-a-scholar/satan.aspx.

Powell, Allan Mark. "Salvation in Luke-Acts." *Word and World* 12.1 (1992) 5–11.

Procter-Smith, Marjorie. *Praying with Our Eyes Open: Engendering Feminist Liturgical Prayer*. Nashville: Abingdon, 1995.

Rausch, David John Jr. "Scapegoat." In *Dictionary of the Bible and Western Culture*, edited by Mary Ann Beavis and Michael J. Gilmour, 471. Sheffield: Phoenix, 2012.

Ray, Darby Kathleen, ed. *Deceiving the Devil: Atonement, Abuse, and Ransom*. Cleveland: Pilgrim, 1998.

———, ed. *Theology That Matters: Ecology, Economy, and God*. Minneapolis: Fortress, 2006.

Reinhartz, Adele. *Bible and Cinema: An Introduction*. New York: Routledge, 2013.

———, ed. *Bible and Cinema: Fifty Key Films*. New York: Routledge, 2013.

Remez, Lisa. "Oral Sex among Adolescents: Is It Sex or Is It Abstinence?" *Family Planning Perspectives* 32 (2000) 298–304.

Roach, David. "Heaven Tourism Books Pulled from Nearly 200 Christian Bookstores." *Christianity Today*, March 2015. Online: http://www.christianitytoday.com/gleanings/2015/march/heaven-tourism-books-pulled-lifeway-90-minutes-in-heaven.html.

Robert, Fuller C. *Naming the Antichrist: The History of an American Obsession*. New York: Oxford University Press, 1996.

Robert, Johnston K. *Reel Spirituality: Theology and Film in Dialogue*. Grand Rapids: Baker, 2000.

Ross, Susan A. *Extravagant Affections: A Feminist Sacramental Theology*. New York: Continuum, 1998.

Ruether, Rosemary Radford. *Christianity and the Making of the Modern Family*. Boston: Beacon, 2000.

———. "Ecofeminist Philosophy, Theology, and Ethics: A Comparative View." In *Ecospirit: Religions and Philosophies for the Earth*, edited by Laurel Kearns and Catherine Keller, 77–93. New York: Fordham University Press, 2007.

———. *Religion and Sexism*. New York: Simon and Schuster, 1974.

Said, Edward W. *Orientalism*. New York: Vintage, 1978.

Salmon, Marilyn J. *Preaching without Contempt: Overcoming Unintended Anti-Judaism*. Minneapolis: Fortress, 2006.

Schneider, Laurel C. *Beyond Monotheism: A Theology of Multiplicity*. New York: Routledge, 2008.

Schüssler Fiorenza, Elisabeth. "Between Movement and Academy: Feminist Biblical Studies in the Twentieth Century." In *Feminist Biblical Studies in the Twentieth Century: Scholarship and Movement*, edited by Elisabeth Schüssler Fiorenza, 3–17. Atlanta: Society of Biblical Literature, 2014.

———. *The Book of Revelation: Justice and Judgment*. Minneapolis: Fortress, 1998.

———. *Jesus: Miriam's Child, Sophia's Prophet: Critical Issues in Feminist Christology*. New York: Continuum, 1995.

Schweitzer, Don. *Contemporary Christologies: A Fortress Introduction*. Minneapolis: Fortress, 2010.

————. *Jesus Christ for Contemporary Life: His Person, Work, and Relationships.* Eugene, Oregon: Cascade, 2012.

Segal, Alan F. *Life after Death: A History of the Afterlife in Western Religion.* New York: Doubleday, 1989.

Smith, Mark S. *The Early History of God: Yahweh and Other Deities in Ancient Israel.* Grand Rapids: Eerdmans, 2002.

Sölle, Dorothee. "Between Matter and Spirit: Why and in What Sense Must Theology be Materialist?" In *God of the Lowly: Socio-Historical Interpretation of the Bible,* edited by Willy Schottroff and Wolfgang Stegemann, 86–102. Maryknoll: Orbis, 1984.

Sommer, Benjamin. "Monotheism in the Old Testament." *Bible Odyssey.* Online: http://www.bibleodyssey.org/people/related-articles/monotheism-in-the-hebrew-bible.aspx.

Stanton, Elizabeth Cady, and the Revising Committee. *The Woman's Bible.* Seattle. WA: Coalition on Women and Religion, 1885.

Stern, David H. *Jewish New Testament Commentary.* Clarksville, MD: Jewish Christian New Testament Publications, 1992.

Stone, Brian P. *Faith and Film: Theological Themes at the Cinema.* St. Louis: Chalice, 2000.

Stuckenbruck, Loren T. "Messianic Ideas in the Apocalyptic and Related Literature of Early Judaism." In *The Messiah in the Old and New Testaments,* edited by Stanley E. Porter, 90–113. Grand Rapids: Eerdmans, 2007.

Sugirtharajah R. S. *Asian Biblical Hermeneutics and Postcolonialism: Contesting the Interpretations.* Sheffield: Sheffield Academic, 1999.

Sullivan, Kevin. "The Watchers in *1 Enoch* 6–16 and the Rise of Demons." In *The Watchers in Jewish and Christian Traditions,* edited by Kim Harkins, Angela Bautsch, Kelly Coblentz, and John C. Endres, 91–106. Minneapolis: Fortress, 2014.

Tracy, David. *Plurality and Ambiguity: Hermeneutics, Religion, Hope.* San Francisco: Harper & Row, 1987.

Turner, Mary Donovan. "Reversal of Fortune: The Performance of a Prophet." In *Performance in Preaching: Brining the Sermon to Life,* edited by Jana Childers and Clayton J. Schmit, 87–98. Grand Rapids: Baker, 2008.

Tye, Karen. *Basics of Christian Education.* St. Louis: Chalice, 2000.

Unterman, Alan, ed. *Dictionary of Jewish Lore and Legend.* New York: Thames and Hudson, 1991.

Valenti, Jessica. *The Purity Myth: How America's Obsession with Virginity is Hurting Young Women.* Berkeley, CA: Seal, 2009.

Vitic, Jessie. "*The Virgin Suicides*: A Biblical Film Analysis". Student paper, RLST 365.3, St. Thomas More College, The University of Saskatchewan, March 15, 2016.

Von Kellenbach, Katharina. "Anti-Judaism in Christian-Rooted Feminist Writing: An Analysis of Major U.S., American and West German Feminist Theologians." PhD diss., Temple University Graduate School, 1990.

Weber, Hans-Ruedi. *Experiments with Bible Study.* Geneva: WCC, 1981.

Whitehead, James D., and Evelyn Eaton Whitehead. *Holy Eros: Recovering the Passion of God.* Maryknoll: Orbis, 2009.

Wink, Walter. *Naming the Powers: The Language of Power in the New Testament.* Philadelphia: Fortress, 1984.

Westerhoff III, John. *A Pilgrim People: Learning Through the Church Year.* Minneapolis: Seabury, 1984.

Wirzba, Norman. *Food and Faith: A Theology of Eating*. New York: Cambridge University Press, 2011.

Wolters, Al. "The Messiah in the Qumran Documents." In *The Messiah in the Old and New Testaments*, edited by Stanley E. Porter, 75–89. Grand Rapids: Eerdmans, 2007.

Filmography

Aménabar, Alejandro. *Agora*. Directed by Alejandro Aménabar. Madrid: Mod Producciones, 2009.

Arcand, Denys. *Jesus of Montreal*. Directed by Denys Arcand. Paris: Centre National de la Cinématographie,1989.

Armstrong, Vic. *Left Behind*. Directed by Vic Armstrong. Toronto: Entertainment One, 2014.

Axel, Gabriel. *Babette's Feast*. Directed by Gabriel Axel. Copenhagen: Nordisk Film, 1987.

Baxley, Craig R. *Left Behind III: The World at War*. Directed by Craig R. Baxley. St. Catharine's, ON: Cloud Ten Pictures, 2005.

Coppola, Sofia. *The Virgin Suicides*. Directed by Sofia Coppola. San Francisco: American Zoetrope, 1999.

Corcoran, Bill. *Left Behind II: Tribulation Force*. Directed by Bill Corcoran. St. Catharine's, ON: Cloud Ten Pictures, 2002.

Donner, Richard. *The Omen*. Directed by Richard Donner. Los Angeles: 20th Century Fox, 1976.

Gibson, Mel. *The Passion of the Christ*. Directed by Mel Gibson. Santa Monica, CA: Icon Productions, 2004.

Gluck, Will. *Easy A*. Directed by Will Gluck. Beverly Hills, CA: Olive Bridge Entertainment, 2010.

Hallström, Lasse. *Chocolat*. Directed by Lasse Hallström. Paris: Bac Films, 2000.

Hyams, Peter. *End of Days*. Directed by Peter Hyams. Universal City, CA: Universal, 1999.

Jones, Terry, and Terry Gilliam. *Monty Python's The Meaning of Life*. Directed by Terry Jones and Terry Gilliam. Universal City, CA: Universal, 1983.

Kaminski, Janusz. *Lost Souls*. Directed by Janusz Kaminski. Los Angeles: Castle Rock Entertainment, 2000.

Macarelli, Robert. *The Omega Code*. Directed by Robert Macarelli. Hollywood, CA: Gener8Xion Entertainment, 1999.

Miyazaki, Hayao. *Princess Mononoke*. Directed by Hayao Miyazaki. Tokyo: Studio Ghibli, 1997.

Miyazaki, Hayao. *Howl's Moving Castle*. Directed by Hayao Miyazaki. Tokyo: Studio Ghibli, 2004.

Miyazaki, Hayao. *The Wind Rises*. Directed by Hayao Miyazaki. Tokyo: Studio Ghibli, 2013.

Miyazaki, Hayao. *Spirited Away*. Directed by Hayao Miyazaki. Tokyo: Studio Ghibli, 2001.

Moore, John. *The Omen*. Directed by John Moore. Los Angeles: 20th Century Fox, 2006.

Polish, Michael. *90 Minutes in Heaven*. Directed by Michael Polish. Atlanta, GA: Family Christian Entertainment, 2015.

Robbins, Tim. *Dead Man Walking*. Directed by Tim Robbins. University City, CA: Polygram, 1995.

Sarin, Vic. *Left Behind*. Directed by Vic Sarin. St. Catharine's, ON: Cloud Ten Pictures, 2000.

Snyder, Zack. *Man of Steel*. Directed by Zack Snyder. Hollywood, CA: Warner Brothers, 2013.

Soisson, Joel. *The Prophecy V: Forsaken*. Directed by Joel Soisson. New York: Dimension Films, 2005.

Treays, Jane. *The Virgin Daughters*. Directed by Jane Treays. London: Granada, 2008.

Trenchard-Smith, Brian. *Megiddo: The Omega Code II*. Directed by Brian Trechard-Smith. Hollywood, CA: Gener8Xion Entertainment, 2002.

Wallace, Randall. *Heaven is for Real*. Directed by Randall Wallace. Culver City, CA: TriStar Productions, 2014.

Webb, Mark. *Spiderman II*. Directed by Mark Webb. Los Angeles: Columbia Pictures, 2003.

Wells, Simon, Brenda Chapman, and Steve Hickner. *Prince of Egypt*. Directed by Simon Wells, Brenda Chapman, and Steve Hickner. Universal City, CA: DreamWorks, 1998.

Index of Authors

Subject Index

Scripture Index

Old Testament

Genesis

1	68	7	5
1:1—2:4a	1, 2, 81	7:1–24	5
1:2	83	7:11	68
1–3	2	9:1, 7	5
1:6–8	5	13:9	xiii
1:6–8a	68	14:18	82
1:26	8, 81, 114	15:15	69
1:26–27	2	16:13–15	82
1:26–28	128	17:1–4	82
1:27	114	17:7, 9	68
2	3, 6	20:12	129
2:2–3	3	21:17	68
2:4b	82	22:11, 15, 17	68
2:4b—3:24	1, 2	24:7	68
2:4b—3:28	3	24:29	69
2:7	9	27:36, 38	61
2:24	37, 119, 139	28:12, 17	68
3	9, 24, 86	28:16–18	99
3:1–24	20	34	133
3:15	20	38	61
3:19	11	47:30	69
3:28	35	48:13–18	xiii
5:24	70	48:13–22	xiii
6:1–4	89	50:15	87
6:2	82		

Deuterocanonicals

Luke

John

1:1–4	6, 83
1:1–5	1, 8
1:2–3	8
1:3	36
1:14	6, 8, 51
1:18	115
1:29	148
1:29, 36	147
1:38	37
1:49	37
2:14–16	146
2:23	146
4:22	18
4:42	18n
4:45	146
5:1	146
5:24	77
5:45, 46	35
6:1–14	39
6:4	146
6:32	35
7:2, 10	146
7:19, 22, 23	35
7:30	54
7:33	135
7:35	57
8:43–47	41
9:6	11, 99
9:22	52
10:22	146
12:42	52
13:1	146
16:2	52
19:14, 31	147
20:28	52

Acts

1:8	18
1:13	134
2:36	153
3:13–16	152
3:22	38
4:12	18
5:31	18
7:51–53	41
7:60	19
11:26	54
13:23	18
13:26, 47	18
15:5	40
15:19–21	40
16:17	18, 82
17:7	100
17:28	8
20:28	21
23:6	21
23:8	72
26:5	21
26:28	54
28:28	18

Romans

1:16	21
1:26–27	xiii, 131
3:25	14
5:12	23
5:18–21	21, 75
6:5	139
9:3	54
9:4–5	55
9:13	61
11:1	54
11:29	52
13:11	21
16:20	88

1 Corinthians

1:22–24	117
1:23	149
6:9	131
6:11	85
6:17	139
7:1, 7–9	131
7:10–16	131
7:31	56
7:38	135
8:5–6	84
8:6	118
11:2–16	134
12:4–6	85

Hebrews *(continued)*

12:2	118, 147
12:16	61
12:18–24	118
12:22–24	147
12:25–29	56
13:4	131

1 Peter

1:21	85
3:1–6	134
3:18	30
4:1	30
4:16	54

2 Peter

1:16–18	39
2:4	89

1 John

2:18	102
2:22	102
4:2	102
4:3	102

2 John

1:7	102

Jude

6	89

Revelation

1:9	11, 76
2:3, 10	11, 76
2:7	9, 75
5:6	147
6:1–17	6
6:9–11	11, 76
6:10–11	75
8	16
8:1, 6–13	6
9:1–21	6
11:15–19	6
11:18	16
12	90
12:4	90
13:18	103
14:4	131
14:12–14	11, 76
15:1—16:21	6
17:7–9	88
19:11–15	27
20:7–10	88
20:10	108
21:1—22:4	2
21:1—22:5	75
21:23–27	76
21–22	1, 76
22:1–2	15
22:2	11
22:17	15

Pseudepigrapha

Jubilees

4:15	89
5:1	89
7:21–25	89
10:7–9	88

www.ingramcontent.com/pod-product-compliance
Lightning Source LLC
Chambersburg PA
CBHW030836270326
41928CB00007B/1072